Film, Form, and Culture

Robert Kolker
University of Maryland

Boston   Burr Ridge, IL   Dubuqu⌐   ⌐⌐, WI
New York   San Francisco   ⌐⌐⌐is
Bangkok   Bogotá   Caracas   Lisbon   London   Madrid
Mexico City   Milan   New Delhi   Seoul   Singapore
Sydney   Taipei   Toronto

McGraw-Hill College

A Division of The McGraw·Hill Companies

FILM, FORM, AND CULTURE

Copyright © 1999 by The McGraw-Hill Companies, Inc. All rights reserved. Printed in the United States of America. Except as permitted under the United States Copyright Act of 1976, no part of this publication may be reproduced or distributed in any form or by any means, or stored in a data base or retrieval system, without the prior written permission of the publisher.

 This book is printed on acid-free paper.

2 3 4 5 6 7 8 9 0 DOC/DOC 9 3 2 1 0 9

ISBN 0–07–290227–2

Editorial director: *Phillip A. Butcher*
Executive editor: *Cynthia Ward*
Marketing manager: *David Patterson*
Project manager: *Karen J. Nelson*
Senior production supervisor: *Melonie Salvati*
Freelance design coordinator: *Laurie J. Entringer*
Senior New Media developer: *Matt DiLorenzo*
Supplement coordinator: *Linda Huenecke*
Compositor: *Shepherd, Inc.*
Typeface: *10/12 Palatino*
Printer: *R. R. Donnelley & Sons Company*

Library of Congress Cataloging-in-Publication Data

Kolker, Robert Phillip.
    Film, form, and culture / Robert Kolker.
      p. cm.
    ISBN 0-07-290227-2 (alk. paper)
    Includes bibliographical references and index.
    1. Motion pictures. I. Title.
PN1994.K573   1999
791.43—dc21   98-39950

http://www.mhhe.com

PREFACE

Film, Form, and Culture welcomes a variety of readers who want to understand how films make stories and how those stories fit into our culture. This book is for film lovers who are curious about how editing and shot composition make us see the things filmmakers want us to see. It is for students in both film and cultural studies courses who are discovering that film narratives are as important and intricate as literary ones and for students of popular and mass culture who are learning about the large-scale production and consumption of images. Anyone interested in how and why moving images have an effect on so many people, and how movies are interpreted and influenced by the people who see them, will find this book useful.

Our guiding principle is that movies do not come out of thin air. They have a history, just as we and our society do, and the histories of film, our culture, and ourselves are intimately entwined. Films have a historically determined form and structure that create meaning and they have a complex set of conventions to communicate meaning and make it accessible. We as viewers have helped create the structure and conventions of films by enjoying what we see on screen and wanting to see more of the same. Like all aspects of popular culture, films develop out of a curious kind of negotiation process, in which filmmakers attempt to understand what we want to see, and we let them know if they are right by buying tickets and renting videos.

Film, Form, and Culture examines these negotiations and their results—the form and structure of the moving image, the economies, both cultural and monetary, of visual narratives, and their ability to reproduce in us the desire to see more of them. Examples for discussion are drawn from a wide variety of American and international films, the analyses of which will provide the tools to analyze others. The book concludes with a chapter on other screens, television and the computer, and the new communities of popular culture, forming on the Internet.

Throughout the book, we will be thinking about how and why we take so much pleasure from what we see on the screen. Our purpose will be to increase that pleasure by revealing complex textures of the moving image through an investigation of its various components, the operation, the economies, the business, and the culture that make it possible. We will examine things as small as the shot and the way shots are edited together to make a story; as large as the economics of filmmaking that help determine what we see and enjoy; as basic as the fundamental stories that films tell us again and again; and we will put all of this within a cultural context. We will define the work of the individuals who make film: the producer, writer, director, cinematographer, production designer, editor, composer, and the actors. We will analyze the founding stories that films tell us again and again, always to our amazement. And we will think about the viewer—you and I—who will appreciate films more when all the parts are explored and reassembled.

Unique to this book is an interactive CD-ROM in which clips from films are analyzed closely, more closely than can be imagined through the still images common to most film texts. Through images, interactively designed with explanatory text, stills, and animations, the reader will come intimately to terms with the basic elements of editing and montage, shot structure, point of view, mise-en scène, lighting, and camera movement. The CD-ROM stands alone, but can also be linked to sections in the text, where small icons indicate that material in the CD-ROM further illustrates and expands the analysis.

Many people were involved in the making of *Film, Form, and Culture*. My film students, patiently working with me over the years (most especially those in my fall, 1997, Intro to Film class), helped me hone and clarify my ideas. Mike Mashon indirectly provided the name of the book. Marsha Gordon did important research on its behalf and Devin Orgeron helped check out the facts. David and Luke Wyatt read the manuscript and their comments made it better. Stanley Plumly made me feel better with his encouragement. Other University of Maryland colleagues, particularly Sharon Gerstel, Elizabeth Loiseaux, Barry Peterson, Jenny Preece, Ben Shneiderman, helped with conversation, ideas and facts. Marta Braun, of the Ryerson Polytechnical Institute, Toronto, supplied the image by Etienne-Jules Marey that appears in the text. Paul Schrader, Oliver Stone, and William Blakefield helped make the CD-ROM possible. Robert Lieberman, my agent, saw the book's potential and helped bring it to publication. At McGraw-Hill, Cynthia Ward (one of the best editors it has been my pleasure to work with) kept a steady eye and an even hand. She was ably assisted by Kari Grimsby and Allison McNamara. Laurie Entringer designed the cover, Karen Nelson managed the production of the book, and Matt DiLorenzo shepherded the CD-ROM through its production process with an amazing patience. David Patterson found the right words to get people to notice. Margaret Manos and Peter deLissovoy copyedited the manuscript, giving it form and coherence. The manuscript's outside reviewers—Terry Byrne, College of New Jersey; Jeanne Hall, Pennsylvania State University; G. Thomas Poe, University of Missouri, Kansas City; Deborah Schaffer, Montana State University—helped with their comments. The errors that remain are mine alone.

CONTENTS

Introduction   xi

1   Seeing Is Not Believing   1

Image and Reality   1

Representation   4
Perspective and the Pleasures of Tricking the Eye   5
Photography and Reality   6
Photography and the Thing Itself   7
Reality as Image   8
Manipulation of the Image   9

From the Photographic to the Cinematic Image   10
Moving Images   11
The Intersection of Photography and Film   11
Economic Processes   12
The Economics of Realism   12

Notes and References   14

2   Formal Structures: How Films Tell Their Stories   16

From Image to Narrative   16

The Economics of the Image   19
The System Develops: Buster Keaton and Charlie Chaplin   20
From the Individual to the Studio   22

The Making of the Classical Hollywood Style   24
   Fabricating the Image   24
   The Whole and Its Parts   28
   Making the Parts Invisible   29
   Ideology at Work   30
   Form and Content   31

The Shot   33

The Cut   34
   The Development of Continuity Cutting   35
   Shot/Reverse Shot   37
   Dialogue Cutting   38
   Sight Lines   40
   Arbitrary Conventions   41
   The Hollywood Economical Style   42

Departures from the Classical Hollywood Style   43
   Eisenstein Montage   44
   Attending to the Shot   46
   Mise-en-scène   47
   The Long Take in Citizen Kane   48

Expressive Use of Mise-en-scène and Editing   50
   John Ford   50
   Robert Altman   50
   Stanley Kubrick   51
   Alfred Hitchcock   51
   Martin Scorsese and Point of View   52

Movie Conventions   54
   Gender Specificity   55
   Convention and Consciousness   57

Notes and References   58

3   Film as Cultural Practice   60

Popular Culture   60

Definitions of Culture   61
   Subcultures   62
   The Roots of Cultural Differences   63

How Popular Culture Becomes Mass Culture   64
   Radio and Print   64
   Television   65

Theories of Culture   65
  The Frankfurt School   66
  The Frankfurt School in America   67
  Masscult and Midcult   68
  Benjamin and Aura   69

Cultural Studies   72
  Text and Context   73
  Negotiation   73
  Judgment and Values   74
  Intertextuality and the Postmodern   74

Cultural Criticism Applied to Cinematic Texts   76
  Cultural Studies and Film   76
  Vertigo *and* Die Hard   76
  The Cultural Mix: Film and Television   78
  Bruce Willis versus James Stewart: The Function of the Star   80
  Vertigo *and the Culture of the Fifties*   82
  Vertigo *and* Die Hard: *Men in Film*   85
  Stories of Modernity   88
  Stories of Postmodernity   90
  The Buddy Film   92
  The End of Redemption   93

Notes and References   96

4   The Stories Told by Film   98

Master Narratives and Dominant Fictions   98
  Internal Tensions   98
  Closure   99
  Narrative Constraints   100

Genre   102
  Subgenres   102
  Generic Limits   102
  Genre and Gesture   103
  Generic Origins   103
  Genre and Narrative Economy   105

Genre Analysis   107

Melodrama   107
  Griffith   108
  Ideological Norms   117
  The Western   118

Film Noir   120
   Expressionist Roots of Noir   120
   Noir's Climax   126
   Noir's Rebirth   128
   Genre Resilience   129

European and Other Cinemas   130
   Italian Neorealism   130
   The French New Wave   133
   The Influence of Brecht   138
   Visual Pleasure   139

Notes and References   141

5   The Story Tellers of Film   144

Who Makes Movies?   144
   Individuals and Creativity   144
   The Ideal Viewer   145
   Film and the Individual Talent   146
   Collaboration as Creativity   146

Moviemakers   148
   Craftspeople   148
   Production Designer   148
   Cinematographer   149
   Editor   150
   Composer   151
   Screenwriter   154
   Actors   156
   Collaboration Reconsidered   159
   Producer   160

The Auteur   162
   European Origins   162
   The Birth of the Auteur   162
   The Auteur Theory   163
   Auteurism Today   173

Notes and References   175

6   Other Screens: The Future of the Image   177

Television   178
   Commercial Structures   179
   The Television Gaze   179

The News and the Gaze   180
Narrative Programming   181
Flow   182
Televisual Pleasure   184

From Analogue to Digital   184

The Third Screen   187
Other Narratives   187
Film, Form, and Culture, The CD-ROM   192
The Computer and the Text   193
Modernity and the Internet   194

Notes and References   198

Index   201

For Linda

INTRODUCTION

There are many things in our lives that we don't want to take seriously. Movies are one of them. We go to the movies to be entertained, scared, grossed out; to make out, spend time, have something to discuss afterward. But we don't often want to think about movies as a serious part of our emotional or intellectual lives, or even treat them with the same intensity we use when we discuss sports or politics. Outside of a film studies course, we rarely hear other people engaged in a discussion of films that goes much deeper than plot or characters.

Even the people who review movies on television or in the papers are rarely serious about their subject. They make jokes and puns, stick their thumbs up or down, tell us the plot and whether the characters are believable. They are part of the show, a kind of overture to the film we may go to see or bring home on video. They are another element of the entertainment.

This book takes another tack, asking you to think seriously about film, as seriously as you would about literature. It's a book about form and structure, content and contexts, history and business. It will give you a sense of film's history and its place in the greater scheme of things, especially in that envelope of words and deeds, money, art, artifacts, and daily life that is our culture.

I take as our basic premise that film is not only entertainment but is a part of industrial and political culture. International policy is sometimes at stake, which can lead in turn to aesthetic consequences. After the end of World War II, in 1946, for example, a major agreement was drawn up between France and the United States: the Blum-Byrnes Accords. This agreement came as an unequal compromise in the face of France's concern over getting its films shown on its own screens. The French public wanted American films. The Accords forced France to accept American films in an uneven ratio: it could show sixteen weeks of its own films, thirty-six weeks of anything else. The Accords changed the way the French made films because some filmmakers decided that the best way to meet the quota was to make high quality films through the adaptation of literary works. Other French filmmakers hated these adaptations and started to experiment with new cinematic forms, resulting in a revolution of filmmaking in the late fifties that was called the French New Wave. The result, in turn, was a change in film form all over the world. French resentment over the influx of American film and other media surfaced again in the 1990s. The General Agreement on Tariffs and Trade (GATT) was delayed over France's concern about America pirating their culture by filling their French movie and television screens with American product. The United States' recognition of the new Russian government in the early 1990s was held up because Jack Valenti, the head of the Motion Picture Association of America, Hollywood's powerful lobby, was concerned that the Russians were pirating American films. Trade negotiations with China in the mid-nineties broke down because of intellectual property rights issues, again involving video (and computer software) piracy.

All nations, our own included, understand the power of film and television to influence their people, to propagandize values and ideologies. Film may be a bargaining chip in foreign policy, the subject of the politician's wrath at home, and consequently the subject of study of many different kinds of academic courses in which its power and complexity are acknowledged and analyzed. We will talk some about the politics and the business, because film is a big business and its creation, its form and its content are about power, the core of politics. But mostly we will talk about the form and content of film. We will come to all of this from the perspective of textuality and find out how film, its production and reception, its place in our culture, makes up a large, coherent construction of meaningful and interrelated elements that we can analyze—a text that we can read.

A major part of this analysis involves the study of form, of the way film and the viewing of film are constructed. Let's go back for a moment to our paper tigers, the film reviewers. The first thing any reviewer does is talk about—usually summarize—the film's plot. "Charlie Kane is an unhappy newspaper man. His wife leaves him, and he looses all his friends." "*2001* opens with a number of shots of animals out on the desert. Then one tribe of apes attacks another until, in the middle of the night, one of the tribes discovers this strange monolith in the middle of their camp. There isn't much dialogue, but the apes look real enough."

Film reviews are almost always evasions, and what they evade is one of the few realities of film itself, that it is an artificial construct, something made in a special way for specific purposes, and that a film's plot or story is a function of this construction, not its first principle. By "artificial" I don't mean false; I'm using the term in its root sense, made by art, or, often in the case of film, by craft. Film is an artifice, and it becomes an artifact, made in specific ways, using specific tools, fashioned to produce and create specific effects—pleasing the audience who pays to see it. Film reviewers and most everyday discussions of film try to ignore the artificial, constructed aspect of film—its form—and instead talk about it as pure story. The characters of its story become, somehow, "realistic," as if they might "really" exist rather than result from a construction of the film itself.

There is no doubt that filmmakers and the development of film form over the last century play a role in this deception. Filmmakers assume that most viewers are not interested in the construction principles of their work and have accomplished a remarkable feat, making the structure of their films invisible. In other words, one reason we don't pay attention to the form and structure of film is that the form and structure of film disappear behind the very story and characters they produce. It is a great act of prestidigitation and one of the main reasons film has become so popular. It has a presence of being, an emotional immediacy that seems unmediated—simply there, without a history, without apparatus, without anything actually between us except the story.

In the discussion that follows, we will demystify this apparent act of magic. As we come to understand that film has a complex and flexible form and that story and characters are created by that form, we will become more comfortable with the notion of film as something carefully and seriously *made*. From that point we will be able to move on and understand that the making has a history and the history has a number of parts and branches. One branch—the largest—is the commercial narrative cinema of Hollywood, the major subject of our study. There are a number of national cinemas, some of them, like India's, almost as large as America's, but without much influence outside the nation's borders. Still another is a more experimental cinema, often found in Europe, Asia, Africa, the Middle East, and Latin America but occasionally cropping up in the United States, which explores and experiments with the potentials of film form in the way a good novelist or poet or computer programmer explores her language in order to create new meanings, new structures of thought and feeling.

Understanding film history will help us to understand the conventions of form and content. Clearly, films change over the course of time. Visual structure, acting styles, story content all seem different now than they were ten or a hundred years ago. But, in many ways, these changes are only superficial. It would be only a small exaggeration to say that, in fact, the structure of film and the stories and characters created by that structure have remained mostly unchanged, or have changed in only a gradual way, during the course of film history. Technical methods have indeed changed, aspects of style (especially acting style) have changed; but by and large the stories film tells and the ways it tells them follow a continuum almost from the very first images shown to the public. And yet film is always publicizing its uniqueness and originality. "For the first time on the screen . . ." was a popular publicity phrase in the forties and fifties. "The funniest," "most unique," "unlike anything you've ever seen," "the best film," "you've never seen anything like it," remain useful nonsense phrases for film advertisements. In truth, every commercial, theatrical film is in one way or another like every other commercial, theatrical film, and all are consciously created to be that way! In order to get a film made in Hollywood, an agent or a producer or a studio head has to be convinced that the film you have in mind is "just like" some other film "only different." Watch the first half-hour of Robert Altman's *The Player* (1992) for a hilarious representation of what "pitching a story" to a Hollywood producer is like.

"Just like . . . only different" is the engine that drives film. Hollywood cinema in particular (but all cinema in general) is based upon the conventions of genre, *kinds* of stories, told with styles and cinematic elements that are repeated with major and minor variations throughout the history of the genre. Through genres films are influenced by history and, very rarely, influence history in return. Genres, as we will see, are complex contractual events drawn between the filmmaker and the film viewer. We go to a horror film or a thriller, a romantic comedy or a science fiction movie, a Western or a melodrama with certain expectations that the film must meet. If it doesn't meet them, we will be disappointed and will not like the film. If a film masquerading as a genre turns out to attack or make fun of it, one of two things can happen. If other historical and cultural events are in sync with the attack or the parody, it is possible that the genre will wither and all but disappear. This happened to the Western in the late sixties and early seventies. Three moving and disturbing films that questioned the historical and formal elements of the Western—Sam Peckinpah's *The Wild Bunch* (1969), Arthur Penn's *Little Big Man* (1970), and Robert Altman's *McCabe and Mrs. Miller* (1971) —joined with the negative response to the Vietnam War and some profound questions about American imperial interests and the myths of manifest destiny to bring the Western down from its enormous popularity to a point from which it has barely recovered.

The more likely response to a film that mocks its generic construction too forcefully is that no one will go to see it. This happened with Altman's late seventies' Western with Paul Newman, *Buffalo Bill and the Indians* (1976); the Bruce Willis action film *Hudson Hawk* (1991); and the Arnold Schwarzenegger film *The Last Action Hero* (1993). Of course, one ironic and self-mocking Bruce Willis action film, *Die Hard* (1988), was very popular (we will analyze it closely in Chapter 3). When Willis and then Schwarzenegger took the mockery too far, however, and the action hero stereotype was made too obviously like a cartoon and too self-conscious, viewers rebelled.

Stereotypes, the expected character, the unsurprising story, the hoped-for conclusion, the invisible style are all part of our contract with the movies, what their makers believe we demand of them. Such demands are certainly not restricted to the movies: in television, pop music, news reporting, politics, we tend to be most comfortable with what we've most often heard. We are wary of the new. Our popular culture is, more often than not, an act of affirming already held ideas, of defining, delimiting, and limiting what we accept as the real.

The worst thing we can say about a film is that it is "unrealistic." "The characters weren't real." "The story didn't strike me as being real." Reality is always our last resort. If someone thinks we're not being serious, we're told to "face reality." If our ideas are half-baked, overly narcissistic, or even just silly, we're told: "get real!" If we are college teachers or teenagers, we're told we'll find things different "in the real world." Reality can be a threat, the thing we're not facing, or not in, or not dealing with. But it can also be a verbal gesture of approbation. "That was so real." And, of course, it's the greatest compliment we can give a film.

In fact, reality, like all other aspects of culture, is a social construct. In other words, through a complex integration of subjective and communal negotiations, we agree on the major elements of what we will call real. Maybe, as some people have argued, the only dependable definition of reality is that it is something a lot of people agree upon. This is not to argue that there aren't actual, "real" things in the world. Natural processes, states of matter (heat, cold, the relative solidity of physical things), the fact that, in temperate climates, plant life dies off in the fall and returns in the spring: these constitute a "reality," perhaps because they happen without our presence. But no matter what natural events and processes occur, they have little meaning without human interpretation, without our speaking about them within subjective or societal contexts.

From the natural comes the mythic; from myths come culture; from culture comes the notion that what was invented by the human imagination is real, even natural. In the end, reality is what we make out of what goes on in the natural and human worlds, what we invest with meaning and incorporate into our culture. Science is one meaning-making narrative; so are myth and literature. Film is another.

I was once teaching a film by the late German director, Rainer Werner Fassbinder, whose films are bitter, ironic, cool, and distanced observations of everyday German working-class life, told in mock melodramatic fashion. I suggested to my class that, of all filmmakers, Fassbinder made movies that at least spoke to some of the realities of the world. A class member took exception. She liked a current film of the time called Broadcast News. It was about a romantic triangle. It was closer to her life than a Fassbinder film, because she was experiencing a similar romantic situation. She chose to make melodrama a reality because she was in a melodramatic moment of her life. She didn't see that she was in a melodramatic moment because she had learned about such moments from the movies. She responded to the romantic melodrama of Broadcast News not because the film responded to her emotional life but because her emotional life was responding to romantic films.

We find films realistic because we have learned certain kinds of responses, gestures, attitudes from them, and when we see these gestures or feel these responses again in a film or a television show, we assume they are real—because we've felt them and seen them before. We've probably even imitated them. (Where do we learn the way to kiss someone? From the movies.) This is reality as an infinite loop, a recursion through various emotional and visual constructs, culturally approved, indeed culturally mandated, that we assume to be "real" because we see them over and over again, absorb them, and, for better or worse, live them.

Here is where the reality factor is joined with genre, history, culture, convention, and the invisible structure of film that we talked about earlier. What we call "realistic" in film is, more often than not, only the familiar. The familiar is what we experience often, comfortably, clearly, as if it were always there. When we approve of the reality of a film, we are really affirming our comfort with it; our desire to accept what we see. Desire is an important word here, because filmgoers aren't fools. No one literally believes what they see on the screen; we all desire and in a certain sense covet, and in a greater sense want to *will* our response to what we see. We want to accept it uncritically, respond to it emotionally. Our culture keeps telling us over and over that emotions don't lie. If we feel it, it must be so.

In the discussion that follows, we will steer our way through the thickets of desire and try to find why we want so much from movies and how the movies deliver what they and we think we want. By examining form and the ways in which our responses are culturally determined, we will attempt to denaturalize our responses in order to understand what we are really getting when we ask for realism—and why we should be asking for it at all.

Cultural determination is an important idea in this book. We will use culture in a broad sense, perhaps close to what the French think about when they worry about their culture being at stake because of the influx and popularity of American movies. As defined here, culture doesn't mean "high-toned" or refer to works of high art that are supposed to be good for us. Rather, culture is the complex totality of our daily lives and acts. Culture is the form and content of our subjective selves and our communal lives, our social and economic class, our entertainments, our politics and economics. Culture is the way we act out ideology. Ideology is the way we agree to see ourselves, to behave, and to create the values of our lives.

Of course, cultures might be more appropriate, because neither culture nor ideology is singular or monolithic. Consider popular music. Hip-hop and rap emerged from African American popular culture in the seventies and eighties. Rap moved from the streets to the recording studios and into the wider population by the mid-1990s, and then separated into a number of strands. One strand, Gangsta Rap, became a way for male African American teenagers to express anger at middle-class white society. But its language of violence and misogyny also disturbed parts of African American culture and signified class and economic divisions within that culture. It brought down the wrath of some of the white establishment as well. Rap as a whole quickly transcended the music world into the larger cultural arena where art, industry, politics and promotion are intertwined. It became sound, fashion, aggression, record sales, movie deals, police busts, highway noise, and big business. Attraction for many and irritant to some, rap became a phenomenon of the culture, a practice of one subculture (a term used to define one active part of the entire culture), and a representation of all of the culture.

Culture is made up of expressions and intersections, representations, images, sounds, and stories. It is local and global, moving and changing, depending upon the needs of individual and groups. It can be as peaceful as family churchgoing or as violent as Serbian weekend warriors, who dress up like the movie character Rambo and set out to kill those they believe are their ancient enemies.

Culture is the sum total of the intricate ways we relate to ourselves, our peers, our community, to our country, world, and universe. It is made up of the minutiae of our daily lives: the toothpaste we use; the music we like; the political ideas we hold; our sexual orientation; the image we have of ourselves; the models we want to emulate. Culture is more than ourselves, because our selves are formed by a variety of means, influences and agreements. So culture is also made up of the general ideological components of the society we live in. Politics, law, religion, art, entertainment are all part of our culture.

And that includes film. We will look closely at the cultural contexts of film: where it fits in the culture, what constitutes its popularity, and why popularity is sometimes used to condemn it. We'll also, in the last chapter, have a look at more recent cultural events that are visual in nature and that tell us and our culture stories: television and the computer.

Finally, a word about the films we will discuss. We will be thinking about and analyzing theatrical, narrative, fiction film—films that tell stories that are meant to be seen by relatively large numbers of people. While we will refer to documentary and to some avant-garde practice, our concern here is with the kinds of film that most people see most of the time. We will talk a lot about American film, because that is the dominant cinema around the world. But there are other very important and very wonderful cinemas and individual filmmakers outside Hollywood, many of whom make their films in response to Hollywood. We will talk about world cinema, the roles it plays, its individual filmmakers and their films.

But doing all this raises a problem. What particular films should we discuss? Within the context of a book, it is impossible to mention (not to say analyze) everyone's favorites, or to deal with films that everyone has seen or wants to see. Adding to the problem is the fact that there is not really an established canon in film studies. Of course, there are great films. Everyone agrees that *Citizen Kane* (Orson Welles, 1941) is among the most important films ever made, and we will discuss it here. (In the first reference to a film, I've followed the convention of giving the title, director's name, and date of release.) But every film scholar and film teacher, like every filmgoer, has his or her favorites. I am no exception. The choice of films I discuss and analyze is therefore often very subjective. I've tried to follow the principle of part for whole. My hope is that the analyses here can provide tools for thinking, talking, and writing about other films, and that each discussion of film, genre, or larger theoretic principle will serve as a template for work on other films, other genres, and other related interests.

No matter what the film, I have tried to set the discussion in the context of culture, response, ideology—those larger issues of which film is a part. You will be asked to connect things and to refuse to believe that the experience of any one thing exists in isolation from any other experience. This book therefore invites you to look at the movies (and, by extension and example, television) as one item in the enormous palette of your own experience and the wider experiences of the culture we all belong to. It invites you to think of a film narrative as seriously as a literary narrative and to understand that the array of images and stories, beliefs and prejudices, love and rejection, peace and violence that we learn about in literature we can learn in very different ways from film. In effect, this book is about the end of film innocence; it is an invitation to discover a world in which nothing is simple, nothing is "just there," and nothing can be dismissed without, at least, your being conscious that dismissal has consequences.

NOTES AND REFERENCES

For the Blum-Byrnes Accords and a history of French cinema, see Alan Williams, *Republic of Images: A History of French Filmmaking* (Cambridge, Mass.: Harvard University Press, 1992).

1

SEEING IS NOT BELIEVING

IMAGE AND REALITY

Oliver Stone's violent, hallucinatory film *Natural Born Killers* (1994) contains a scene in which the homicidal Mickey is caught by the police in front of a drugstore. The media are present; television is capturing Mickey's capture. The police get Mickey on the ground and viciously beat him with their clubs. The camera assumes a position at some distance from the action, observing it. In a fraction of a second we realize that Stone has recreated, in a fictional space, the infamous videotape of the beating of Rodney King by the Los Angeles police in 1991. That tape, which has been shown over and over again on television news and been seen by millions of people, is an eloquent example of how a simple image can communicate a violent truth.

A still from the videotape of Rodney King being beaten by the police.

Oliver Stone's re-creation of the beating in his film Natural Born Killers *(1994).*

When the police who took part in the King beating were first brought to trial, their lawyers used the videotape as evidence against the prosecution. The defense lawyers turned themselves into film studies scholars. They showed the tape in slow motion, backwards and forwards, frame by frame. They instructed the jury in the methods of close visual analysis, and they used their analysis to prove to the members of the jury that they weren't seeing what they thought they were seeing. What was really on the videotape, the defense said, was an offender

1

violently resisting arrest. What the police were doing was actually part of an "escalation of force." The jury (predisposed against the victim in the first place) believed it.

There is a curious cultural cliché that says pictures don't lie. It's part of the greater cliché that seeing is believing. Somehow a thing seen directly, or through a visual representation, brings us closer to some actual reality. Words are too obviously not things themselves; words are made-up sounds, represented by made-up letters, put together in a contrived grammar that everyone in a culture uses to communicate. Language is clearly cultural and not natural—it is human made. But vision, sight, brings us the thing itself. Things that are *seen* appear to be and even feel as if they are unmediated; that is, they seem to be conveyed directly to us, not indirectly communicated—or mediated—through a person or a device. This belief in the reality of things seen extends to the images of things. Unlike words, which interpret experience, images appear to be present and immediate: there, whole, and real. Of course all we ever see of actual things are images—two, in fact, focused upside down by the lens of each eye onto the retina, righted and merged in the brain to create the sensation of an object in space. If seeing a thing seems to put us in touch with the real, then an image of the thing will capture the real, leaving its impression for us to return to and depend upon.

Images entrance us because they provide a powerful illusion of owning reality. If we can photograph reality or paint it, or copy it or turn it into a purely subjective rendering, we have exercised an important kind of power. This power is clear in the linguistic tracings of "image": "imagination," "imaginary," "imagining," are all related to "image" and indicate how the taking, making, or thinking of a picture is an integral part of understanding. Through the image we can approach, understand, and play with the material of the external world in ways that both humanize it and make it subjective. At the same time, the image allows us to maintain a real connection with the external world. The image is there and here, outside and inside. We love this visual play of the objective and subjective.

We love to look and see. There's even a word for it: scopophilia, the love of looking, which doesn't have quite the same antisocial, erotic connotation as voyeurism, the act of looking at a subject who is unaware of our look. And we especially love to look at the pictures of things. We take photographs, make videos, and create digital images; we do it as amateurs, often allowing the camera to be our intermediary amidst the chaos of real events, or we enjoy the work of professionals. Images are our memory, the basis of our stories, our artistic expression, our advertising, and our journalism. Images have become an integral part of popular music since MTV, and they are, of course, the core of movies.

Images are so much an object of desire that we begin to exchange them for the objective world. We so believe in the presence and reality of images that we may take them at face value. They are, we often think, exactly what they are (or what someone tells us they are). We invest them with emotion and meaning; we may forget that they are *images*—mediations—and create a kind of short circuit: if the image of a thing is close enough to the thing itself, perhaps we can neglect the thing itself—those events actually going on in the world—and merely indulge in the image. The emotions we attach to an image can be simply set in motion by the image, and we can ignore the origin and the formal properties of the image itself. We can cut ourselves off from the events that made the image possible—the material of the external world—and make that short circuit, accepting the cliché that pictures never lie. If pictures never lie and are worth a thousand words, they must be dependable, true, if not the thing itself, at least a suitable substitute. This is what Oliver Stone is thinking about when he imitates the Rodney King videotape in *Natural Born Killers.* The videotape was an image of an event, taken without the knowledge of those who were participating in it, which is the closest thing image-making can get to objective recording (an argument used by documentary filmmakers, who try to maintain the illusion that their images are closer to objective reality than those made by fiction filmmakers). But that footage is not "objective"; it exists because of the economics of video recording, the relative cheapness and ubiquity of amateur equipment; the willingness of an onlooker with a camera to turn it on as the beating was in progress, rather than do something to stop the beating; the willingness of television news programs to show over and over again any kind of novel, violent imagery they can find. The footage exists because of the desire of people to watch.

What about the "objectivity" of the image itself? Anyone who took to heart the cliché "seeing is believing" saw a man being beaten by the police, in the fuzzy gray wash of an underexposed, amateur videotape taken at night. The trial lawyers, however, who analyzed the image from their own perspective in their desire to debunk the evidence in order to free their clients, proved to a jury—willing to believe them—that they didn't quite see a man being beaten, but an aggressive person the police were trying to restrain. In Oliver Stone's re-creation, the police are brutally restraining a brutal, aggressive person, an unthinking, amoral killer. The image is a complete fabrication, done in the studio or in a carefully controlled location. Most likely the "star" of the film, Woody Harrelson, isn't even in the shot, replaced by a stunt man. There is, in a sense, nothing there, only the re-creation of another image—this time fully exaggerated as representatives from television news (including Japanese television, with an excited commentator whose remarks are translated through subtitles) look on, make their images, make comments, while the sound track is filled with the music of Carl Orff's *Carmina Burana.* The re-creation is twisted with irony, begging us to provide a more complex reaction than we might have given to the original videotape or the trial lawyers' interpretation of it. The recreation makes sure we take the side of the character being beaten even though the film has clearly defined him as a homicidal maniac.

At the end of *Natural Born Killers,* in a closing montage of contemporary violence, Stone shows clips of Rodney King's televised plea to end the violence during the Los Angeles uprising of 1992. King's image, however, is diminished by the illusions of violence created throughout the film. This result is somewhat unintended; the real victim seems somehow less real in comparison to the artfully organized and aesthetically charged images of violence that have occurred in the course of the story, and in the course of King's own story shown filtered through the video of the beating. Stone has asked us to think about the construction of images, something that few films attempt to do because their value is built upon our desire not to ask what images are made of and what they might really mean. We love to look; movies love to show us things. Perhaps we don't want to know what we're looking at. Indeed, for many people, Stone's ironies were lost. They found *Natural Born Killers* too violent. Unwilling to decipher the complex visual structure of the film and understand what that structure was trying to say—that images of violence are manufactured to play upon our desire to see and enjoy violence at a safe distance—they took the images too literally and were repelled. They believed what they saw.

All of which leads us to the central question of this chapter: When we look at an image, and especially when we look at the images that make up a movie, what do we see? What's there, what do we think is there, and what do we want to be there? We can begin an answer by examining the development of painting and photography, because film is so much an extension of the latter and borrows some effects of the former.

REPRESENTATION

People painted before they wrote. Painting is among the earliest artifacts we have of prehistoric civilizations. A hand, a deer, images of the human figure and the naturalized world, things reflected and caught and seen; and then, in the case of the deer, eaten. There's elemental magic in these early images that suggests that if you make an image you have gained some control over nature and over yourself through imagination. The painted image came, in different ways in different cultures, to express not merely seeing but an interpretation of what is.

By the neoclassical period (from the late-seventeenth to the mid-eighteenth centuries in most of Europe) the ideological thrust of art was to be as "true" to the natural world as possible. Interpretation and inspiration were, in theory at least, subordinated to imitation and to the capturing of the image, to reproducing it, proclaiming that nature could be taken and owned whole by the imagination.

The *camera obscura* came to prominence in the seventeenth century: a box with a pinhole through which light could pass, it projected an upside-down image on its opposite side. Some painters called a version of this contraption a "Claude Glass," after the admired French landscape painter Claude Lorrain (1600–1682). They would enter the box and trace the image of the outside world that was reflected through the pin hole. The Dutch painter Jan Vermeer

(1632–1675) actually reproduced in his paintings the lighting effects that were created by the camera obscura.

The camera obscura was a sort of prephotographic device, designed to make possible the urge to capture the real world with as little apparent mediation as possible. When photography itself came along in the mid-nineteenth century, painting was put in crisis. The photograph, it seemed, did the work of imitating nature better than the artist ever could. Some painters made pragmatic use of the invention. There were Impressionist painters who used a photograph in place of the model or landscape they were painting. But, by and large, the photograph was a challenge to painting and was one cause of painting's move away from representation and reproduction of a direct kind to the abstract expressionism of the twentieth century. Since photographs did such a good job representing things as they existed in the world, painters were freed to look inward and represent things as they were in their imagination, rendering emotion in the color, volume, line, and spatial configurations native to the painter's art.

Photography was not wholly responsible for the development of abstract painting. The important point is that photography introduced to modern culture another form of image making, of visual representation, one apparently more "real" than painting because it seemed to capture an image of the world out there and bring it, framed, composed, and contained, before our eyes.

An important principle of representation (and mediation) is that an image is not *the* thing itself but *a* thing itself. This sounds perfectly obvious until we recall the phenomenon of short circuiting we discussed earlier. We tend to look at a painting or a photograph not as a thing in itself but rather as a thing that uniquely represents another original object and that acts as a trigger mechanism for an appropriate emotional response. When we look at the family photo album, we don't ask how the images were constructed and what the construction is saying about the subject of the photograph. We desire to see and feel something through the image. So we look at the images and feel nostalgia or joy or pain about the family represented in the photographs. When an image becomes opaque and we can't pass through it to a comfortable thing, meaning, or emotion—as happens in abstract expressionist painting or in photographs we can't recognize—our first question is, "What is this about?" We want our images to be transparent so we can look through them; we want them to be *about* something. They exist to transmit the real world and to trigger emotional response.

Perspective and the Pleasures of Tricking the Eye

Images are not transparent views of the world. We take them for such only through or own willful, learned acts of evasion. What we evade are the technical, cultural, and political structures that make up an image, the fact that they are not the world but the products of human creation. Let's consider painting first. A painting is an interpretation of something seen that has been executed

Perspective was a mathematical invention that allowed a vanishing line to be created on a canvas and thus presented the illusion of depth on a two-dimensional surface. Photography and film adopted the principle. Photographers and cinematographers set up their cameras to show the vanishing line, and we can see it at work here, in one of the earliest films we have, the Lumière brothers' 1895 film of a train arriving at a station.

by the artist's hand. A painting is pigment on canvas articulated through a combination of color, shape, volume, and spatial organization. The way space is organized and the subject represented in a painting are very specific to a given culture and time, though they also bear traces of a particular artist's style and personality. Perspective, for example—the illusion of depth on a two-dimensional surface—is hardly a universal way of organizing space on canvas and did not always exist. Asian painting has never used it. Western painting didn't use it until the early fifteenth century. It was developed by the Florentine architect Filippo Brunelleschi (1377–1446) and the painter Masaccio (1401–1428). Perspective is based on mathematical principles of linear convergence, the way lines can be drawn so they appear to vanish at a single point in space. People have theorized that perspective was invented for ideological and cultural reasons, because it allowed the wealthy patrons who sponsored artists to be given a privileged place in viewing the canvas. That is, perspective allowed the viewer a sense of ownership, a sense of standing before a space that was made for his gaze. He stood outside the painting, occupying a position that seemed to be at the convergence of an imaginary set of lines that opened into the canvas and then appeared to converge again behind the canvas. These "vanishing lines" created the illusion that the space of the painting completed the patron's gaze—indeed any viewer's gaze. The double convergence creates an important effect, for if sight lines converge toward the back of the image on the canvas, they also converge in the imaginary space in front of the canvas, a space that is filled by the controlling look of the spectator. This phenomenon would have tremendous repercussions in the development of film in the twentieth century.

Photography and Reality

Photography was invented in the second half of the nineteenth century out of experiments that, like those involving perspective, were both scientific and aesthetic. At its most basic, photography is a chemical process, during which a light-sensitive material is altered when exposed to light. When this altered material is chemically treated, the exposed particles wash away, creating transparent or translucent spaces where the light fell. The negative image (light for dark) is reversed during printing. The chemistry hasn't changed very much since the middle of the nineteenth century, although digital imaging will very soon render chemical processing obsolete. The aesthetics and politics are a different matter.

The great French film theorist, André Bazin, speaks about the *inevitability* of photography. What he means is that art has always been motivated to capture and maintain the reality of the world, to hold its images eternally. Photography is the climax of that desire because, Bazin believes, it is the first art in which, at the exact instant during which the image is transferred to film, the human hand is not involved. For Bazin, the taking of a photograph is a pure, objective act. He puns in French on the word *objectif,* which means both "objective" and "lens." Bazin was deeply committed to the concept of film and photography as the arts of the real, but he was also aware that the reality of film and photography was "artificial," made by art. He was intrigued by the paradox. He was well aware that in the seemingly automatic passing of a thing to its image, some human intervention always occurs. So, of course, even though the image passes through the lens to the film in the camera without the intervention of the human hand, that intervention has already occurred: in the crafting of the lens and the chemical manufacture of the light-sensitive film emulsion; by the photographer who chooses a particular lens and a particular film for a particular shot; in the way the photographer lights and composes the shot. Every photographer is a composer: think of the basic, practically universal gesture of an amateur picture taker, waving her arm to signal people in front of the lens to move closer together, to get in the frame. The professional photographer and the photographer as artist make more elaborate preparations for a shot and, after the shot is composed and taken, manipulate the image in the darkroom.

Photography and the Thing Itself

The photographic image is not the thing itself. It is a photochemical representation of a composed, lit, lens-mediated transmission onto film of the thing itself. But even when we acknowledge the intervention of optics, chemistry, and the photographer in the recording and developing of the photographic image, we still haven't considered all the mediation that goes on. An image of the thing is not the thing. The subject of a photograph is not neutral: the subject—a person or a thing—is first chosen to be a subject, and then poses or is posed for the camera, assumes a camera-ready attitude often dictated by the culture (smiling, for example). Even a subject caught unawares by the camera has been changed by the very act of having been caught unawares. By the very event of being captured on film, a subject unaware of the presence of a camera has been frozen in photographic time and space, turned into an image, made into something he wasn't when the camera snapped his picture. The natural object—a landscape, for example—is marked by the fact of its being chosen, as well as by the time of day during which it is photographed, the way the

photographer composes it for shooting, chooses an appropriate lens, and manipulates the quality of light, first with the camera and then in the darkroom.

INTRODUCTION Here is a core issue for everything discussed in this book.
People *never* perceive "the thing itself." Whether in a photograph,
in a movie, or on television; whether on the page, from someone's
own mouth, or from a teacher and her textbook, what we hear, see, read, and
know is mediated by other things. Recall the way the Rodney King video, a
videographed record of "the thing itself," was made to mean what various
people, in various contexts, decided it should mean.

I am not arguing for what philosophers call solipsism, the notion that
things exist only when we see them. Nor am I asking the clichéd question, "If
a tree falls in the forest and nobody hears it, does it make a noise?" Of course
it makes a noise, on the basic physical level of causing air molecules to vibrate.
To *hear* and, perhaps, respond to the noise requires an animal present. To *understand* the noise and any complex significance it might have requires a
human presence. Understanding, perception, analysis, comprehension, meaning are human activities, complex, and often ambiguous.

Reality as Image

Our argument is that reality is always a mutually agreed-upon, social construct. Our ideas of truth, beauty, morality, sexuality, politics, and religion; the
ways we interpret the world and make decisions on how we act in it are determined by a complex process of education, assimilation, acculturation, and assent that begins at birth. It is a cliché that human beings are out of touch with
nature, and that more than a few of us are out of touch with reality. The fact is,
even when we are in touch, it's not with some given natural world or some objective, existing reality. Being in touch with nature means acting upon a learned
response to the natural world. In fact, responding with awe in the face of natural beauty dates back only to the eighteenth century and became a major cultural event only in the nineteenth. Before the late seventeenth century, people
in Western Europe did not pay much attention to nature's grandeur; they were
not moved by it nor did they care much to contemplate it. A mountain range
was something in the way. A complex shift in sociological and aesthetic responses occurred in the early eighteenth century and can be traced in its development through travel literature and then in poetry, fiction, and philosophy.
By the mid-eighteenth century, wild, mountainous landscapes became the site
of grand, overwhelming emotional response. The mountains had not, themselves, changed; cultural response had. The "Sublime," the effect of being
transported before nature's wildness *and* in front of representations of that
wildness in painting and poetry, was born. With it came nineteenth-century ro-
manticism and attitudes toward the natural world that remain with us still.

Reality is not an objective, geophysical phenomenon like a mountain. Reality is always something *said* or *understood* about the world. The physical
world is "there," but reality is always a polymorphous, shifting complex of

mediations, a kind of multifaceted lens, constructed by the changing attitudes and desires of a culture. Reality is a complex image of the world which many of us choose to agree to. The photographic and cinematic image is one of the ways we use this "lens" (here in a quite literal sense) to interpret the complexities of the world.

Reality becomes a kind of cultural baseline upon which we can build a variety of responses. One response is a feeling of security. We feel safe in front of something that strikes us as "real" or realistic. Another response is to dismiss someone who doesn't seem to be operating from this same base. We bless something (a film, a painting, a novel, a political program, a way of life) with the name of realism if it comforts us with something we desire or are familiar with, or have been told we should desire or be familiar with. We ask or are asked to face reality when we or someone else acts in unfamiliar ways. We say "that's not realistic" to dismiss someone or something that does not fit into our range of beliefs, hopes, or desires. "Get real," we say. "Get a life."

So, when the critic André Bazin said that the history of art is equal to the history of people's desire to save an image of the real world, he quickly modified this idea by saying that the desire to capture reality is in fact the desire "to give significant expression to the world. . . ." In that phrase "significant expression" lies the key. It's not the world we see in the image but its significant, mediated expression. For Bazin, such expression becomes very significant in photography and film because of the apparent *lack* of interference from a human agent. This is a peculiar paradox. The image is a significant expression of the real world; it almost *is* the real world because its image is formed without human interference—recall Bazin's theory that, at the instant of transferring the image to the film, the photograph occurs without human intervention. As we have seen, this theory has a kernel of truth, but is deeply compromised by all the manipulation that goes on before and after the image is actually made (and even while the image is being made, because lenses are not neutral). Out of the paradox comes many of our confusions over what the photographic and cinematic image actually is and actually does.

Manipulation of the Image

During its relatively brief existence, photography has taken on many culturally and economically determined forms. In the very early days, in order to overcome a perceived inferiority to painting, photographers adopted a painterly style. Some of them handcolored their work, after composing a figure or landscape in poses or compositions similar to those used by the Impressionist painters. As photography found its independent path, many other styles emerged, all of them depending upon some kind of manipulation of the image during the picture-making process. These included the creation of "abstract" photographs, images that reveal only patterns, shapes, and volume. This style flourished in the twenties at the same time that Dadaist and Surrealist artists incorporated the photographic image into their work. When, again in the twenties, photography became more common in journalism and advertising, manipulation of the image became extreme. Removed from the status of art, with all its implications of personal style, subjective vision, and revelation, the photograph became a tool for representing specific points of view with the purpose of selling commodities and focusing opinions. Shifting from one cultural realm of style and ideological determination in which individual expression counted strongly, photography became part of another, a corporate style in which the image of a politician making a speech, or a group of strikers in a menacing posture, or a woman assuming a conventional pose of seduction while wearing a particular brand of makeup or clothing, has specific designs on the viewer and asks for specific responses.

Images like these are obviously determined by external, cultural, economic, and political needs. But the image in the cause of economics and politics is different from the image in the cause of art only in its purpose. All images, all stories, all creations made by people have designs, in all senses of the term. The particular designs of journalism and advertising photography are narrow and focused, wanting the viewer to respond by putting money into circulation, in a word, by paying for the product. This kind of photography does not primarily imitate, reveal, or show. Rather, it exhorts, cajoles, and manipulates. It exploits fully the one abiding reality of representation and mediation: a call for some kind of response from the viewer. Something does indeed come between the thing itself and the image. In the case of the work of art, that "something" is a form and structure that ask of us an emotional and intellectual response meant to help us understand the artist and the way she feels about the world. In the case of the journalistic, advertising, or political image, that something is a form and structure that ask us to agree to the general values of our culture and the various commodities it creates, to form an opinion, to spend money or cast a vote. In the case of movies, form and structure ask us to respond to many of these requests simultaneously.

FROM THE PHOTOGRAPHIC TO THE CINEMATIC IMAGE

The alleged reality of the cinematic image is, in reality, a mechanical event. In a sense, film is a reality machine. Time and space—the coordinates of Western art, story, and life—are represented by the vertical strip of images that travels through the projector. Twenty-four photographs, or frames, go past the projector lens each second. A simple, very nineteenth-century mechanical process pulls the film strip down, one frame at a time, while a shutter in the shape of a Maltese cross opens and closes the lens so that each frame is projected on the screen in its turn. The resulting illusion is extraordinary. Because of the operation of the shutter, the screen is actually dark for a total of almost thirty minutes during an average two-hour film. And because of a cognitive desire to attach the events of one image to the next, and thanks to perceptual optics that cause our eyes to see images fused together above a certain rate of flicker, the series of stills projected on the screen is interpreted by our brains as a continuous flow. Space and time appear unified and ongoing.

Moving Images

Historically, the moving image and the photograph developed separately, merging in the very late nineteenth century. Projections of painted images, sometimes called magic lanterns, had been around since the seventeenth century. Various devices that created an illusion of figures in motion, or the sense of moving images in a large space surrounding the viewer—devices with wonderful names like zoetropes, phenakistoscopes, thaumatropes, panoramic views, cycloramas—had been around since the eighteenth century and reached their apogee in the nineteenth. These were mostly toys or sideshows that, in various ways, placed painted images in progressively different positions of movement on the inside of a revolving drum. By peering through slits in the side of the turning drum, or—in the case of cycloramas—standing in front of an unrolling canvas, the figures or painted landscapes seemed to elide into each other in a semblance of continuous motion.

The Intersection of Photography and Film

Magic lanterns, zoetropes, and photography intersected in the late nineteenth century in a quasi-scientific way through the work of two photographers, Eadweard Muybridge and Etienne-Jules Marey. Muybridge was born in England and did much of his work in America. Marey was French. In their work, the nineteenth-century curiosity about mechanical invention, industry, and the ways in which both could overcome the limitations of time and space met and pointed to the development of movies—a time and space machine that rivaled the locomotive and the telegraph.

Before the moving picture, photographers began analyzing motion into its component parts through multiple exposure. One of the most important of these experimenters was Etienne-Jules Marey (1890).

Muybridge and Marey photographed human and animal movements in ways that analyzed the motion into its component parts. Marey actually used a gunlike photographic mechanism to "shoot" his photographs (and the term "shooting a picture" originates from that machine). With its aura of scientific investigation, their work situates one branch of photography in that tradition of Western culture that seeks to analyze and quantify nature. The discovery and implementation of perspective in painting during the fourteenth century is part of that movement, itself a part of the larger movement to comprehend, own, and control the natural world.

Stanford's Wager   Leland Stanford, a former governor of California, who liked both horses and science, invited Eadweard Muybridge to help him settle a wager concerning whether at one point in a horse's gallop all four hoofs leave the ground. Muybridge proved it by taking a series of photographs at high speeds. Muybridge and Stanford went on to publish photographs of animals in motion in *Scientific American*, and Muybridge parlayed this into a career of public lectures in which he demonstrated his analytic series of shots of animals—as well as naked people—in motion. He published a version of his work in 1887, the eleven-volume *Animal Locomotion*. (Marey had published his animal locomotion studies, called *La machine animale*, in France in 1873.) Muybridge further combined his analytic photographs with the old kinetiscope-zoetrope toy to create an illusion of movement of his animals and people and, by 1881, was projecting them on a wall to a large audience. Scientific investigation, commerce, and spectacle merge in the projected image.

Economic Processes

The image was becoming a commodity. The rapidity of this event was accelerated during the last decade of the nineteenth century when Thomas Alva Edison's employee, William Dickson, developed a way to record moving images on a Kinetograph and show them on a Kinetoscope. Edison had wanted to make moving images as an accompaniment for his phonograph, but decided to concentrate on the image alone. The work of Edison's company in the late nineteenth century led to a slow but steady proliferation of moving images in peep shows, in which "flip cards" or a film loop were viewed through a viewer in a machine; in nickelodeons, where working-class people paid a nickel to go into a small room and see a short film projected on a sheet; and finally by the 1920s in the movie palaces built as part of the successful attempt of moviemakers to create a "respectable" middle-class audience for their images. By the late twenties, in an economic slump, the movie studios revived Edison's original notion of synchronizing image to sound and made "talking pictures" to the delight of audiences and a resulting rise in box office receipts.

The steady progression from the individual photographers, inventors, and entrepreneurs who developed the moving image, to the film studios, which were actually large-scale factory operations that mass-produced these images, may seem, at first, a big leap, but it took less than twenty-five years.

The Economics of Realism

The immediate emergence of movies as a popular, commercial art was just slightly in advance of the great boom of popular culture that would take place in the twenties. Film's invention came with the great nineteenth-century technologies that included telegraphy and the railroads. Its beginnings coincided with the growing influence of newspapers. It completed its growth as a mass medium in the twenties, at the same time as radio, and shared its popularity.

In the end, film infiltrated the imagination more than any other nineteenth-century invention because it told stories with images. It also made its story-tellers rich.

The consolidation of art, science, and capital in the service of moving images was not only rapid but in retrospect inevitable. Scopophilia—that "desire to see"—caused people to devour images as fast as they could be made. Scopophilia, especially when it receives satisfaction through images that narrate stories, is so powerful that it causes people to want to pay to be satisfied. The promise of seeing more, along with the promise that you would also feel more because of what you saw, had a profound popular appeal. Once the reality machine of moving pictures was set in motion no one ever wanted to stop it, only refine it to make it run more smoothly and increase its profit-making potential.

The popularity of movies was so great that, shortly after the turn of the century, demand for films soon exceeded supply. Various theater owner-entrepreneurs on the East Coast—most of them first-generation immigrants from Eastern Europe who had engaged in wholesale and retail selling before entering the business of film exhibition—decided that the best way to supply their theaters with product was to manufacture it themselves. They would make the images they needed to sell. They fought with Edison, who attempted to control the patents on his motion picture machines and who sometimes employed thugs to beat up the filmmakers and take their equipment away (constituting what film historians call the "patent wars" of 1910–1913). The filmmakers went to California to escape Edison's reach, settled in Los Angeles, and rather quickly established their own tightly knit companies that, by the late teens, evolved into the studios that centralized all facets of motion picture production and which exist, in modified form, to this day.

In the history of film, the first quarter of the twentieth century was a particularly active period of creativity on all levels: the development of visual narrative structure, the creation, the buying, and the selling of studios and talent, the invention of the star system, the integration of the entire production and distribution of images through theaters owned by the studios. This is the history of production that moved from an individual, director-based activity into a huge industrial operation, headed by an executive who delegated individual films to producers, and which was peopled by an enormous in-house staff of writers, directors, composers, designers, electricians, actors, and other craftspeople.

The speed of the process by which moviemaking developed into commerce was, as I have said, driven by the willingness of audiences to look and look and look and want to see more and more, for whom the movie theater was the most convenient place to get access to those images. Movies supplied a visual imagination and narrative flow for the culture at large. They extended basic stories of popular culture—stories of sexuality and romance, captivity and release, family and heroism, individualism and community—into visual worlds that were immediately comprehensible, almost tactile. In the movies, time and space appeared as if intact. Human figures moved and had emotions. Life seemed to be occurring. The moving image was a febrile, story-generating, meaning-generating thing. More than literature, painting, or the photograph, moving images eloquently expressed popular desire and apparently expressed what many, almost most, of the people across economic and social classes wanted to hear and see. The fact that what they were hearing and seeing was an illusion in every respect seemed not to matter. It might, in fact, have contributed to film's popularity. Seeing and feeling in the secure knowledge that no obvious consequences are involved is an important aspect of our response to any aesthetic experience. The moving image was a particular attraction to everyone who wanted to see more, feel more, and do it in the safe embrace of an irresistible story. It still is.

NOTES AND REFERENCES

Image and Reality   Basic resources for information on the way we perceive image and reality are Rudolph Arnheim, *Art and Visual Perception* (Berkeley and Los Angeles: University of California Press, 1974) and E. H. Gombrich, *Art and Illusion* (Princeton: Princeton University Press, 1969).

Representation   In the 1970s and 80s painters called photorealists took Polaroids of their subjects—a human face, a city street, a diner, a motorcycle. They placed a grid over the photograph and a corresponding grid over the canvas and then copied the photograph, square by corresponding square, onto the canvas. When you look at a photographic reproduction of a photorealist painting, you often can't tell that it's a painting.

Perspective and the Pleasures of Tricking the Eye   Professor Sharon Gerstel of the University of Maryland supplied information about the history of perspective. Erwin Panofsky's *Perspective as Symbolic Form*, trans. Christopher S. Wood (New York: Zone Books, 1991) is a good source for the theory of perspective. Professor Elizabeth Loizeaux of the University of Maryland offered ideas about the camera obscura. Michel Foucault's essay "Las Meninas" argues the theory of perspective as a means of owning the space of a painting. It is in *The Order of Things* (New York: Random House, 1970), pp. 3–16.

Photograph and Reality   The references to and quotations from André Bazin are from *What Is Cinema?* vol. I, trans. Hugh Gray (Los Angeles and Berkeley: University of California Press, 1968), p. 12. This is an invaluable book for understanding the theories of reality and the moving image. See also Bill Nichols, *Ideology and the Image* (Bloomington: Indiana University Press, 1981).

    For an emotional and theoretical discussion of photography, see Roland Barthes, *Camera Lucida : Reflections on Photography*, trans. Richard Howard (New York: Hill and Wang, 1981).

    A classic work on the Sublime in literature is M. S. Abrams, *The Mirror and the Lamp: Romantic Theory and the Critical Tradition* (New York: Norton, 1958).

Moving Images   Anne Friedberg, *Window Shopping: Cinema and the Postmodern* (Los Angeles and Berkeley: University of California Press, 1993), offers a good reading of nineteenth-century technology and the development of mass media.

The Intersection of Photography and **Film** and **Economic Processes**   Material on early movie machines, Marey, Muybridge, and Edison can be found in Charles

Musser, *The Emergence of Cinema: The American Screen to 1907* (New York: Charles Scribner's Sons, 1990), pp. 15–132. For Etienne-Jules Marey, see Marta Braun, *Picturing Time: The Work of Etienne-Jules Marey (1830–1904)* (Chicago: University of Chicago Press, 1992). David A. Cook's *A History of Narrative Film* (New York: W. W. Norton & Company, 1996) and Kristen Thompson and David Bordwell's *Film History: An Introduction* (New York: McGraw-Hill, 1994) are excellent sources for information about the development of film as art and industry. See also Scott Bukatman, "Gibson's Typewriter," in *Flame Wars: The Discourse of Cyberculture*, ed. Mark Dery (Durham: North Carolina University Press, 1984), pp. 73–74.

The Economics of Realism   Thomas Elsaessar's collection of essays, *Early Cinema: Space, Frame, Narrative* (London: British Film Institute, 1990) is a good source of information on the formation of the film industry. See especially pp. 153–59.

2

FORMAL STRUCTURES: HOW FILMS TELL THEIR STORIES

When Oliver Stone restages the Rodney King video in *Natural Born Killers*, he is addressing the ease with which the image flows from fact to illusion and from illusion into story, and the ease with which we accept the flow. The original videotape was a representation made because an onlooker was present with a camera, desired to observe the action through the lens rather than interfere or take any preventative part in it, and then offered the videotape to television stations, which gladly showed it over and over again. The lawyers who defended the cops who delivered the beating also showed it over and over and reconstructed the mediating processes of the image to argue that people were not actually seeing what they thought they were seeing. Stone further removes his representation by mocking it up, imitating it, and putting it in the service of his own story.

Movies are always about putting images in the service of the story they attempt to tell, and about the economics of doing this. From the beginning, filmmakers understood on an intuitive level that images, because they were, in a sense, hand-made mediations between the world and the viewer, were profoundly manipulable. Even more, these filmmakers knew that by manipulating the image, the image in turn would manipulate how and what people saw and the way they responded to what they saw. As sophisticated as the Renaissance painters, who plotted the sight lines in their paintings to create the illusion of depth and presence, filmmakers would plot all aspects of the image for very similar purposes. Sight lines, plot lines, character, spectator position, are all planned to reduce the sense of distance between spectator and image and optimize an illusion of participation.

FROM IMAGE TO NARRATIVE

The evolution of the photographic image into the moving, story-telling image is itself a narrative of the making and comprehension of illusions. It is a narrative that runs as smoothly as a good Hollywood film, because it is driven by the desire to see and to accept what is seen. Filmmakers learned the structure of their art and craft; filmgoers learned how to decipher it because they wanted to. They did not even have to learn to accept it, only to love it.

If we take a moment and stay with the early development of the moving image and its stories, we will more easily understand the structuring of illusions and the formation of conventions—those structures of form and content that, once invented, are used over and over again. This chapter will start with an examination of how image and narrative structure were formed and then move into a discussion of how that form and its variations were perpetuated throughout the history of film. We need to understand the formation of image and story and then go on to its meanings.

In 1888, Eadweard Muybridge, the photographer, visited Thomas Alva Edison, the inventor. Muybridge urged Edison to combine Muybridge's image projector, the zoopraxiscope, with Edison's phonograph. In 1889, Edison met Etienne-Jules Marey, who had developed a moving-image film strip, in Paris. In 1891, Thomas Edison's assistant, W. K. L. Dickson, demonstrated a viewing machine in which could be seen a smoothly moving image of a man—Dickson himself. In France, in 1895, Auguste and Louis Lumière projected a short film they had made of workers leaving their factory. The French magician, Georges Méliès, who had watched the films of the Lumière brothers, projected his first film in 1896. (Moving-picture projection was developed almost at the same time in the United States, France, England, and Germany.)

The Edison Company's early attempts at filmmaking were of single, staged events: a co-worker sneezing; a couple kissing—the erotic image emerging in cinema at its very start. The Lumière brothers shot events going on in the world: their workers leaving their factory, a train arriving at a station. But they soon began staging incidents: a child squirting a gardener with a water hose; brother Auguste feeding his baby. The magician, Méliès, on the other hand, worked largely inside his studio, mocking up images, creating trick shots on film. He showed people disappearing in the middle of a scene; people underwater; men traveling to the moon. Before distributing the finished film, Méliès had his factory workers hand-paint each frame, creating an illusion of color.

The Lumière brothers filmed things happening in the world and also made things happen for the benefit of their cameras. From its earliest moments, film was attracted to slapstick comedy, based on physical interaction of people and objects. Watering the Gardener (*Louis Lumière, 1895*).

This greatly reduced history may give a faulty impression. While we know the history of Edison's work, as well as what was happening in France and in other countries where similar inventions were occurring at the end of

Film and the erotic are linked in some of the earliest images we have. The Kiss *(Thomas Edison, 1896).*

the nineteenth century, it grows increasingly difficult to develop a coherent history of film's very rapid early development after this point. It is especially hard to say who was the "first" to do anything for the simple reason that approximately three-quarters of all films made during the silent era are lost. But the Lumière brothers, Méliès, and the Edison factory do provide us with models for certain lines of development in film, lines by no means straight or uncomplicated. What they developed leads to a notion—a theory, actually—that three fundamental conventions of filmmaking emerged from their work. From the work of the Edison factory came both the Hollywood studio system, with its division of labor, and the Hollywood narrative style, based on character and action. The Lumières pointed the direction to the documentary, to film's power to record events that would occur anyway, even if the camera were not present. From Georges Méliès' magic trick films came the cinema of fantasy, of science fiction and the wondrous voyage, which would, of course, become an important part of Hollywood filmmaking.

Another French filmmaker, Jean-Luc Godard, who, throughout his career as critic and director from the 1950s to the present, has been interrogating the nature of the film and television image, came to a different conclusion. He suggested (through a character in his 1967 film, *La Chinoise*) that the Lumière brothers, those presumed documentarians, and makers of *actualités*—events filmed as they were happening, which *would* be happening even if the camera weren't there—were not necessarily the originators of the documentary. From the prospect of a century, Godard suggested that what the Lumières really made constitutes our fantasy images of what Paris looked like in the late nineteenth century. Their images constitute the imaginary—the shared image fantasy—of the way things were, through the images of film. Méliès, on the other hand, seems to be the documentarian of the fantasies of late nineteenth century, middle-class France.

This is a neat turning of things on their heads. More than an intellectual puzzle, Godard's proposition gets to the root of the question of the image. Just because the Lumière brothers turned their cameras on events in the street does not make them recorders of things as they were. Indeed, we know that they set up many of their shots in advance. Because Méliès made trick shots in his studio does not make him a mere fantasist. Each was involved in different kinds of early cinematic mediation, of putting on the screen images that were not about reality but about different ways of constructing reality cinematically, different ways of seeing and interpreting the world. The same is true of the work of the Edison factory. Though always working toward the commercial exploitation of his inventions, Edison made moving images that moved people's imaginations. His work prefigures the Hollywood paradox in which commodities are manufactured for profit while at the same time demonstrating the imagination's ability to fashion images that are eloquent and moving.

Ultimately, cinema did not evolve simply into two or three separate paths, but into various branches, growing out of basic impulses, almost never pure, to see, manipulate, and represent the world in images. Whatever the origin of the moving image, whether it is a recording of what is already there in the world or made up in the studio, imagination, culture, ideology, and economics intervene. They mediate and form what we finally see on the screen; we, as viewers, mediate in turn, interpreting the images to make them meaningful to us.

THE ECONOMICS OF THE IMAGE

As cinema developed, the impulses of the Lumières, Méliès, and Edison were joined in intriguing ways. From the Edison factory came the economic impulse, the urge to treat the image as commodity, to own it, rent it, sell it, profit from it. From the Lumière brothers came the urge to reveal, to present an image of what appears to be the world as it is, but always turns out to be the world as it is seen in a particular way on film. They also sold and profited from their images. From Méliès came a sense of the image as the space of fantasy; he also developed a concept and methods of image fabrication that finally came to form the basis of American film production, part of its economy of manufacture. Méliès also sold his images and profited from them.

The work of Méliès was about control, crafting every element of the image, putting it together, element by element, for specific effect. Whereas Auguste and Louis Lumière allowed a certain serendipity to occur when they exposed motion picture film to the outside world, Méliès arranged and accounted for every element in the shot. Working in the studio, using stop action (shutting off the camera, removing or putting something in the scene, then starting the camera, so the person or object seemed to pop into or out of view), working with miniatures, painted backdrops, and then hand-coloring the film, he and his factory allowed nothing to occur by chance and little of the outside world to intrude. Even though legend has it that the first stop-action event in a Méliès film occurred by accident, in fact the elements of his image making were calculated,

The triumph of artifice. Human figures (on the right) are combined with drawings. A Trip to the Moon *(Georges Méliès, 1902).*

created and circulated by the filmmaker and seen by the viewer in a closed accounting system in which nothing appeared by chance. This was to prove to be the future of the Hollywood system of image making, where "reality" is a product manufactured in the studio, and economy means not only the calculation of profit and loss, but the entire circulation of imagination, production, distribution, and exhibition, each calculated to create the maximum return of emotion and grosses at the box office.

The System Develops: Buster Keaton and Charlie Chaplin

INTRODUCTION Before the studio system, filmmakers experimented with different attitudes toward the external world and the economics of the image. Many filmed outdoors, where light was available and backgrounds were ready-made. Much of the pleasure of watching the films of the silent comedian, Buster Keaton, for example, comes from seeing images go by of the world of early twentieth-century America. This world is not foregrounded. Keaton's images are not documentary, not about chance, but rather about his body in flight, running, falling, endangered, engineered into precarious situations. One of the great moments in silent film comedy comes in Keaton's *Steamboat Bill, Jr.* (1928). Keaton stands in the midst of a terrific storm and the facade of a house behind him suddenly falls. It is a full-sized house, or at least the front of one, towering over the still figure of Keaton. When it falls, the sense of his fragility is marked. He will be crushed. But the engineering of the trick is such that the facade of the house falls straight over him so that the cut-out of the window in the middle of the top floor neatly falls around his body. He stands stock-still without a flinch, and then he runs away.

MISE-EN-SCÈNE The essential physicality in this stunt is unthinkable in any other medium. It is a trick of space, of two-dimensionality, of weight, structure, and the body, of the figure in a landscape. Manipulated, used, and also *there*, figure and landscape are part of the mise-en-scène of a film by Keaton or any great physical comedian, including the much maligned Jerry Lewis. Mise-en-scène, an element of any good film, comic or not, refers to the way space is organized and perceived in a film, including the way figure and background are composed. Mise-en-scène also includes lighting and movement, the use of black and white or color, the distance between camera and figure—everything that happens within the frame, including the frame itself. In almost any Keaton film we see Buster and the streets, curbs, houses, cars, and people around him. Space is used generously, and Keaton himself becomes one of the many elements that occur within that space. At any time, any one of these elements may be called upon to become a prop for a gag or a stunt. As in the case of the house facade in *Steamboat Bill, Jr.*, parts of the world may be built specifically for the gag. But even the apparently spontaneous appearance of people and streets in a Keaton filmed are part of its preconceived presence, its mise-en-scène. Our response to Keaton's images are—

Keaton loved to place himself within the physical world, allowing the camera to observe the body caught and triumphing. The General (Buster Keaton and Clyde Bruckman, 1926).

The subject of his own mise-en-scène, Chaplin understood that viewers were interested in seeing him; and he obliged. Modern Times (Charles Chaplin, 1936).

as Jean-Luc Godard said of the Lumières—the response of our fantasy of what the world might have looked like. Even in Keaton, though we do not see the world itself. We see its image. Its memory. And, even when the house falls on him, we are in the presence of a visual trick: we are set up, surprised, and delighted.

Keaton's great rival in silent comedy, Charlie Chaplin, worked somewhat closer to the Méliès method of studio shooting. Chaplin had less use for the outside world than Keaton did. He worked almost exclusively in the studio and reduced the mise-en-scène to himself. The main signifying element in a Chaplin film is Chaplin. He might indeed engineer a complex gag, as when he gets caught in the gears of an elaborate machine in *Modern Times*. (*Modern Times* is a post–silent film made in 1936, but Chaplin doesn't talk.) Constructed in the studio, the process of the gag highlights Chaplin and his combat with the guts of the machine rather than the mad confluence of physical structure and the body as in Keaton and the falling house.

Foregrounding his own persona, making that persona, the Tramp, a representation of character, attitude, and sentiment, a figure onto which the viewer could overlay his or her own desires, vulnerabilities, and feelings of social or economic inadequacy, Chaplin could demand that focus be kept on his body. Here he was quite unlike either the Lumière brothers or Méliès and closer, perhaps, to the tradition of Edison. The latter foregrounded characters and faces in his early films, Méliès and Lumière worked with a larger mise-en-scène in which human figures were often only one element of many. For them, the moving image represented intersections between subject, foreground, and background. For Méliès, those intersections were crafted together in the studio, parts of them literally by hand, whereas Chaplin's studio work uses little of the potential sleight of hand offered by the camera, by paintings, and by trick shots. His was the cinema of personality, of the star.

From the Individual to the Studio

The different styles of Keaton and Chaplin represent, in a sense, the next level in the culture of the image, in the processes of cinematic representation and the transition from film as craft to film as commodity. Their work also puts another turn on our investigation of the reality of the image. As comedians, the images they made and the stories they told exaggerated the world and the place of the human figure in it. Though their styles were quite different, both filmmakers indulged in the comic movements of falls and chases, pursuits and being hit by blunt instruments. Keaton saw his cinematic world as a place for combat between his body and the physical things of the world. Chaplin saw it as a site of sentimental triumph, of the cleverness of the "little guy," conquering odds and winning the heart of a simple woman. Image making for him provided the vehicle to carry his character of the Tramp through misadventures to redemption and the triumph over class; from despair to a measure of self-possession. He wanted all this to take place in a world whose presence was immediate and apparently unmediated. He wanted his audience's hearts. That is why he made his images as neutral as possible. Keaton was entranced by the reality of the image itself and the ways it could suggest other realities still. Chaplin was entranced with the representation of his own image conquering odds.

Again the parallels with Méliès are interesting. Like Méliès, Keaton understood how he could manipulate the components of the shot to best effect. Keaton liked to make the artificiality of the image part of the joke of his films. In *The Playhouse* (1921), Keaton plays with multiple exposure, performing an entire vaudeville act by himself, with himself as every member of the audience. In *Sherlock, Jr.* (1924), Keaton is a movie projectionist, who dreams himself into the screen, into the image, and is overcome by its conjuries. Scenes change; the weather changes; the flow of images confuses him and causes him to take pratfalls.

This sequence in *Sherlock, Jr.* is among the great statements and admissions of how artificial the film image actually is. Keaton, in all his films, is either doing or being undone by things that happen around him. Objects and people in the image conspire; Buster flees and then cleverly gets the better of them. In *Sherlock, Jr.*, he is conspired against by the very medium in which he works. The image itself turns against him. Chaplin, however, appears as the master of the image and intends to subdue it to his comic persona. Together, Chaplin and Keaton reflect what is happening as filmmaking grows to industrial proportions and, in the course of that growth, reconciles or fudges the boundaries between illusion, realism, presence, audience response, and corporate need. Both very independent filmmakers, their styles reflected and incorporated the complex, sometimes contradictory parts of art and commerce that would form filmmaking both in America and abroad. Even their professional careers pointed to the directions filmmaking moved in the twenties.

Late in the twenties, Keaton, who successfully operated his own production company, signed with MGM, already one of the giants among film studios. By doing so, by signing with a studio that developed and promoted the producer system in which the director had only a small role, Keaton lost much of his creative control and creative edge. Earlier, in 1919, Charlie Chaplin, together with two of the biggest stars of the silent period, Douglas Fairbanks and Mary Pickford, and D. W. Griffith, the great film director, formed United Artists, a film finance and distribution company. Keaton did not have Chaplin's foresight to remain in control of his work.

Two of the greatest comic players in silent film went in different directions as movies became a corporate endeavor. Keaton, who was thoughtful about the image and the ways it could represent objects in the world, manipulating them into comic representations of the body under siege, lost out, in effect, to Chaplin, who was thoughtful about his own image, and manipulated his films into a representation of his own ego, which was then extended into larger areas of production via United Artists. But Chaplin proved to be only a momentary victor. United Artists remained an important backer and distributor of films until the early 1980s, though it never reached the ranks of the major studies, such as MGM and Warner Brothers. Chaplin himself matured as an artist, and some of his films of the later thirties and forties were somewhat less sentimental than his earlier work, though no less centered on Chaplin himself as the focusing agent of the image. Because more serious and didactic, they were also not as popular as his earlier work. Because of his left of center politics, and the fact that he never became an American citizen (he was British by birth), Chaplin was denied reentry to the United States in 1952, at the height of America's anti-Communist hysteria. He never made another commercially successful film. Keaton, on the other hand, enjoyed something of a revival in the sixties. He made new films and his old ones were rediscovered. He appeared often on television. Meanwhile, Chaplin maintained a mythic reputation despite his ups and downs as a commercially viable filmmaker and his role as political scapegoat.

Chaplin and Keaton used and were used by the Hollywood system in different ways. Chaplin's privileging of his own star presence, making his figure the sentimental focus of a studio-bound construction in which everything is made in order to foreground the star and his story, became, in fact, the dominant mode in American filmmaking. Becoming part owner—with two other big movie stars and a pioneering director—of a studio, Chaplin further helped the studio system to come into dominance. Keaton's individual talent was swallowed by the studio system. The image that represented the world outside was subdued to the image of the world made within the studio's confines. The image made in the studio became, in turn, subdued to the attractiveness of story, star, and, always, economics. Mediated by story and star, and by the viewer's willingness to see what the story asked her to see, the image became "realistic." That is, it became transparent, invisible. It became the classical Hollywood style.

THE MAKING OF THE CLASSICAL HOLLYWOOD STYLE

Fabricating the Image

Let's first repeat and then elaborate some basic principles. What you see when you look at a movie is not what you actually see. What you are actually seeing on the movie screen is the reflection of a strong beam of light sent through a moving ribbon of plastic. Embedded in this plastic are dark and clear areas formed by the chemical residue of a previous exposure to light. These make up the images. The screen reflects the projected images back to you, and you interpret them as objects and figures, still or in motion. This means of projecting and perceiving moving images has not changed much since the late nineteenth century when it was invented. Newer technologies, the ones employed when a film becomes a videotape or laserdisc, are more complicated. The original images have been transformed into analogue electromagnetic waves, which are then recorded onto tape or burned into the grooves of a laserdisc, which are then read and reconverted into electrons. When they bombard the red, green, and yellow phosphors of a television screen, a representation of the original image is created on the reverse side of the tube: an electronic representation of what was originally a representation made from light and chemicals.

Our perception of cinematic narratives is an illusion, made up of fragmentary elements of light and shadow, pieced together and then interpreted as coherent, ongoing wholes. The studios who make the films were pieced together from a number of small moviemaking and movie distributing businesses in the 1910s and 1920s. They created an economy of the visible, an organized, rationalized, commodity-driven form of production that depended upon the manufacture of a film out of various pieces, each one made by different groups of people in the studio hierarchy. The finished product depended upon the audience's willingness to interpret and decode those pieces, reading and responding to the story they told. In order to accomplish the manufacture of up to two films a week during the peak years of studio production, from the late twenties through the early fifties, the studios had to streamline production processes. They followed essential manufacturing processes by dividing up the work. At the top, the studio boss in Hollywood communicated with his financial officers in New York, who, by controlling the money, actually held the reigns of the studio. The studio head in Hollywood settled on the stars and properties (books, plays, scripts) that were handed along to the producers. The producers in turn assigned writers, a director, and other crew to the film. By the time shooting was begun, everyone's role was laid out: shots were sketched on storyboards, sets were built, the script, usually the product of many hands, was largely finished. The work of making the film was and remains largely a process of executing a plan in precise, piecemeal fashion, so determined as to allow as few mistakes, as few time and cost overruns, as possible.

Part of the planning involves creating the images themselves as a staged process. Very often, a shot—which is any length of an unedited, or uncut,

The lyricism of artificiality. Within the studio, filmmakers can pull resources together to create images that suggest more than they show. Here, the idea of a moon and some water, with the camera behind the man's back (in the film, the camera gently tracks behind the man as he walks) have a lyrical and foreboding effect. Sunrise (F. W. Murnau, 1927).

piece of exposed film—is built bit by bit over a course of time, with many different hands contributing to the construction process. In studio film-making, very few of the various elements of a shot—the human figures, the background, foreground, sky, scenery, buildings—need to be present at any one time in its creation. The economics of the image require that the studio break the shot elements into the smallest, most manageable units, just as they break the entire production process down into manageable units. Everything that can be done indoors is. Space is therefore restricted. It's not possible to put up tall buildings in a studio, but it is possible to build the lower part of a building facade and compose the shot so that the character is standing in front of a structure that appears to be large because we are inclined to want to imagine a whole even though we see only a part. If more of the building needs to be in a shot, it can be added in the special effects lab, or painted on glass and put in front of the camera. Swamps are difficult places to shoot in; but a mound of dirt, a pool of water, some vegetation strewn carefully about, combined with careful lighting and composition, will convey the image of swamp. The swamp sequence in the German director F. W. Murnau's American film, *Sunrise* (1927), with a spotlight standing in for the moon, and the camera gracefully moving around the characters on a movie set, remains one of the most lyrical shots in the history of film, despite its utter artificiality.

Going to sea to shoot a film is an expensive and tactically difficult proposition. It is cheaper to send a second unit crew out to shoot some boats in the ocean and then do the rest in the studio. A large tank of water with a skillfully built model boat can substitute for the full-scale event out in the vagaries of the natural world. A set of the captain's deck constructed on hydraulic lifts that rocks back and forth will serve for the dialogue shots in which the characters need to be seen talking. For added realism, the set can be placed in front of a large movie screen with a projector behind it. On the screen, a film of waves and stormy sky shot by the second unit or taken from the studio library of stock shots can be projected while the dialogue scene is being shot. Rear-screen projection is the most common means studios used—and still use—for scenes shot in moving cars. A cut-out model of a car is put in front of the screen, the driver and passenger sit and deliver their dialogue, and the street is projected on the screen behind them. In older studio films, rear-screen projection would sometimes be used to show two people simply walking down a street.

These are relatively straightforward image manipulations. More complicated are the paintings or models or mattes of backgrounds and foregrounds that, well executed and well lit, and integrated with the human figures in the frame, give the illusion of a complex and articulated world. The paintings, the models, and the actors need not be in the same place at the same time, and the painting may have openings cut out for the human figures to be projected into. A process called a "blue screen matte" or "traveling matte" allows the various parts of the shot to be photographed in front of a blue screen. The various shots that will eventually make up one completed shot are projected one after the other through an optical printer, which is simply a projector and camera that can be carefully calibrated. The blue color drops out, resulting in an image of illusory wholeness, even of illusory motion, when the matte shot includes a figure in motion: Superman flying, Bruce Willis falling down an elevator shaft in *Die Hard* (1988), the SAC bomber flying over arctic wastes in *Dr. Strangelove* (1963).

Indeed, we usually think of such highly wrought special effects in relation to action or science fiction films, and we take a special pleasure in seeing the results of "f/x." We enjoy the reality effect of such shots while acknowledging their artificiality. But the fact is that all Hollywood studio films, no matter what their genre, use special effects much of the time.

And it is an old tradition. In 1903, Edwin S. Porter made a short film called *The Great Train Robbery.* An early Western and among the first films in which the story shifts back and forth between narrative sequences, it contains a sequence in a railroad car where the scenery going by outside is actually matted in—taken at another time and then matched with the set of the railroad car either through rear-screen projection or optical printing. The difference between this sequence and a film by Méliès is that the trickery is not supposed to be noticed. It is not meant to be part of the visible appeal of the film. Neither are those shots of people driving in front of movie screens or walking up roads whose surroundings have been painted and matted in long after the actors have gone on to other films.

This railroad car is a set. The image of the outside rushing by is created possibly by projecting the image on a screen just behind the cutout of the door in the railroad car. The Great Train Robbery (*Edwin S. Porter, 1903*).

Are there shots in films in which everything we see was present when the shot was made? Certainly. This is part of the appeal of documentary films, for example, in which the camera observes, with a minimum of intrusion, a sequence of events that might have occurred had the camera not been

The gangster on the street. In Stanley Kubrick's The Killing *(1955), Johnny Clay gets a suitcase to pack the stolen cash. The move to on-location shooting in the fifties marked an important break with the studio tradition. Many independent filmmakers, like Kubrick, working on a small budget, took their cameras outside, away from the studios. The visual texture of the mise-en-scène began to change.*

Shot on location in Calcutta. Satyajit Ray's The World of Apu *(1959) is the last of a trilogy of films (including* Pather Panchali, *1955, and* Aparajito, *1956) in which a culture is explored by seeing characters in their landscape.*

there. The documentarist looks for or tries to recreate a whole, ongoing event. The post–World War II Italian neorealist movement, which we will discuss in some detail later on, was based on making films in the street, observing people in their surroundings with an immediacy that was powerful and sometimes shocking. Hollywood took immediate notice. In the late forties and early fifties, American films used some exterior, on-location shooting, especially in low-budget gangster films. American theatrical films in the sixties and seventies, responding to yet another European innovation, the films of the French New Wave, tended to move away from the synthetic image, at least for a while. Sequences in cars were actually shot in cars moving along the street. Crews spent more time at locations, with actors and their surroundings present within the shot as the shot was taken. Historically, in European cinema, there has been as much dependence on constructing an image from component parts as there is in American filmmaking. But abroad and at home, there have been and continue to be individual filmmakers willing to go outside the studio and shoot in the world. When that happens, in the streets and countryside of Calcutta in Satyajit Ray's Apu trilogy (*Pather Panchali*, 1955, *Aparajito*, 1956, *The World of Apu*, 1959) or the streets of New York in so many American gangster films of the 1950s, the image and our relationship to it changes. The closed and secure world generated by the studio opens into a more detailed, textured, less manageable image of the world outside.

In Hollywood today, the artificial construction of the image has made a major comeback. All the old practices of rear-screen projection, matte work, and other forms of image manufacture are now being done by computer. Through digital manipulation, the image is put together bit by bit. Characters

are placed in the middle of crowds, the members of which are digitally dupli-
cated, or on mountaintops, or in outer space. Dinosaurs are graphically rendered and made to leap across a plain as humans look at them; a gigantic
spaceship hovers over New York; a huge ocean liner hits an iceberg and sinks;
incredible acts of transformation and destruction are possible with no location
necessary other than a computer terminal. Anything and anyone can be placed
anywhere and made to do anything. The same holds true for sound. Digital
sound allows intricate sonic mixes to be made in which every single sound,
from footsteps to the human voice, is built and processed to achieve the best
effect. The purpose of digital image and sound manipulation is the same as
old fashioned optical work: to save the filmmakers money, give them the
greatest amount of control possible, and engineer the viewer into the image
and then beyond it into the story. With the digital, there is a seemingly unlim-
ited possibility to substitute spectacle for substance.

The Whole and Its Parts

The economy of the image is entwined with the economy of perception. We
read the bits and pieces of image and story as if they were whole. The
process extends to all other aspects of the filmmaking process. Film acting,
for example, is built piece by piece. A performance in a film is not a continuous process, but is put together out of many parts. A film is not shot in sequence, nor is a sequence shot completely in one take. To do so would be
time-consuming and a waste of money. Therefore, an actor has to perform in
spurts, in short spasms of emotion, guided by the director and a staff member called the continuity person (or, in older Hollywood parlance, the script
girl), whose job it is to keep tabs on everything from the position of a neck-
tie, to a half-completed gesture, to a facial expression that must be held from
shot to shot.

Any given part of a film can be made at any time. The middle may be shot
first, the third sequence last, the end at the beginning, the next-to-last sequence
just before the middle. (By "sequence," I mean a unit of the story, self-
contained, yet connected to the sequences that proceed or follow it. "Sequence" and "scene" are often used interchangeably. However, a scene is more
of a descriptive unit, something we separate out of the flow of the story.) For
example, if a number of scenes throughout a film take place in the same room,
it is more economical to shoot all of those shots at the same time, rather than
leave the set unused and then return to relight or rebuild it. If a high-priced,
in-demand actor is involved in a film, it is more economical to shoot all the
scenes in which that actor is involved rather than recall the actor to the set
again to shoot a scene that will occur later in the narrative. If a location—that is,
a site, usually out of doors, at a distance from the studio—is involved, all the
scenes that take place at that location will be shot together, no matter where or
when they appear in the film. There is a story about the making of the film
Blow-Up (1966), directed by the Italian filmmaker, Michelangelo Antonioni. He

wished to make his film in chronological order. Two major parts of the film, one early, the other at the end, took place, a day or two apart in the story, in a London park. Actual filming began in spring and concluded in the fall. When director and crew returned to the park for the last sequence, the leaves had changed color. They had to spray them green to re-create the earlier effect. An American filmmaker would have shot all the sequences in the park at one time and worked out the temporal arrangements during the editing process. Quite possibly, the American filmmaker would have had a tree and some grass put up in the studio, matting in the rest of the environment in the effects lab or, these days, on a computer.

Making the Parts Invisible

With relatively few and important exceptions, films from all over the world are constructed on a principle of radical self-effacement—of rendering their form invisible and causing as little trouble as possible to the filmmakers in the creative and manufacturing process and the viewers during the process of reception. The reception process is made possible through a set of conventions and assumptions by means of which the viewer will accept the illusion of transparency and see the film as an ongoing whole, a story played out in front of her eyes. Form and structure, the artifice of the image, the fragmentary nature of screen acting will all melt away and come together in apparent wholeness.

This effect is not unique to movies. Recall our discussion of perspective. Although perspective is based on carefully calculated mathematical structures, the result of perspective in painting was to naturalize the image, to give the illusion of three dimensions on a two-dimensional surface and, by so doing, provide a window through which the viewer's gaze could own the contents of the image. Painting presented "content," represented things in the outside world, until late in the nineteenth century. When photography and film took over this job, painting began to represent its own form, to speak about surface, color, form, and texture. When it did, it created obstacles. Looking at abstract art, people keep wanting to know "what is it trying to show."

Music depends upon its ability to link itself effortlessly to emotional response. Few people understand the mathematical complexities of harmony and counterpoint, what a hemidemisemiquaver is, or can explain the sonata form. In the early twentieth century, a group of composers rebelled against the transparency of musical form and wrote atonal music based on the mathematical principles of the twelve-tone scale. They sought less a pathway to emotion than an expression of musical form. Their work demanded knowledge of how music works and attention to something other than the emotions of the sounds. This music was not very easy to listen to or very popular.

Prose writing also has an invisible form. While we read, we rarely pay attention to the structure of language in prose fiction and instead concentrate on what the writer is saying and what his characters are doing, which correlates with our desire to see what the painting is about or feel the emotions of the music. Those writers who concentrate on form, who foreground the structure of their prose and how it makes meaning—Henry James, James Joyce, Samuel Beckett, Jorge Luis Borges, Toni Morrison—become the focus of academic study. In ordinary reading, though, the greatest compliment we can give to a book is that it is a "page turner." The phrase implies the reader moves past page, prose, form, and style into the movement of story and character.

There is no equivalent phrase for film, probably because there are so relatively few films that are *not* the equivalent of "page turners" and because, while we are watching, the "pages," the images, are turned for us. The assumption is that the structure and style of any film will be invisible, allowing the viewer to enter and move into the story and the emotions of the characters. The point is for us to be carried away by plot and the motivations of the characters. Image structure and editing, the way the story is put together, are subservient to the story and the characters' lives.

Ideology at Work

It is important to note that ideology is at work here. We have agreed, across our culture and, increasingly, across the world, on what film is supposed to be and not supposed to be. We have agreed that film is story: no work should be involved in getting access to that story, and no conscious process of reading and interpreting that story should be required. Film should give all and demand little. It should not—we mentioned earlier—be serious, demanding, or "deep." There are many levels of assumptions here, and they need to be unpacked.

As we have said, the work of imagination, no matter what its face—painting, music, novel, or film—is not a simple mirror image of reality, pure emotion, or pure story. Imagination requires mediation, of color and shape, of sound (carefully, even mathematically determined, in the case of music), of words, of moving images. In all cases content—story, characters, emotions—is never simply there, waiting for us to see it. Content is generated by the form and structure of the imagination's work and is specific to the kind of work being done. The form and structure of painting are different from that of novel writing or filmmaking. In all cases, some kind of interpretive work is involved on the part of the viewer or listener. On some level, reading is involved, reading in its most general sense of engaging the form of a work, comprehending it, interpreting it, comparing it with other, similar examples of its kind, contextualizing it, in short, making sense of it. Sense is not a given. It must be made.

Making sense out of film is not automatic. We have to learn how to read narrative images, a job that is easily and quickly accomplished at an early age. Around the turn of the century, early filmmakers had to begin learning how to make images legible, how to structure them so that they would be easy to read and the stories they told immediately comprehensible. "Learning," however, is not quite precise, because early filmmakers did not have a body of knowledge to absorb. "Intuiting" is a better word, because these filmmakers were really guessing, in a haphazard manner, how image and narrative structure would work best. By the late 1910s, their guesswork was largely done. They accomplished a task they did not even know they were beginning: the creation of a universal, legible structure of image, movement, and narrative that would dissolve into pure story in front of its viewers. The components of that structure have not changed very much. They are routine and repeated in film after film. As with any routine, the more we do it, the less we are aware of it, and the more automatic our responses to it become. When we watch a film, we are part of a great process of assent to its presence and wholeness, even though it is absent and made up of fragments. The assent is an ideological event: what we want to see, what we are asked to see, takes precedence over the "reality" of what we are actually seeing.

There is a kind of logical passage in the history of filmmaking and film viewing, intuitively reached and driven by the need to create images and stories that people would literally buy. Under the ideological banner of pleasure without toil, of leisure activity that demands only a positive emotional response, filmmakers and filmgoers are joined in the process of making images and stories that are immediately understood and enjoyed, so immediately that they appear *there,* ready-made and unique, even though they are not there and are made with a great deal of artifice, put together in bits and pieces, and so far from unique that they have been repeating themselves, form and content, for over a century.

Form and Content

We should try, then, to bring the form and structure of film, its means of production, construction, and comprehension, back into consciousness and make them visible. To start, let's redefine the word "story" that we've been using to describe what we see and respond to in a film. Story is what the film tells us, the process of events the characters go through and enact. Plot is the abstract scheme of that story, what we summarize after we've seen the film; what film reviewers on TV and in newspapers give us. Narrative is the actual telling of the story, the way the story is put together, formed and articulated.

Narrative is the story's structure. If someone asks me about Steven Spielberg's *Jaws* (1975), I might give them some plot: a great white shark terrorizes a beach town, kills people, and is finally hunted down by three men in a boat. I could elaborate that into something closer to the story, although it would be more description than story, and in any case would be *my* story, derived from the film, because I am giving it narrative structure: Sheriff Brody is pulled from a peaceful, domestic life by the intrusion of the terrible creature into the town he has been hired to protect. The shark attacks people, but the elders of the town want it kept quiet so as not to ruin holiday tourist business. There is tension between Brody and the elders, and also uncertainty. Brody has been hired to do the bidding of the town, but he has a moral responsibility to protect the innocent. And so forth.

On the level of plot, Brody is looking out for the shark. But the structure of this sequence does more than tell us that: it draws our gaze to the character's and, by alternately looking at him and assuming his own point of view, creates expectation and excitement— especially when that point of view is blocked. Jaws (Steven Spielberg, 1975).

I could also elaborate this way: the presence of the shark is indicated by music—low, almost staccato chords played on bass fiddles, a mirror of the high staccato strings used in *Psycho*. When the shark is ready to attack, the film allows us to look as if through the shark's eyes, moving in the water toward its prey. Suspense is further created by playing with the gaze of Sheriff Brody on the beach. He looks and looks at the water. People move in front of him, and he has to bend and rise to see. There are false alarms, and our tension keeps rising. The intercutting of shot/reverse shot from Brody to what he sees reaches a climax when Brody finally does see something in the water. At this point, Spielberg uses a device that Alfred Hitchcock developed. By combining two movements of the camera—a tracking shot in one direction and a zoom in the opposite—he shows Brody as if space were collapsing around him, thereby heightening our awareness of some exciting and terrifying event.

In this brief analysis, I began by recounting plot and then moved from plot to structure, that is, from content to form, describing some of the ways the narrative is put together to tell us its story. This analysis also puts the structure into a context by revealing that Spielberg didn't invent everything, but borrowed and developed some stylistic devices from another filmmaker. The point is that all aspects of a film are based on formal, structural principles, and meaning is always communicated by structure. Meaning does not exist without a form to communicate it. We never simply "know" something, or see something, or are told something. When we respond emotionally to a film, there is always a formal structure driving that response.

THE SHOT

Film form can be reduced to two basic elements, each of which can be used in a great variety of ways. They are the shot and the cut. A shot is any unbroken, unedited length of film. That length can be the entire magazine of film in a 35mm camera (20 minutes or more), or the length of tape in a videocamera. A shot can also be brought into existence in the editing room when an otherwise unedited length of film has some unwanted material trimmed from either end. In its purest form, a shot may not have anything cut or edited into it. If it does, it becomes two shots, one shot broken by another that has been spliced into it. The shot is determined by its physical existence as an unbroken entity—or its appearance as such.

As we know, nothing is what it appears in a film. At the end of the infamous shower sequence in Alfred Hitchcock's *Psycho* (1960), Marion Crane's lifeless body is slumped over the side of the bathtub. The camera moves from a close-up of her eye, past the bathroom door, to the adjoining bedroom, resting on her pocket book on the night table, where she had put the stolen money she planned to return the following day. The movement is deeply ironic, for Marion's dead eye sees nothing, and we are left with the emptiness of her murder and its disconnection from the robbery she committed. The movement from eye to purse seems to be one shot. However, close examination reveals a trick. As the camera passes by the bathroom door there is a very quick dissolve (a dissolve occurs when the end of one shot fades out as the beginning of another fades in). What apparently looks like one shot is actually two.

LONG TAKE The first sequence in which the reporter, Thompson, goes to visit Susan Alexander in Orson Welles's *Citizen Kane* (1941) begins with a dramatic boom shot, in which the camera arcs over the roof of the nightclub where Susan is performing. (A boom shot occurs when the camera moves on a crane and covers a great amount of space.) A storm rages, the camera moves through the nightclub's rooftop neon sign, heads down and through the skylight into the room where Susan sits at a table. The effect is powerful, but it's a big illusion. The rooftop is a model. If you look closely at the sequence on a laserdisc, this becomes apparent, and you can even make out the separation in the construction of the model of the neon sign, which would have been pulled away by technicians as the camera approached. Obviously it would have been impossible (or impractical) to send that camera through a skylight on an actual roof. As Hitchcock does in *Psycho*, Welles uses a dissolve, here hidden by flashing lightning and the sound of thunder and pelting rain, to connect two shots. The first part begins on the model rooftop; the second starts at the top of the studio set and booms down to the characters below. These shots create the illusion of one continuous shot.

In film, an illusion of an unbroken length of film is as good as the real thing, and the shot remains cinema's unit of internal continuity. It allows film to represent space and time as connected and ongoing: it composes space and either guides the viewer's eye within its space or offers a reflective, meditative gaze at that space. What happens in a shot can be as simple as the camera gazing at a character or as complex as a movement in which the camera follows a character across a long and articulated space. In Welles's *The Magnificent Ambersons* (1942), the camera watches for many minutes as a character standing in a darkly lit, turn-of-the-century kitchen falls into hysteria while talking about the decline of her family and her home. The intensity of the sequence grows from the camera's unflinching gaze and the power of the actress's performance. This is a rare moment in film in which a performance—in the usual sense of an ongoing and developing process—is allowed to develop on its own, and Welles's unwillingness to give us any other view, to cut into or away from the action, gives us no option but to watch it unfold. In *Weekend* (1968), Jean-Luc Godard creates an intricate, long, circular track and pan of a farmyard, to the accompaniment of a Mozart sonata. (When the camera tracks, it moves on its base, linearly or diagonally through the scene; when it pans, it pivots on its base from side to side or up and down). Godard moves around the circle, one way and then the other, four and a half times; people move in and out of the shot; we see the piano player, who is playing the concert in the farmyard itself; people listen and move on; a man walks past. The result of this complicated shot is to provide a kind of visual analogue to the form of the music. Martin Scorsese creates a four-minute tracking shot in *Goodfellas* (1990), during which the camera follows the main character and his fiancée as they walk from the street into a nightclub, down the steps, through an enormous and busy kitchen, onto the main floor, over to a table, which is set up for them as they approach, and sit down and talk as a comedian begins his act on stage. The shot is an extreme expression of cinematic energy; an affirmation of the camera's ability to create and traverse space and time.

THE CUT

CONTINUITY Editing also addresses time and space, by building the temporal structure of a film and breaking apart and reordering its spatial construction. The formal expression of editing is the cut, a literal severing of the shot. If a shot is an actual or apparent unbroken length of film, editing is what breaks it. But editing joins together as well as cuts apart. Through editing, filmmakers build the structure of a movie by arranging its shots. At its simplest, editing is what is done to a shot. Editing is cutting; but *an* edit usually refers to the joining together of two shots. There are a number of editing styles, the most dominant of which is the classic continuity style of American filmmaking—a major component of the classical style—the main purpose of which is to link shots in such a way that the act of linking vanishes and the illusion of coherence and unity is foregrounded.

A reasonable question would be, why edit at all? Why not just create the sequences of film each in one shot, so the unity of time and space would be maintained without having to trick perception into believing that parts are wholes? The answer to the question lies deep within the culture of Hollywood studio filmmaking and speaks to the development of the classical style. Very early in film history, at the time of Edison, the Lumière brothers, and Georges Méliès, and lasting until just after the turn of the twentieth century, films were short and usually made in one or a few shots. There was not much camera movement, and the space defined by the composition of the shot was frontal and static. People have theorized that this frontal, static gaze was an attempt to represent the view of a stage from the point of view of the auditorium, a perspective most early filmgoers would have understood and found comforting. Over the course of a relatively few years, as spectators became more comfortable with the spatial arrangement of the shot and the composition of the image, filmmakers began experimenting with the construction of story—the narrative—of films. The single shot seemed not to provide enough flexibility.

The Development of Continuity Cutting

Imagine this problem: A film calls for two events to happen simultaneously. A woman is held captive by a man of evil intent. Her fiancé knows where she is and is coming to rescue her. How can this information be structured for maximum effect? One method might be to show each action in a single shot, each complete in itself, one after the other. This method would extend the single-shot construction that was the mainstay of early cinema, but it would not provide temporal control. In other words, the action of the story would be at the mercy of the linearity of the shots, not the rhythm of the action: the heroine is held captive; the hero rides to her rescue; the hero arrives and saves the heroine.

The successful solution of the problem created an illusion of simultaneity by editing the sequences together so that a shot of the woman in captivity and a shot of the fiancé coming to her rescue were intercut in an alternating sequence. Intercutting two sequences, often called parallel editing or cross cutting, provides a means to integrate story parts with finesse and flexibility. Early filmmakers discovered that suspense could be created by changing the lengths of these alternating shots, perhaps shortening them as the hero approached the captive heroine. Audiences accepted this structure with ease, and it became one of the foundations of the classical American style.

Edwin S. Porter's *The Great Train Robbery,* made in 1903, is an early example of a film that intercuts sequences, and it pointed the way to great flexibility in narrative construction. For a short time in the early part of the twentieth century, the control of this flexibility extended to film exhibitors— the owners of the movie houses! *The Great Train Robbery* includes a famous shot of one of the robbers pointing a gun toward the camera and firing as if at the audience. Exhibitors were at liberty to put this shot at the beginning or at the end of the film.

Other elements of cutting were developed during the period between 1905 and the early 1910s, all of them crucial to the continuity style and to a cinema being created to entice and hold the viewer's gaze. One element was a solution to a seemingly simple problem. A filmmaker might need to get a character up from a chair and out of a room, catching her again from the outside of the room as she passes through the door. With a mobile camera, it would be quite possible, and very dramatic, to do a backward track, dollying the camera (moving it on tracks or another device) away from the person as she gets up and moves through the door. During the early period, however, cameras were not very mobile. Since they needed to be hand-cranked, they couldn't be moved easily, unless apparatus and operator were placed in a moving vehicle, not useful for the closed space of a room. Beyond the physical limitations, there was also, I think, a desire for a rhythmical structure in film that could only be attained by cutting, a rhythm that would keep the viewer's attention through changing shots as opposed to continuous unbroken shots. Narrative rhythm became an important driving force in the development of editing.

Cinema, early and late, is full of shots of people getting up from seated positions, leaving a room, getting into a car, going to their destinations. These are essential narrative transitions. During the pre-1910 period, however, these movements were not always cut together in consistent ways. In an early film, it is quite possible to see a person rising from a chair in the first shot and, in the second, the person rising from the same position she had already occupied before the cut. The effect is seeing the person getting up from the chair twice. This is not incompetence, but rather the sign of a cinematic grammar incompletely standardized, as if one didn't know (or care) that the clause on either side of coordinate should be different and instead said, "She got up out of the chair and she got up out of the chair." There were no conventions of continuity cutting, no rules; they had to be invented and used over and over again before they became conventions. But, as we noted earlier, "invented" is not quite accurate. The individuals who developed the grammar of continuity cutting were not theorists and were certainly not scientific. The process was an intuitive one, and you can see it developing across the period and especially in the short films D. W. Griffith made for the Biograph company between 1908 and 1913. He made almost five hundred of them, a number of which have survived to supply us with a textbook of the emerging classical style.

Griffith and others learned how to match shots, so that the analysis of a single movement—the person getting out of a chair and leaving the room— would appear not to be the fragments of an action that they actually are, but the illusion of one continuous action. Even the hard part, synchronizing the cut of the woman leaving the room to the shot of her exiting the door on the other side, becomes smoothed and timed to achieve the right sense of forward, purposive motion, not only of the character but of her story as well. Coordinates become, in effect, commas. Hiding the cut by editing on a continuous movement, distracting the viewer with something else going on in the frame and, from 1930 on, using dialogue or sound as a cover, became a major function of the continuity style.

Shot/Reverse Shot

CONTINUITY   One element of continuity cutting is, in many ways, its most important, because it establishes a basic structural principle for the way narrative is created in film. This involves the concept of the gaze, the way characters look at one another and the way we look at, and get caught up in, the looks of the characters on screen. We are connected to a filmic story largely through the orchestration of looks, and the prime conductor of the process is the shot/reverse shot. Making the fragments of the editing structure invisible and creating the illusion of an ongoing action depend upon building the gaze of the spectator into the story-telling or narrative space of the film. Our glance is directed, woven, sewn into the visual structure. In fact, critics often use a surgical metaphor, calling the process in which our gaze is stitched into the narrative the "suture effect."

When our gaze is so woven, a two- or three-way pattern is formed in which we, like the viewer of a perspective painting, are given pride of place and the illusion of ownership of the narrative space. Things happen for our eyes, and as our eyes are entangled with the gazes of the characters in the film, we feel a part of events, an element of the narrative. Like every other aspect of continuity cutting, the shot/reverse shot sequence achieves complex results from quite simple means. A character is seen talking or registering a response to something (this is the shot). Cut to the person being spoken to or the person or object that caused the character to respond (the reverse shot).

Near the end of *Psycho,* Lila Crane, the sister of Marion, who was brutally murdered in the shower, goes into Norman's mother's old, dark house to visit with the old lady. From the moment she starts up the stairway leading to the house, Hitchcock constructs the sequence from a series of shot/reverse shots during which we look at Lila as she registers a response of fear or curiosity and then cut to the object of her gaze: the house, a room, a fixture, a bed. Through this construction, Hitchcock so synchronizes our expectations and fears with Lila's that he can play two jokes. The first one is on both the character and on us. Lila enters Mrs. Bates's room and approaches the bureau, her eyes caught by—as the camera zooms in on—a bronze sculpture of two folded, smothering, hands. As she stands by the bureau, her reflection in the mirror is bounced back from another mirror behind the one she is looking at, so that there are actually three Lilas. We look from behind and see Lila's back. In the mirror before her, we see her reflection and, in the second reflection, we see her back. These images occur very quickly, so that before we can actually make out her reflections, she is startled by them, shrieks, turns, and we shriek with her. As she turns, Hitchcock cuts to the mirror behind her, now object of her gaze and ours; she sees that the figure who startled her was her, so do we, and we both relax.

*Using the shot/reverse shot sequence to play
a joke. Lila Crane examines Norman Bates's
room. Her gaze is caught by something.*

*She goes to the bookcase, pulls out a book,
and looks at it. As she is about to turn the
page . . .*

*There is a reaction shot—a shot of her
reacting to what she sees.*

*But, instead of cutting to the point-of-view shot
that would show us what Lila is seeing,
Hitchcock cuts to an action occurring elsewhere
in the motel, where Sam is confronting
Norman. We never get to see what's in the book.
Psycho (Alfred Hitchcock, 1960).*

The joke that's played on us alone occurs when Lila examines Norman's
room. Again, Hitchcock cuts from Lila looking to what Lila sees: Norman's
bed, a stuffed doll, a record of the *Eroica* Symphony on Norman's phonograph. Lila takes a book off the shelf and registers the fact, which we see in the
reverse shot, that it has no title on its spine. She looks at the pages and registers surprise tinged with a bit of horror in the reaction shot that follows. But
Hitchcock refuses a final reverse shot. He does not show us what Lila has just
seen in the book. For a moment, the suture is cut, and we are left on our own.

Dialogue Cutting

The shot/reverse shot convention is such a powerfully established part of the
institution of making and watching cinema that a clever filmmaker can tinker

with it to provoke a specific reaction. But the tinkering is rare enough, especially in Hollywood cinema. Its normalization is what allows filmmakers to work quickly and within budget and us to understand the narrative easily and quickly without our attention's being diverted by the way the narrative is formed. Perhaps the most insistent, unvarying version of the shot/reverse pattern occurs in the presentation of a simple dialogue sequence between two characters.

CONTINUITY This structure has been so common for so many years that if you watch any movie or dramatic or news interview television program, you are guaranteed to see the following: two people begin a conversation with the camera framing them together in a two-shot. This shot will last perhaps ten or twelve seconds. The sequence will then cut to a shot over the shoulder of one of the participants looking at the other. After a very few seconds, the sequence will cut again to a reverse of this, over the shoulder of the second participant, looking at the first. These reverses, each one lasting perhaps three to six seconds, will continue, perhaps punctuated with one-shots, that is shots of one of the participants alone in the frame, for as long as it takes the dialogue to conclude. And it will conclude with the original two-shot of both figures.

Because this cutting pattern is so universal, rather than take an example from a film, I will create an abstract example that can be applied as a template to any movie that you are likely to see. Imagine the following scene: a man walks into a room, sits down across the table from a woman, and starts a conversation. A third person in the room is standing and listening. The editing structure might be as follows. Each entry indicates a shot you might see on the screen:

1. The woman looks up toward the door.
2. Shot of the door opening as man enters.
3. The woman looks up, surprised.
4. The man approaches and sits down at the table.
5. Shot of the third person in the room, who raises his eyebrows.
6. The man and the woman talk in two-shot (both are together in the frame).
7. Cut to an over-the-shoulder shot from the woman to the man.
8. Reverse shot over the shoulder from the man to the woman.
9. Repeat this pattern three times, then return to
10. The two-shot of the two people talking.
11. A shot of the third person smiling.

This core of this sequence might actually have been constructed out of six separate shots. For example, the woman looking toward the door, registering surprise, and then smiling might have been filmed in one shot. The man entering the room, approaching the table, and sitting down might constitute the second. The two-shot of the man and woman talking at the table would make up a third, and the change in camera position from over the shoulder of one of the participants to the other would make up the fourth and fifth shots. All of the onlooker's reactions would be shot together, as would the two-shots of the couple at the table and the over-the-shoulder shots. Although six shots are used to construct the sequence, many more than five would actually have been taken. Each of the shots actually used would be chosen from a number of takes, in which the same setup, dialogue, and action were repeated, over and over, until the director feels she has enough good ones to choose from. (Bear in mind that, traditionally, only one camera is used in filmmaking, so that each wide shot, one-shot, two-shot, or close-up is done separately.) Out of all of these takes, the shots are cut together to create the continuity of the sequence.

Some of these shots may not require all the participants to be present. The shot of the man entering the room might include all three people, as would the initial two-shot of the conversation. But the shot of the woman looking up would not necessarily require the presence of the other two actors, nor would the shot of the onlooker responding to the conversation (especially if these shots were done in medium or full close-up). In the over-the-shoulder shots that make up the dialogue at the table, it may not be necessary to have present the actor over whose shoulder the camera is gazing. If the shot shows only a little bit of one actor's face, a stand-in performer will do. In television interview programs, it is common practice to shoot reaction shots of the interviewer after the person interviewed has left. These are then cut in to give the impression that the interviewer is responding to the answers given by his subject.

In the editing of a sequence, as in the composition of a single shot from different elements, the filmmakers create and we read what we need in order to understand the forward momentum of the story. In our made-up sequence, it is easy to imagine that a look of anticipation from the woman toward the door makes us anticipate something, and our anticipation is fulfilled by the cut to the man entering. The looks from the bystander serve to seal the participants and the viewer into the content of the sequence and create a dramatic context for what is going on. If the bystander smiles warmly, we believe everything is fine; if the bystander sneers or grimaces, we might suspect an evil deed is about to occur.

Sight Lines

Remember that each of the shots for such a dialogue sequence, or any sequence in a film, is made independently and then cut together during the editing process to create the sequence. It is important for the purposes of constructing the sequence, and for maintaining continuity when the sequence is viewed by an audience, that the sight lines maintained by the characters remain constant. The characters must look in the same direction in each shot, for fear of breaking the rhythm of the viewer's own gaze at the scene. This is called an eye-line match, and it is another constituent of the continuity style. If a character is looking to the left in one shot, that eye line must be maintained in the succeeding shots, and the other character must be continually looking to the right. What's more, as the cutting moves our gaze from one character to the other, the position of the camera must remain along the same plane in

CONTINUITY

front of the characters. This is the critical and, like everything else in this process, absolutely arbitrary 180-degree rule. At no point in the dialogue sequence, or in any other sequence in any film that chooses to follow the rules, is the camera allowed to cross a 180-degree line imagined to stretch from left to right across the scene. You can visualize this by imagining that you can look straight down at a scene of two people and see a line drawn directly behind, or even through, them. The camera may be placed at any point on one side of that line, never behind it (and never exactly 90 degrees in front of it because the space would appear too two dimensional). Such rules came into being out of fear that, if the characters were looking in different directions from shot to shot, if the camera moved to the other side of the 180-degree line, or was positioned at a direct 90 degrees to the figures, audiences would be confused and the artificial structure of cinematic space would be revealed.

Arbitrary Conventions

There are a number of extraordinary things about these structures and their rules, not the least of which is that they began *before* the coming of sound. The standard, over-the-shoulder dialogue cutting pattern was not created to accommodate the sound of two people talking, but simply *to show* two people talking. This method of presenting dialogue, along with the more generally applied 180- and 90-degree rules, is arbitrarily unique to cinema, and later to television. No other dramatic, visual, or narrative form uses these conventions (although they have been modified for use in comic strips), nor does anything like them exist in ordinary experience. They have lasted almost one hundred years and are ubiquitous, so much so that the first thing a filmmaker usually does when he wishes to explore alternatives to the Hollywood continuity style is refuse to do over-the-shoulder shots or obey the 180- and 90-degree rules. As we saw in the example from *Psycho,* an innovative director may exploit them and make them yield different responses. Most filmmakers do them by rote. As viewers, we are so acculturated to these compositional and cutting techniques, we don't know they are happening—which is exactly the point. To film a dialogue sequence is to create an over-the-shoulder cutting pattern. Therefore, to watch a dialogue sequence is to watch the over-the-shoulder, shot/reverse shot cutting pattern. We take it as a given and, essentially, don't notice it—we see right through it. More precisely, we don't respond to the cutting except to move within its secure and comforting pattern, imagining ourselves between the glances of the participants on screen.

Continuity cutting is an industrial standard, like a driver and passenger side door on a car, like the exact tolerances that enable a screw and bolt to fit together. Like any standard, it creates functionality and universality and becomes the means that permit filmmaker and audience to ignore the details of structure while they go about the work of communicating emotions and advancing a story. From the principles of continuity cutting narrative is generated and a story is told. The key element is that the story is told with the least interference from the structure that creates it. Creative energies and viewer comprehension need not be absorbed with formal complexity because the form—as complex as it is—is so conventionalized that viewers look through it, as if observing a story unfolding on its own.

The Hollywood Economical Style

The classical Hollywood continuity style is incredibly economical. Since every filmmaker must know how to shoot a dialogue sequence, or a suspense sequence, or a sequence in which a woman looks at a man and knows she's in love, the setups (lighting, camera position, marks where the actors need to be) are relatively easy to make. The facial gestures and where they will fit in the finished sequence are determined by a thousand such sequences made in other films. Fragmenting a sequence into many different shots makes it possible, as we've seen, not to have all the actors present at the same time, or the entire set built at once. If an intense confrontation between a good guy and a bad guy in a warehouse calls for individual shots (one-shots) of each character threatening the other, only the character in the particular shot need be present. Someone out of camera range (usually the person responsible for keeping track of the continuity from one shot to another) can read the lines of the good guy while a shot is made of the bad guy yelling threats and brandishing his gun. The two parts of the sequence can be cut together in the editing room. Coverage, shooting the sequence from different angles and making numerous takes of those angles, assures that the film can be put together to the producer's liking, in line with conventional cutting procedures in the inexpensive confines of the editing suite. As long as attention was paid to where the eyes of each of the antagonists were looking, as long as the lighting was consistent and nothing changed in the background—a clock, for example, which must not be permitted to indicate the passage of shooting time, but only the passage of narrative time—the editor can match movement, dialogue, and sound so that the intercutting between the two characters will be subordinated to what they are saying.

The economy of the continuity style operates on the side of reception as well as production. As viewers, we have been so acculturated to the style's nuances, that a mere exchange of glances, edited across the gaze of two characters, can tell us volumes. Suspense and horror films, for example, depend absolutely on a character's look of surprise or fright that prepares us to expect to see the object of this agitated gaze. That object can be shown in the following shot or a few shots later. But shown it must be to close the circulation of the look, the expectation, and to satisfy that expectation.

Part of the satisfaction is gender based. Gender-specific stereotypes of the strong man saving the weak and passive woman informed the early development of cross cutting—the editing of captivity/rescue sequences by intercutting shots of the woman in peril with shots of her approaching rescuer. In gen-

eral, the structure of the gaze in film is really the structure of the male character and of the male viewer, gazing at the female character who is built into the
narrative as the object of desire. The exchange of looks in film is very often
erotic, and so the structure of the gaze drives the narrative, drives our emotions, and propels the characters across the cutting and into each other's arms.
Form dictates content, and sexual desire dictates both.

Directed by the looks of the characters, and, on a higher level, by the structure of looks and cuts that are used uniformly over all of cinema, the viewer
need be shown and told quite little. Events, responses, emotions, narrative
movements become coded. Having seen films and television, we know how to
read the structure. Like a computer code, it runs our responses and, within
given limits, can be assigned variables. So, it would be absurd to say that *all*
films are alike, that they all communicate the same meanings and garner from
us exactly the same response. But the ways they order our responses, code
them, and communicate them is indeed quite uniform—so much so that radical variations from the established patterns become visible to us and are accepted or rejected to the extent that they disturb us with their visibility.

DEPARTURES FROM THE CLASSICAL HOLLYWOOD STYLE

Viewers and reviewers remarked how director Quentin Tarantino played with
narrative chronology in his 1994 film *Pulp Fiction.* Chronology is an important
aspect of the classical style, and it has not advanced very far from Aristotle's
classic notion that dramatic narrative construction should consist of a beginning, middle, and end. (Jean-Luc Godard once commented that Aristotle was
quite right, narrative should have a beginning, middle, and end, but not necessarily in that order.) A film narrative must proceed along a recognizable path of
development and must come to closure. Any dissonance, any disruption to the
lives of the characters generated at the beginning and worsened toward the
middle, must be resolved by film's end. *Pulp Fiction* seems to disrupt this
movement. The end of the very first sequence of the film, in which the two
gunmen are caught in the middle of a holdup in a diner, takes place at the end
of the film. In the middle of the film, one of the gunmen, John Travolta's Vincent, is shot to death, coming out of a toilet—meaningless, violent death being
a main narrative anchor of Tarrentino's movies. There he is, alive again, at the
end of the film in a sequence the beginning of which we have already seen.

The structure is less radical than jokey, and actually helps Tarantino tie up
his film and leave audience members less queasy than they might have been.
It gives Vincent a reprise, while also sending him back to the toilet in an attempt at ironic counterpoint to the event that occurred earlier and to further
emphasize the anal references throughout the film. It also offers a mock redemption to Samuel L. Jackson's Jules, who decides to leave his life of crime
and take up religious work. The minor break in narrative continuity is amusing, only provocative enough to make an audience curious. More serious

efforts are found in the work of other filmmakers, most often from outside the United States, where experiments began early and still continue. There is, for example, a British film called *Betrayal* (David Jones, 1983), written by the playwright Harold Pinter, whose narrative runs backwards, starting at the end and ending at the beginning. An episode of *Seinfeld* parodied this narrative trick. In *Last Year at Marienbad* (1961), by the French director Alain Resnais, normal continuity cutting is made non-continuous, and the entire convention of linear chronology in film narrative is called into question. Any reverse shot, in this film about the uncertainty of memory, could possibly take place at another time than the shot that preceded it. Other alternatives to the classical style, classical continuity, and conventional narrative development have occurred throughout the history of film. They were occurring, even as the classical style was in the process of inventing itself.

Eisenstein Montage

MONTAGE The Russian Revolution of 1917 unleashed enormous creative energies across the arts in the former U.S.S.R. Revolutionary artists were driven by a desire to make aesthetics, culture, ideology, and politics interact on a visible, formal level and make them accessible to as many people as possible. In filmmaking, artists such as Lev Kuleshov, Alexander Dovzhenko, Vesevolod Pudovkin, Sergei Eisenstein, Dziga Vertov, and Esther Shub looked to editing—or *montage,* as it is more accurately called when applied to their work—as the means by which the raw material of film, the shot, could be turned into a statement charged with revolutionary energy. They looked closely at Hollywood films, particularly at D. W. Griffith's work, to find out how they worked. What they discovered was that the continuity cutting being developed in the West was a form that led to reconciliation or redemption: men rescued endangered women, bad guys were overtaken by good. There was always climax and closure, in which "good" prevailed. In *Intolerance* (1916), Griffith was not averse to having Christ and the angels descend over the scene to close the narrative and unify it for eternity. The revolutionary Soviet filmmakers had something else in mind. They were looking for perception, not redemption; they wanted to pass on the charge of history to their viewers, not the calm of eternity.

Eisenstein in particular was fascinated by the ways in which montage could be used as an aesthetic and an ideological tool. In his films (*Strike*, 1924; *Battleship Potemkin*, 1925; *Ten Days That Shook the World*, 1928; *Old and New*, 1929; *Alexander Nevsky*, 1938; *Ivan the Terrible*, 1943, 1946) and the essays he wrote about them he formulated a structure of filmmaking that was more than montage; it was an attempt to generate the pulse of revolutionary history in his viewers. Eisenstein believed that the basic unit of film structure was not the shot, but at least two shots cut together. The process of cutting shots together was not to be an operation that repressed the visibility of what was happening in the name of continuity. Rather, montage was form hurled at the viewer. It was to be visible, legible, and powerful, a way of making the viewer sit up and take notice. Eisenstein's filmmaking colleague, Dziga Vertov, who, among many other films, made 23 issues of a newsreel called *Kinopravda* between 1922 and 1925, and *The Man With a Movie Camera* in 1929, referred to his own method of filming and editing as the "kino eye"—the cinematic eye. Dziga Vertov believes in the kino eye, said Eisenstein. "I believe in the kino fist!"

For Eisenstein, the shot was raw material and montage the film artist's tool that allowed him to cut images together in ways that would cause conflict and visual dissonance. Eisenstein would play shots off one another in order to make the viewer see something greater than the individual shots alone. A montage sequence might be built from the rhythmic or dynamic elements of the individual shots: conflicting diagonal lines, the movement of figures in one shot placed against an opposite movement in another; conflicting *ideas,* a woman calling for peace and calm cut against the chaos of advancing soldiers and hysterical crowds. This interaction makes up part of the montage pattern of the great "Odessa Steps" sequence in *Battleship Potemkin,* in which the Czarist navy attacks civilians on shore in retaliation for a mutiny aboard one of their ships. The sequence builds from shots of the people of Odessa demonstrating support for the mutiny to the attack itself, which is rendered in rapid, often shocking cuts of gunfire, the crowd, a lone woman carrying her dead child down the steps as soldiers marching with their rifles at the ready, move up to her in the opposite direction. Masses of people, soldiers, civilians, seen collectively, in groups, one, a few, or many, moving in opposite directions, and cut together in a montage that defines the outrage of the attack and its brutality. In the most famous montage in the film, which has been parodied by Woody Allen in *Bananas* (1971) and Brian De Palma in *The Untouchables* (1987), not to mention the crazy *Naked Gun 33⅓: The Final Insult* (1994), a woman with a baby carriage at the top of the Odessa steps is shot by the troops. As the sequence proceeds, and the montage returns to her every few seconds, she sinks lower to the ground. But these successive shots are not in continuity with one another. That is, each time we see a shot of her falling, she is not in exactly the same position she was in the previous shot. Usually, she is in a more upright position than she was at the end of the last shot. The suspense and agony of her fall is therefore discontinuous, stretched out, repeated.

Working against the codes of continuity cutting being developed in Hollywood, Eisenstein refused to indulge in an illusion of linear time, replacing it instead with an emotional time, the time of suspense and of thought, extending the woman's fall so that the viewer understands the enormity of the crime against her (echoed elsewhere in the Odessa sequence by a brief and stunning shot of an old woman in close-up, who, having exhorted the crowd to reason with their attackers, is shot in the eye). As the woman finally falls, she loses her grip on the baby carriage, which, finally, is released to roll down the steps, against the tide of the oncoming troops and the fleeing crowds, in a montage of accelerated speed toward destruction.

Eisenstein's was a cinema of ideas and huge, political emotion, in which the conflicting patterns of images attempt to represent the conflict of history itself—a Marxist history of class struggle, the overturning of oppression, and the victory of the proletariat. Eisenstein wanted nothing less than to give cinema the form of dialectical materialism, that philosophy of history which sees events and ideas churning in conflict with each other, negating one another, creating new syntheses, constructing the new out of conflicting elements of the old. Nothing suited Eisenstein better than to create Soviet montage as the dialectic to Hollywood editing.

His ambitions outstripped political reality. Eisenstein visited America in the early twenties, shot footage in Mexico, and negotiated with Paramount Pictures to make a film of Theodore Dreiser's novel *An American Tragedy.* He lost ownership of the Mexican footage, and his ideas and politics were too radical for Paramount, which reneged on the deal. He returned to a Soviet Union in the throes of a violent retrenchment. The arts were undergoing the revisions of socialist realism, a state-ordered aesthetic that cut back formal experimentation and promoted a transparent representation of worker and peasant heroes. Eisenstein had already run afoul of Stalin, who was partially responsible for stopping his Mexican film. This gay, Jewish, avant-garde communist filmmaker was permitted to make fewer and fewer films, and he spent much of the rest of his life writing and teaching.

Eisenstein's films have left only the most sporadic influence in Russian cinema or any other. His style can be recognized in some of the documentary films of the thirties, including those financed by the American government, films like Pare Lorentz's *The Plow That Broke the Plains* (1936) and *The River* (1937). In Hollywood, Eisensteinian montage was mostly turned into another variety of special effects and then largely forgotten. But his films and his theories of montage remain an important force in the history of cinema as a response to the Hollywood style. Flashes of Eisenstein are suddenly breaking out in cutting styles of MTV music videos (hardly a revolutionary form) and, in a more interesting way, in the work of Oliver Stone, especially in *JFK* (1991), *Natural Born Killers,* and *Nixon* (1995).

Attending to the Shot

Although there continue to be experiments in the assembling of shots that make up the narrative, it is not in the area of cutting or montage that the most important responses to the Hollywood style have occurred. Many filmmakers who wish to make films that go counter to the Hollywood style concentrate their attention on the shot rather than the cut. First, they locate continuity cutting as the main badge of the Hollywood style they do not wish to wear. But, unlike Eisenstein, their interest is not in the effects achieved by juxtaposing shots. Rather, they examine the expressive opportunities of the shot itself. These filmmakers look to camera movement, lighting, and the complexities that can be achieved in composing an image to achieve their effects. When

they do cut, it is usually to move from scene to scene or to break down a sequence into its most important parts, rather than use the conventional patterns
of editing a sequence. They will often flagrantly disobey continuity rules, cutting to the opposite side of the imaginary 180-degree line, cutting arhythmi-
cally, not attempting to hide cuts by editing on similar actions, and not using
over-the-shoulder cutting at all. Often they will use long shots—much longer
than the average nine seconds of the classical style.

Films as diverse as Murnau's *Sunrise* (1927), Welles's *The Magnificent Ambersons* (1942), Howard Hawks's *The Big Sleep* (1946), Bernardo Bertolucci's *Before the Revolution* (1964), and Terence Davies's *The Long Day Closes* (1992)—to
name only a very few—illustrate the ways filmmakers can work against the
rules of continuity, using long takes, alternative cutting patterns, and unusual
visual and dramatic rhythms to achieve results that differ from those of standard Hollywood practice.

Mise-en-scène

MISE-EN-SCÈNE Directors who depend on the shot more than the cut are called
mise-en-scène directors. We have already examined mise-en-
scène and it is important to summarize the concept. Mise-en-
scène is a French term and originates in the theater. It means, literally, "put in
the scene." For film, it has a broader meaning, and refers to almost everything
that goes into the composition of the shot, including the composition itself:
framing, movement of the camera and characters, lighting, set design and general visual environment, even sound as it helps elaborate the composition.
Mise-en-scène can be defined as the articulation of cinematic space, and it is
precisely space that it is about. Cutting is about time; the shot is about what
occurs in a defined area of space, bordered by the frame of the movie screen
and determined by what the camera has been made to record. That space, the
mise-en-scène, can be unique, closed off by the frame, or open, providing
the illusion of more space around it. In *Travelling Players* (1975), a film by the
Greek director Theo Angelopoulos, a group of people move into the past by
taking a long walk down a street in one shot; time moves backward as they
walk. There is a sequence in the film *Grand Illusion* (1937) by the director (and
son of the Impressionist painter) Jean Renoir in which a group of World War I
POWs receive a carton of gifts. Among the gifts is, unaccountably, some
women's clothing. One of the soldiers puts the clothing on, and the rest stare
at him in stunned silence. Renoir creates their response by gently, slowly, pan-
ning across the men staring. The movement yields up the space the men inhabit, suggests that it extends beyond the frame, and delicately emphasizes
their confused sexual response to this sudden appearance of a man in
woman's clothes. Had Renoir cut from face to face, the effect would have been
quite different, suggesting the isolation of one man and his emotional response from the next person in the group. If he had offered only a wide shot of
all the men together, their individual expressions would have been lost. The

pan joins individual to group, making the revelation of space not only physical but emotional and communal, and the response more generally and genu-
inely human. It allows us to understand the response and not lose our perspective. Closeness and comfortable distance remain.

Editing is a way to form a narrative temporally, both in the making and
the viewing of a film. Editing speeds up the shooting process in ways outlined
earlier: it speeds up the viewing process by creating a rhythm of forward action. Even the over-the-shoulder cutting of a dialogue sequence, which creates
an event that takes place in one space over a short period of time, is moved
along by the rapid shifts of point of view between the participants. Mise-en-
scène filmmaking directs our attention to the space of the shot itself. It slows
things down—especially on the production side, where care must be taken in
performance, lighting, and composition. If a long take is involved—like the
shot in Scorsese's *Goodfellas* that lasts almost four minutes—careful planning is
required to make sure that actors and camera move synchronously. In a long
take, actors must act. There's no chance to save a performance by cutting away
to someone or something else in the scene. If a mistake is made, the entire shot
has to be made again. The economics of Hollywood production frown on such
methods.

For the viewer, a film that depends upon mise-en-scène and long shots
makes special demands. Without editing to analyze what's important in a
scene by cutting to a closeup of a face or an object, the viewer is required to do
the looking around in the shot, to be sensitive to changes in spatial relationships and the movements of camera and actor. Even a film that uses a lot of
cutting may still depend on the mise-en-scène to articulate meaning as each
cut reveals a different spatial relationship. Perhaps a general rule is that films
made in the classical continuity style point to and usher the viewer through
the progress of the narrative. Films that depend on mise-en-scène ask the
viewer to pause and examine the compositional spaces of the narrative. The
classical continuity style is directive, the mise-en-scène style contemplative.

The Long Take in *Citizen Kane*

LONG TAKE There is a sequence in *Citizen Kane* that tells us about Kane's
childhood, concentrating on the moment when his mother signs
over his care to the rich Mr. Thatcher. The sequence concerns the
shifting relationships between mother, son, father, and a new patriarchal figure, who will take the son from his parents and introduce him to the world of
wealth and personal isolation. Welles describes these relational changes not so
much through what the characters say to each other as through the way the
camera and characters move through the space of the sequence. The sequence
begins with Mrs. Kane looking out the window and calling to her son, who is
playing with his sled in the snow (the sled that, at the end of the film, will be
revealed as "Rosebud," Kane's dying memory). The camera pulls up and back
as Mrs. Kane turns around, and as the camera moves, it reveals a figure to her

right. This is the new guardian, Mr. Thatcher. The camera tracks backward in front of them as they move to the other side of the room, talking about signing the papers that will give Thatcher custody of Kane. Through all of this, the child outside in the snow remains visible and audible through the window even as the camera moves back. Welles employs a technique known as deep focus, by means of which everything in the frame, from front to rear, remains equally sharp. As a result of the deep focus and the long backward track of the camera, space expands to the rear of the frame. The small cabin in which all of this takes place is expanded into a larger area of psychological change and uprooting, which is underscored by the appearance of the father in the shot.

As Mrs. Kane and Thatcher continue to move toward the opposite end of the room, Mr. Kane is revealed on the left side of the frame. Throughout the shot, he remains always slightly behind his wife as she and Mr. Thatcher approach the table where the papers are. In their movement to the table, the child, still playing outside the window, is sometimes blocked out by the figure of his mother or father, but throughout the shot a triangulated dynamic is maintained between the three adults and between the adults and the child. After withdrawing her gaze from Kane out in the snow, the mother looks straight ahead and then down at the table. Thatcher's and Mr. Kane's gazes remain fixed on Mrs. Kane. She is the pivotal figure, the one making the choice. The two men are dependent upon her actions while the child is separated from her, almost literally pulled away by the visual effect created as the camera moves from the window to the table.

After Mrs. Kane and Thatcher sit down at the table and Mr. Kane comes closer to the two of them, the camera tilts up, causing the father to appear for a moment as a slightly threatening figure—threatening, at least, to those ready to sign away his child. Note that an unusually low camera position often has the effect of making a character loom over the frame in a threatening manner. However, Welles will sometimes use this position ironically to indicate that the imposing figure is about to fall from power. An unusually high camera position diminishes a character. Hitchcock will often use a disorienting high angle shot to show a character in physical or moral jeopardy. In our sequence from *Kane*, the father's power is weak and diminishing. He's about to lose his son to a man who is practically buying him from his mother. The three adults talk about their business deal while young Kane remains clearly visible through the window, on the other side, far behind them, now forming the apex of the triangle. Mr. Kane relents in his opposition to the deal the moment he understands how much money is at stake. He then goes to the back of the room and shuts the window—as if shutting his son out of his life. Mrs. Kane and Thatcher follow; she opens the window again and, finally, after about two minutes and thirty seconds, there is a 180-degree reverse shot of Mrs. Kane from outside the window.

This complex arrangement and rearrangement of space and figures creates a kind of Oedipal ballet in a small room, a dance of shifting parental relationships and authority that results in both gain and loss for the child. The ballet of camera and character in their dynamic spatial confines is more eloquent than the spoken dialogue and much more descriptive of narrative events.

EXPRESSIVE USE OF MISE-EN-SCÈNE AND EDITING

John Ford

Very few filmmakers depend solely upon shot length and shot content to articulate the narrative space of their films. Many directors combine the shot and the cut together to create a mise-en-scène of space and time that enables them to develop narrative subtleties. This, in turn, permits the viewer to comprehend a range of meaning and emotion in the frame and across the cut. Alfred Hitchcock's films invite us into threatening spaces, but at the same time they allow us ways to look at the characters and the things they do with some detachment, even irony. John Ford, the master of the Western landscape, places his figures in open, outdoor spaces, bounded by the rocks of Monument Valley as a symbol of a mythical West both overwhelming and able to be mastered. He constructs frontier towns on the edge of this landscape and carefully renders, visually and in the stories he tells, how difficult it is to build the borders of civilization, and the cost to the people who build them. Ford's editing is fairly conventional, but in films like *Stagecoach* (1939), *Fort Apache* (1948), *The Searchers* (1956)—to name a very few—his shot construction creates images of a frontier past always diminishing, always on the edge of historical imagination.

Robert Altman

Robert Altman blurs boundaries. His mise-en-scène—in films like *MASH* (1970), *McCabe and Mrs. Miller* (1971), *The Long Goodbye* (1973), *Nashville* (1975), *Buffalo Bill and the Indians* (1976), and *Short Cuts* (1993)—is made up of peripheral spaces and off-hand conversations. His camera restlessly zooms in and out among many faces of many people doing and saying many different things, often at cross purposes to one another. (A zoom shot is created when the lenses change focal length—from wide angle to telephoto, for example—while the camera remains stationary.) What we see in an Altman film is a visually and aurally busy world of people always moving together in opposite directions, whose lives meet and cross in peculiar and often shattering ways. The space of his shots is often compressed through the use of a telephoto lens and Altman will cut from one zoom shot to another using that long lens. Within the busy movement and compressed spaces of the shots and the sometimes unexpected and ironic cuts, conventional continuity is often left behind. We are asked to validate the connections between the shots and comprehend more than the characters, in their fragmentary existence, can see. Altman's style puts more burden on the viewer than conventional films to see how its pieces and its spaces fit together.

Stanley Kubrick

Stanley Kubrick is a filmmaker who creates complex shots, symmetrically designed, cold and powerful, linked together expressively, sometimes astoundingly. Consider the "Dawn of Man" sequence of his 1968 film *2001: A Space Odyssey*. The sequence is built of long shots of an imaginary prehistoric landscape (filmed entirely in a studio), in which apes on the brink of humanity discover a weapon and with it the use of deadly violence. At the end of the sequence, one ape, in a delirium at having learned how to use a bone to kill, hurls it into the air. The camera tracks the bone rising and rising. As it begins to fall back to earth, there is a cut to an image of a spaceship—thousands of years in the future, and looking somewhat like a bleached-white bone—floating through space to the music of "The Blue Danube Waltz."

Eisenstein could not have imagined a more audacious montage in which past and future are sealed in the invisible fracture of the cut, linking together the birth of human violence and the future reawakening of human experience. In this moment, Kubrick turns editing into something akin to a statement about history, philosophy, politics, and metaphysics. Clearly, deciding to use editing for a particularly rich statement was important for this filmmaker who ordinarily depends upon the construction of the shot and camera movement to communicate his ideas.

Alfred Hitchcock

Kubrick is a rare filmmaker, who puts so much thought and concentration into a structural event in his films. Alfred Hitchcock is another. Hitchcock carefully planned every formal move in his work well before filming actually began. Cinematic form and structure, Hitchcock understood, are the means by which narrative is made and emotion generated. Nothing must be left to chance in the structure and no one must interfere with the finished plan when shooting begins. Hitchcock was pleased to say that by the time he went to filming, he never had to look through the camera, because his plan for the film and his instructions on how to execute it were complete. As a result, Hitchcock's best films are made of complex structures in which each composition and cut relates a great deal of information. The space of the Hitchcockian world is created by positioning characters and camera to produce a composition that often ironically comments upon the characters' situation. He will relate figures and objects through a subtle cutting between gazes, creating an interplay between a character looking at something or someone and a shot in motion of the person or object being looked at, so carefully measured that the cutting back and forth builds a sense of threat or vulnerability.

Consider the sequence in *Psycho* when Norman invites Marion into his parlor, just before the shower murder. By cutting between the characters in their isolated worlds—their own little islands, as Marion says—and slowly increasing the visual association of Norman and his stuffed birds, including a terribly threatening, low-angle shot in which a stuffed owl looms over Norman's head, the sequence reveals much of the mystery of the plot. With its emphasis on dark and threatening spaces, fear and withdrawal, its association of Norman first with passivity and anxiety and then, in a shot in which he bends forward in the frame, with a threatening look toward Marion and the viewer, the mise-en-scène of this sequence forms the nucleus of the film. Its visual structure, along with the dialogue, lets us know everything that is going on and will go on—if we care to watch and listen.

MISE-EN-SCÈNE   Early in *Vertigo* (a film we'll talk about in some detail in the next chapter), Scottie goes to visit Gavin Elster, the man who will set in motion an enormous ruse that will ruin Scottie's life. Scottie is already reduced and weakened. His fear of heights has resulted in a fellow police officer's being killed and his own retirement from the police force. In Gavin's offices—large, ornate, overlooking the San Francisco waterfront, with a huge construction crane moving outside the window—Scottie is made to look small, sometimes almost cowering. Throughout much of the scene, Hitchcock has him sit, scrunched down in a chair composed in one corner of a frame, as Gavin, standing on a raised portion of the floor in his office, dominates him and the viewer. Through the spatial arrangement developed by the construction of the set and the camera, whose placement and movement keep diminishing Scottie's presence, we are allowed to comprehend undercurrents that are not articulated in the dialogue. Gavin tells Scottie a story about how Gavin's wife is possessed by a spirit from the past. In fact, Gavin is using Scottie in a plot to kill his wife, a plot that will eventually lead to Scottie's total breakdown. Scottie will become the diminished figure we see in this sequence. Like the parlor sequence in *Psycho,* this sequence in *Vertigo* gives away a lot of the film through the ways in which Hitchcock has us see his characters as part of his eloquent mise-en-scène.

Martin Scorsese and Point of View

POINT OF VIEW   Martin Scorsese is a great admirer of Hitchcock, always thinking about his films and filtering them into his own work. Sharing with Hitchcock a sharp sense of mise-en-scène and the skill in developing an articulate cinematic space, Scorsese is especially taken with the way Hitchcock creates point of view. Commonly, point of view in cinema means the representation of a what a character sees, and it is built out of the basic cinematic units of shot and cut. If a shot of a character looking at something is followed by a shot of an object or another person, we assume (because film almost never gives us reason to assume otherwise) that what we are now seeing is what the character is seeing. This is the closest film ever gets to the first-person effect in written fiction. The "I" in cinema becomes, almost literally, the "eye." We are asked to believe that we are seeing through the eyes of the gazing character. There have been very few experiments in creating film that is structured entirely in the first person. Welles wanted to make his first film—an adaptation of Joseph Conrad's novella, *Heart of Darkness*—a first-person narrative, but couldn't make it work. The actor Robert Montgomery attempted to mimic the detective novelist Raymond Chandler's first-person style in his film adaptation *Lady in the Lake* (1946). The result was a wooden, silly-looking film in which the camera got punched in the nose and coffee cups were lifted up to the lens to mimic the character drinking. The only time the main character is seen is when he looks into a mirror.

The first-person effect in film is best achieved by means of the interplay of gazes created through the intercutting of characters who look and the people or things they're looking at. Film, therefore, is mostly narrated by a mute third-person voice, the overseeing eye of the camera and the controlling movements of the cutting. First-person points of view are built into this general third-person structure, articulating it with the intensity of the individual gaze. Hitchcock, as we've noted, achieves this by cross cutting a character looking with what the character is looking at, most often with the camera in motion. For example, when Marion's sister, Lila Crane, approaches the old, dark house in *Psycho*, Hitchcock shows her climbing up the stairs with the camera moving back at a slightly high angle. (Breaking compositional symmetry by putting a character in an odd position, too low, too high, or just off center in the frame is a favorite Hitchcock method of communicating disorientation and unease, even a sense of dread.) He intercuts her climb with images of the house moving closer, almost suggesting the point of view of the house itself, gazing back at the approaching figure. The sense of expectation and menace is extreme.

Scorsese embroiders upon these effects in interesting ways. *Taxi Driver* (1976) is a film whose essential theme is about point of view: how a character sees and interprets his world. In this case, the point of view is restricted to the consciousness of a psychotic cab driver. Scorsese achieves his effect by creating an exclusive point of view in which the world articulated on the screen is a reflection of what Robert De Niro's Travis Bickle, the crazy cabbie, sees. The mise-en-scène of *Taxi Driver* is expressionist, the exterior representation of a disturbed mind. We see the world as Travis experiences it: the nighttime streets of Manhattan filled with hookers and gangs, crazy people yelling as they walk by, a homicidal lunatic (played by Scorsese himself) sitting in the back of the cab. Scorsese will emphasize Travis's disorientation and madness even when the camera is looking at him. As Travis walks down the street, there will suddenly be a dissolve—an optical effect which is conventionally used as a narrative device to create a transition in time and place—though here nothing changes. Travis continues to walk down the street. The dissolve is suddenly given new meaning as an indication of the slippages in Travis's own mind. The famous "Are you talking to me?" sequence, with its jump cuts (removing little bits of the sequence, creating a skipping effect, as if the character's own attention was sparking on and off) and mirror shots, continues the perception of a narrow, obsessive, decaying mind.

Travis, like many other Scorsese characters, is menacing and sees menace around him. Paranoia rules. When Travis (or Jake La Motta in *Raging Bull*, 1980) looks at the world, the world looks back as a threatening place. Another way Scorsese manages this sense of threat is to generate the point-of-view shot in slow motion, so that the character's world appears as if it were a hallucination. Scorsese has perfected this technique so that he will change the speed of the motion in the course of a shot. The figures seen by the main character will move slowly and then subtly speed up, until they move at a normal pace. This technique, which is a refinement of Hitchcock's method of intercutting a character in motion with an object or person the character is looking at, also in motion, is disturbing because it plays against the stability of the shot/reverse shot we have come to expect. It generates an unstable space and reflects the perceptions of an unstable character. With it, point of view and the mise-en-scène are joined in an expressive definition of character and the emotional state, the emotional *space*, he inhabits and we are asked to observe.

One of Scorsese's favorite point-of-view techniques is to use the camera as a surrogate for one of his tough-guy characters as he moves along a bar in a club. He does this in both *Mean Streets* (1973) and *Goodfellas* (1990). The latter film employs a long moving camera shot as the character, Henry Hill, introduces us to his fellow thugs. At the end of the shot, Henry himself emerges, but from the left side of the frame—not from where the camera is positioned. With this slight disruption of expectations, Scorsese brings into question who is actually seeing what, whose point of view we can really depend on. The question is central to this film, which is largely about whose stories we believe and why we believe them (we will explore *Goodfellas* in detail later on); but it's applicable to all film, where point of view is yet another artifice that we accept on the faith of convention.

MOVIE CONVENTIONS

The construction of mise-en-scène is one of the most complicated things a film and its makers can undertake, which may account for the reason that coherent, complex mise-en-scène is rarely seen in films. It takes thought, time, and money. The majority of films made in the classic continuity style are shot simply and unexpressively in a shallow space, with bright, even high-key lighting, the camera set quite still at eye level to the characters. The burden of narrative is carried by the dialogue. Currently, thrillers and horror or science fiction films made in the classical style may use an expressive dark-blue, smoke-filled lighting for nighttime. Some horror films use exaggerated point-of-view shots to allow us to "see with" the eyes of the monster. But these have all become conventions; we expect to see them and we know what they mean when we do. These elements of the classical style have become, like all the others, invisible and, at the same time, heavily coded. On one level, we take no notice of them, but on another level, these conventions communicate to us, succinctly, economically, what we need to know to understand the story being told and to feel the emotions that must be felt.

The Hollywood style depends upon our having seen films in which the same formal devices are used over and over again so that we know what they mean as soon as we see them. They speed narrative along and place us squarely in the story. But, in a curious way, they are telling another story. In many ways the classical style constitutes its own narrative. It tells its own story of stimulus and effect, action and reaction, our desire to see and respond to the continuous stream of images and movements, characters, and stories that satisfy our seemingly endless desire. The formal devices of the classical style communicate meanings, transitions, elements of story that are the same from film to film.

When the camera dollies in to a close-up of a character whose eyes are slightly raised and, after the dolly in, there is a dissolve with wavy lines from one shot to another, we know what's coming: a dream, a daydream, a memory, or a fantasy sequence. Someone steals into an apartment or warehouse or underground parking garage and hides in the shadows. A woman follows, going about her business as if nothing has happened. Our gaze is privileged by so many other sequences just like this; therefore, we see more than the woman does. Trained to move across the cuts, we know that women in dark spaces inhabited by a villain unseen by them are vulnerable. We experience unease and fright in anticipation of what might happen. No matter what is going on in the rest of the story, this combination of shots tells a story of its own. The characters' point of view doesn't matter, only ours. Whenever a camera moves around in an arc or rapidly dollies forward toward an object, our emotions surge (perhaps because otherwise the camera is so often still). Facial expressions or body movements, edited in counterpoint to each other, tell volumes. A nod of a head, a stiff smile, parted lips, narrowing eyes, hands held up to a wide-eyed face with mouth agape; a shot of a hand moving down toward a pocket; shoulders hunched or hands held away from the body; a head buried in open hands or a hand cupping a chin—these and dozens of other stock movements and gestures make up the rhetoric of narrative codes used by film.

Gender Specificity

Many of these facial expressions and body movements are gender specific and much narrative material is expressed through the gender of the person who uses them. Only women put their hands up to their faces to express horror, fear, sadness. Men may jerk their shoulders back or put an arm out—often a protective arm if a woman is with them. A man will allow his head to fall on his forearm in a moment of stress or pull it down between his shoulders to express anger. Women cast eyes upward for a variety of sexually related reasons; men work their mouths, usually in a self-contained smile or smirk. Men may raise their eyes, but usually as a look of annoyance. Faces, hands, props, camera movement, lighting, cutting patterns are used over and over again to assure that we understand perfectly what is going on. The curious and fascinating thing about all of this is that these repetitions of style and gesture are not taken as a joke when they are seen in context, unless they are self-conscious, stilted, their timing is off, or some other ineptitude is committed by the filmmaker, or they are being used to parody their own conventionality. The reason, in part at least, is that we are not about to laugh at something that helps us so easily to understand what's going on in the scene and in the film. We are not about to laugh when these stock gestures and movements are carrying us forward through a story that has captured our attention to itself and away from the ways it is being created.

The classical style is therefore invisible and highly visible at the same time. Its visibility and invisibility can play counterpoint. A film dependent on ordinary structures of shot/reverse shot, eye-line matches, conventionally expressive gestures may suddenly indulge in a surprising camera movement or an unusual spatial composition. A filmmaker may wrench the invisible into the foreground by exaggerating a movement or a gesture, as Hitchcock does with the cross-tracking effect discussed earlier, or with the leap to a high-angle shot that he so often uses to express the diminished, vulnerable state of a character who has just made a terrible discovery or is in terrible danger. Some

Breaking the 180 degree rule. In setting up the shot/reverse shot pattern for this dialogue sequence in Before the Revolution *(1964), Bernardo Bertolucci places his camera on the other side of the 180 degree line.*

filmmakers, outside of the Hollywood system, make up new codes, new meanings to movement and gestures, shots and cuts, or turn the old ones on their heads. Orson Welles and Stanley Kubrick use tracking shots to turn space into expressive containers of their characters' loss of power and diminishment. The Italian director, Bernardo Bertolucci, flaunted the conventions of the Hollywood style in his early films. A sequence in *Before the Revolution* (1964), in which two men converse on a park bench, is constructed out of cuts that break the 180-degree rule. Each cut places the camera 180 degrees on either side of the two men. A dialogue sequence in *The Spider's Stratagem* (1970) is punctuated by fades to black. The fade to black is a convention of the Hollywood style that signifies the end not only of a scene but of a particular narrative moment.

But here, when the scene fades back in, the characters are in the same place, and their dialogue is continuing. *The Spider's Stratagem* is about a young man caught in history, tricked by politics, betrayed by his father, and lost in time. The strange fades to black in the sequence communicate the character's dilemma, his inability to know where his own story begins and ends. Like Scorsese's use of the dissolve in the middle of a shot in *Taxi Driver* that does *not* act as a transition to another place or time, Bertolucci's fades to black make us conscious of how coded the elements of classical style are by turning the codes against themselves.

Convention and Consciousness

Perhaps the complexities of the classical continuity style and the responses to it can be summed up by a notion of unconsciousness and consciousness. The classical style asks that we be unconscious of form and structure but conscious of their effects. That is, most films want us to understand them immediately, directly, without mediation. Filmmakers who wish to explore the language of cinema and make its form and structure expressive in their own right—the way some painters and novelists use the language of their art to draw attention to its own devices—want us to be conscious at all levels. They want us to know when they are cutting and to ask why; to be aware of a camera movement and think about its purpose; to look *at* the way people and objects are arranged in the frame and not look *through* that frame as if it were some kind of open window or mirror.

However, in the end, we have to be conscious of everything in every film. To be lulled by the classical continuity style into a trance of identification with light and shadow on a white screen is not useful. Assenting to the ideology of the invisible may be relaxing, but, in an interesting way, it is not safe. To look through form and structure does not mean that form and structure are actually invisible. They *are* present, working to create the meaning and generate the feelings you experience during a movie. To ignore them means that they and the corporate communities that created them are given permission to continue on their way doing what they want, telling stories that may or may not be beneficial to us in our dealings with the world. But to *read* them, consciously, analytically, with as much attention as we read those films that do not use the classical style, means that we are not only entertained, but that we understand why and how we are entertained.

Analyzing the illusory nature of film does not discredit it or diminish the pleasure of watching film. Quite the contrary. The more you know about what you are and are not seeing, the richer the experience is, and the more reflective. It's exciting to respond emotionally and intellectually to film; to feel the story and understand how that story is being constructed; to see through the images to the characters and their turmoil and at the same time observe and understand what the images themselves are doing. It's possible and important to feel and understand, to synthesize and analyze.

We can extend this process of analysis and synthesis beyond the individual film to a wider context and consider the role of film and other popular forms of entertainment in the culture at large. How do films reflect larger cultural events? Why does the culture support the conventions of storytelling in film and other forms of mass entertainment? Why do films keep telling us the same stories?

NOTES AND REFERENCES

From Image to Narrative   The story of Muybridge and Edison, and the information about early projection is from Charles Musser, *The Emergence of Cinema: The American Screen to 1907* (New York: Charles Scribner's Sons, 1990), pp. 62–68, 91.

Linda Williams discusses the early development of the image and its relationship to the body in *Hard Core* (Berkeley & Los Angeles: University of California, 1989, pp. 34–57.

The Making of the Classical Hollywood Style: Ideology at Work   There are a number of essays and books that discuss the ideology of the classical Hollywood style. Two excellent and accessible essays are Robin Wood's "Ideology, Genre, Auteur" and Colin McCabe's "Theory and Film: Principles of Realism and Pleasure" in Gerald Mast, Marshall Cohen, and Leo Braudy, eds., *Film Theory and Criticism* (New York: Oxford University Press, 1992). Bill Nichols, *Ideology and the Image*, cited in the previous chapter, is another good resource. For a detailed history of the Classical Hollywood Style, see David Bordwell, Janet Staiger, and Kristen Thompson, *The Classical Hollywood Cinema: Film Style & Mode of Production to 1960* (New York: Columbia University Press, 1985).

The Cut   In addition to Thomas Elsaesser's collection of essays *Early Cinema*, cited in the previous chapter, two other books present a broad and stimulating examination of the early developments of the classical Hollywood style, concentrating on the development of cutting and narrative patterns: Noël Burch, *Life to Those Shadows*, trans. and ed., Ben Brewster (Berkeley and Los Angeles: University of California Press, 1990); and Tom Gunning, *D. W. Griffith and the Origins of American Narrative Film* (Urbana and Chicago: University of Illinois Press, 1991). Porter's 1903 film *The Life of an American Fireman* used to be considered the "first" film to intercut sequences. In fact, a more reliable print of the film was discovered in which the scenes were linked in a linear fashion, leading to the conclusion that the intercut version was a *later* edition, made by someone after intercutting had become the norm. See Stephen Bottomore's essay "Shots in the Dark—The Real Origins of Film Editing" and André Gaudreault's "Detours in Film Narrative: The Development of Cross-Cutting" in Elsaesser's *Early Cinema*. The standard work on the concept of the "suture," the stitching of the viewer's gaze into the narrative, is Daniel Dayan's "The Tudor-Code of Classical Cinema" in *Film Theory and Criticism.*

The Cut, Dialogue Cutting   The notion that cutting on a look to the thing looked at will create the appropriate emotional response is an old one. The story of the "Kuleshov effect" has it that, in the early 1920s, the Russian filmmaker Lev Kuleshov took a strip of film showing a neutral close-up of an actor. He then intercut that shot with one of a plate of food, a coffin, and children playing. When the film was shown, people were amazed at the versatility of the actor, who showed hunger at the food, sadness at the coffin, pleasure at the children.

The Cut, The Hollywood Economical Style   For the male gaze, read Laura Mulvey, "Visual Pleasure and Narrative Cinema," in *Film Theory and Criticism,* and widely reprinted.

Departures from the Classical Hollywood Style, Eisensteinian
Montage   Eisenstein's essays are collected in two volumes, *The Film Form: Essays in Film Theory,* ed. and trans., Jay Leyda (San Diego: Harcourt Brace Jovanovich, 1977); *The Film Sense,* ed. and trans., Jay Leyda (New York: Harcourt Brace Jovanovich, 1975).

Departures from the Classical Hollywood Style, Mise-en-scène   An excellent discussion of composition and the construction of open and closed worlds occurs in Leo Braudy's *The World in a Frame* (Garden City, N.Y.: Anchor Press/Doubleday, 1976). André Bazin addresses the contemplative nature of the long shot throughout his essays in *What Is Cinema?* cited in the previous chapter.

Departures from the Classical Hollywood Style, The Long Take in *Citizen Kane*   Deep focus, or "depth of field," is a result of camera optics. A lot of light and a very small aperture opening (which translates as a high f-stop) create the effect. It is hard to do, expensive, and tends to call attention to itself, three reasons why it is rarely used in filmmaking. There are examples of faked depth of field, in which a special lens is used to focus two spatial planes. You can see it in Martin Scorsese's *Cape Fear* (1991).

3

FILM AS CULTURAL PRACTICE

How and where does film fit into the larger cultural scheme of things? We have seen that film is a part of industrial production (the making of films follows principles of mass production, and, in purely economic terms, is now one of the largest commercial endeavors in Los Angeles). We have started to examine how film creates and satisfies its consumers' desires. But unlike other industrial goods, and conforming more closely to what we usually think of as art, movies have emotional and moral designs on us. They ask us to respond with our feelings and to think of the world in moral certainties, to assume there are good people and bad, ethical acts and unethical ones. They even suggest ethical solutions to the problems of how we should act in the world. Yet when compared to a novel or a painting or a symphony, the emotional demands made by a film seem shallow and unambiguous. Unlike the traditional high arts, film does not demand great intellectual powers to understand it. Quite the contrary: Hollywood film eschews intellect, seems to demand no analysis at all, and invites us to pass through it into the illusion of unadorned, unmediated story.

POPULAR CULTURE

Film, to circle back to where we began our discussion, does not want us to take it seriously, despite its emotional and moral demands. Unlike other consumer goods, it is created only for leisure-time use, which, as historically defined by a culture that values work above everything else, means that it is unimportant. In fact, there is a double prohibition against seriousness at work here. Consumer goods are purchased, often at some expense, to make our work and our domestic lives easier. Movies are purchased very cheaply, though they are very dear to make, and they seem to have no use at all for the people who consume them other than to offer them a temporary escape from the real world where money is made and spent. People understand that a temporary escape from the stresses of daily life is good; but the movies and the television programs that allow that escape are still held suspect and often devalued.

Cheap to purchase and cheap in form and content, movies and other works of mass or popular culture have therefore usually been considered trite and banal, without complexity, authority, or value. The works of popular culture are often marked as age or gender or race specific, and such compartmentalization almost always carries implied pejorative judgments. Rock and roll is the province of teenagers and is so mindless that it will harm them. Rap belongs to African American teenagers and promotes immorality and violence among this potentially dangerous audience (the racial stereotyping is obvious and extreme). Romance fiction is the debased reading of middle-aged women who have nothing better to do than nourish their hopeless fantasy lives. Sports is for jocks. Movie fans—the targeted audience between ages 15 and 35—need sexual titillation and have a deep need for vicarious experience delivered in the most banal and violent way while middle-aged moviegoers may prefer a romanticized, simplified adaptation of a Henry James novel. In almost all cases, the judgment of some people toward popular culture is clear: those who admire and enjoy popular culture are being pandered to and willingly enjoy the bad effects of the pandering. That willingness somehow reflects a debasement of the culture. Fear that cultural standards are being lowered by popular culture and mass media causes distrust, which is followed by condemnation. But condemnation seems to have no effect. We still love movies; we still watch television and listen to rock and roll and rap. Distrust then turns to cynicism.

The negative view of the popular is further nourished by the fact that mass culture is commercial culture ("commercialized" would be the popular, pejorative term). Movies, television, rock music, romantic novels, newspapers are commodities, objects of commercial desire. The companies that manufacture them seek a profit. Popular culture commodities are the product not of the individual imagination but of the calculations of the large organizations that construct them to appeal to the largest part of their audience. The results are then positioned for the most appropriate segment of that audience, marketed according to age, gender, race, class, and promoted and sold accordingly. The commodities and their audience become part of the cost/price, profit/loss, asset/liability, manufacture/distribution structure that makes up industrial practice.

DEFINITIONS OF CULTURE

There is an element of truth in everything negative that is said about popular culture, although blanket condemnations are not useful in helping us understand its complexity. It will be useful to attempt a broader definition that takes into consideration its commercial, even its pandering, aspects and that contextualizes the popular in all its seriousness and playfulness. In this larger view, culture can be seen as the text of our lives, the ultimately coherent pattern of beliefs, acts, responses that we produce and comprehend every day. The idea of culture as text means, firstly, that culture is not nature; it is made by people in history, the product of all they think and do. Even the unconscious or semiconscious acts of our daily lives can, when observed and analyzed, be understood as sets of coherent acts and be seen to interact with each other. These acts, beliefs, and practices, along with the artifacts they produce—the music we listen to, the clothes we wear, the television we love, the films we watch—have meaning. They can be "read" and understood. People drive cars and select certain makes of cars, go to school, open bank accounts, make paintings, watch television, accept racial and sexual differences (or don't), hate Democrats or Republicans (or don't), believe in free will and a free economy (or don't), behave well or badly, love classical music or rock, and somehow make perfect sense of most of this behavior. With a little study and an open mind, we can understand the sense we make of it and the needs that are fulfilled by the choices we make and the things that entertain us. We can understand why and how our entertainments affirm or deny our beliefs and that none of this is natural. It is all born of class, gender, race, education, acculturation.

Subcultures

Now, our culture—or that part of our culture that makes divisions between high and low, serious and popular art—defines culture much more narrowly than we just have. It defines as culture those serious works made by independent imaginations that are complex, difficult to understand, and acceptable only to the few who have, want, or like "culture." In other words, culture segments and segregates itself. The culture's culture is what we normally think of as the difficult, personal art we have to engage deeply in order to understand: paintings in museums; symphonies played in concert halls; poems and novels analyzed in the classroom. If other kinds of imaginative products are allowed to fit within this definition, they are referred to as "low" or "popular" culture and relegated to the margins. Popular culture is scorned by admirers of "high" culture; and the high is scorned by the popular. This mutual antagonism is sometimes expressed through allusions to stereotypes. Classical music, art, and poetry lovers are the effete, the intellectual elite, with all the implications of class and sexual otherness this implies. People who enjoy the popular arts are sometimes represented as working-class slobs, or women without a life, or people of color who threaten dominant values. There are even wider, more profound, and potentially dangerous splits between subcultures who enjoy the products of popular culture itself. Religious and political differences mark divergent interests in radio programs, kinds of music, and films. People who listen to National Public Radio are identified as different from those who listen to right-wing talk shows—both by themselves and by others. People who watch action movies are seen differently—even by the moviemakers themselves—from those who watch adaptations of Jane Austen novels. In such divisions, the resentment and anger felt by one group toward another are marked and unsettling.

The Roots of Cultural Differences

The roots of all this are complex and indicate how any narrow definitions of culture are insufficient to describe the strong and changing elements of the larger culture we belong to. What follows is a very abbreviated sketch of some complex events and movements that created subcultures within larger cultural groups, but it will give an idea of how culture keeps generating itself, how vital groups within it create its art, and how that art changes and transforms the culture.

In European culture, the "serious" production of music and painting and literature goes back to the Middle Ages, when it belonged to the royal courts. The "lower classes," illiterate peasants, mostly, had cultures indigenous to their country and place, based on crafts and oral traditions, a phenomenon that is true of most non-European cultures as well. The formation of a property-owning and goods-trading middle class began in the Italian Renaissance, and it is this new group that brought high culture out of the palaces and into the villas, the homes of wealthy traders and property owners. Owning or sponsoring fine art was part of the proprietary movement of the burgeoning middle class. Well-to-do Italian merchants become patrons of the arts, commissioning painters, for example, who, in gratitude, would paint an image of their benefactor at the feet of Christ. Ownership was a sign of wealth. Owning or patronizing art was a sign of wealthy good taste. It still is.

During the eighteenth century, the property-owning middle class grew across Europe, small shopkeepers flourished, and an industrial working class began to grow. Each of these classes developed its own cultural forms. The novel, for example, was developed in the early eighteenth century and was originally directed at middle-class women, who read, for example, the romantic adventures of the heroine of Samuel Richardson's *Pamela; Or, Virtue Rewarded* (1740) and *Clarissa* (1747–1748) with a devotion and identification (and, sometimes, a sense of irony) that many people still devote to soap opera. Melodrama, a popular working- and lower-middle-class form, was born of the novel and the theater, especially the late eighteenth-century theater of post-revolutionary France. It started as pantomime with music—melodrama means drama with music—in response to laws that forbade traditional theatrical performances in which actors spoke their lines. Early melodrama in Europe and in the United States was broad, moral, and political, with exaggerated gestures and simplified structures of good and evil—too broad and "common" for upper-class tastes. It was broadly participatory as well, inviting emotional and even verbal response. Melodrama was a form of satisfaction and gratification, a communal expression of a class desire for stability, place, and confirmation of simple moral values. In various forms, it has thrived in many cultures in the West and the East.

Music Hall variety entertainments were, by the mid-nineteenth century, another working class site of comedy, popular music, parody, and gender lampoon (cross dressing in British variety shows remains popular, accepted without embarrassed innuendo). Music Hall was and is performed in a space that encourages lively audience response. The American version of Music Hall, vaudeville, along with melodrama, were to prove enormous influences on the development of film.

HOW POPULAR CULTURE BECOMES MASS CULTURE

In order for popular culture to become mass culture, storage and distribution methods had to be developed. Print culture was well advanced by the eighteenth century, and novels and newspapers enjoyed a fairly wide circulation. In the case of the novel, some transmission occurred through people reading aloud to groups. In order for the music, images, and narratives that were enjoyed by mainly working- and lower-middle-class audiences to become mass culture, other means had to be developed, which they were by the late nineteenth and early twentieth centuries. The new technologies of photography, telephony, the phonograph, and the movies served well those who did not have the time or the means to contemplate the complexities of high culture, and these new technologies quickly became dominant. When this happened, the culture of print, with its demands of education, leisure time, and of access to the quiet and solitude that reading fiction or poetry demands, ebbed.

Radio and Print

We have examined one new form of storage and distribution in some detail: the photographic emulsion on plastic strips, which when exposed to light and developed into a series of high-resolution images, can be cut together in various ways, put in cans, and sent around the country and the world to be projected on movie screens. Electronic transmission was another important nineteenth-century development. The telephone, phonograph, and radio delivered voice and music, news and entertainment, into the most intimate of spaces, the home. To see a movie, people had to go out of the house, with all the planning and expense that entails. By the twenties, radio was omnipresent in the domestic sphere and became the dominant form of entertainment. When sound came to film in the late twenties, a vigorous interchange between the two media began. Radio carried film advertising as well as programming based on current films. Radio stars played in films; film stars appeared on radio.

One version of print media expanded along with movies and radio by becoming integral to them. Newspapers advertised and reviewed radio and film. Movie magazines and newspaper gossip columns extended the work of studio publicity by keeping the stars and their personal lives in the public eye. It would be no exaggeration to say that, by the end of the twenties, an elaborate, integrated network of popular culture had evolved in which listener and viewer had access to an intertextual web of radio, movies, magazines, and newspapers. By intertextual, I mean that all of these elements referred to one another, reproduced or represented each other. Radio broadcasts were used as narrative elements in film; films were turned into radio drama; newspapers reviewed both and printed film publicity and scandal; film music and popular music were connected so that a movie theme was available on record and on the radio. By the 1940s, a film might include a theme song composed especially so that it could be released as a single.

Television

The only thing missing was a means of delivering moving images to the home, and that problem was solved after World War II. With the coming of television (which began development in the thirties), the web of mass-mediated popular culture was ubiquitous, available to anyone who could afford it. By the mid-1950s, almost everyone could. The intertextuality of this cultural web grew as well. Radio ceased being a medium for drama and assumed a major role first as a delivery system for popular music and, recently, as a site for the expression of various political views. Film and television took immediately to one another, even though television cut deeply into film attendance and moviemakers pretended nothing but scorn for the new form. Television became the delivery mechanism for old films and for films made specifically for television. Movie studios bought television outlets and assisted them with product. With the advent of the videocassette and cable television in the late 1970s, movies and television became, on a very important level, functions of one another. Filmmakers depend upon videocassette sales and rentals to round out the profits of a film. Moviegoers balance viewing at home with going to the movie theater.

Meanwhile, the domain of "high" culture shrank. It remains proscribed by class and education and finds a home in museums, concert halls, and bookstores with some airplay on radio and television. But it was always marginalized and is growing more so. The "popular," in particular the American version of the popular, is the dominant form around the world. Within it thrive many varieties and subforms, many national inflections. In almost all cultures, film is ubiquitous, and the most ubiquitous of all, the dominant of the dominant, is American film.

THEORIES OF CULTURE

In order to understand the place of popular culture in general and film in particular within the larger complex of cultural practice, it will be useful for us to look at some theories of culture, in particular those theories that discuss mass media and film. These theories constitute a new and expanding area of work called, appropriately, cultural studies. Cultural studies looks at various kinds of texts within the context of cultural practice, that is, the work, production, and material stuff of daily life, marked as it is by economics and class, by politics, gender, and race, by need and desire. It examines the form and structure of cultural texts as they create meaning or have meaning created by the people who produce them and the people who are entertained by them. Cultural studies thinks about meaning as an ongoing process built out of complex relationships between people in their daily lives and the works of imagination they look to for emotional and intellectual sustenance and release.

The Frankfurt School

An early wave of cultural criticism that took mass media as its subject found it deeply troubling, and for very good reason. The Frankfurt Institute for Social Research was founded in Germany in 1924. Its function was to integrate the study of sociology, psychology, culture, and politics. Among its members and associates—known as the Frankfurt school—were some of the most important left-wing thinkers of the twentieth century: Max Horkheimer, Theodor Adorno, Herbert Marcuse, Erich Fromm, Siegfried Kracauer, and Walter Benjamin. Because they were left wing and, many of them, Jewish, the Institute was closed down by the Nazis in 1933. Many of its members came to America, where they taught and pursued their work.

A core part of that work was the study of film and mass media. Seigfried Kracauer wrote two major studies of film, *Theory of Film: The Redemption of Physical Reality* (1960) and *From Caligari to Hitler: A Psychological History of the German Film* (1946). The latter was an attempt to describe a cultural mood, one that would lead to a cultural and political catastrophe, by looking at the films the culture had produced. Theodor Adorno wrote books and articles on philosophy and music and coauthored with Max Horkheimer *The Dialectic of Enlightenment* (1944). A chapter of this book, "The Culture Industry," along with Walter Benjamin's magisterial essay, "The Work of Art in the Age of Mechanical Reproduction," laid the foundation for future studies of media, culture, and politics. It proved to be a difficult foundation to build on. Given the society they observed, the conclusions about mass culture reached by Adorno, Benjamin, Kracauer, and others of the Frankfurt school were either very negative or ambiguous.

Germany in the 1920s was a society going through a massive political upheaval that would lead to the most brutally destructive regime in modern history. The Frankfurt school viewed the rise of popular culture in this society as part of the growing authoritarianism in Germany's political culture. Instead of a web of interrelated texts in which the listener or viewer is part of a complex structure of commercially produced and distributed music, news, images, and sound, the Frankfurt school saw a vertical, pyramidal structure where government and industry in close collusion with each other dominated the mass of people who watched films and listened to music and radio. The audience for popular culture was an undifferentiated and passive mass, robbed of subjectivity and individuality by an authoritarian government, which swayed the people to its needs by manipulating the popular media.

To the Frankfurt school, the audience for the popular was in fact *created,*
given form, made compliant, turned into a willing tool of the ruling political
party. Again, this view was based in a strong reality. Hitler's Nazi government
was the first to use mass media—radio and film especially (they were busily
developing television)—as a controlled means of communication, fashioning
information, entertainment, and outright propaganda in such a palatable way
that its audience could not, did not want to, resist. The Frankfurt school looked
upon the government and its associates in industry, journalism, broadcasting,
and film as strong and controlling, the audience as weak, willing, and easily
fooled. Horkheimer and Adorno wrote: "Life in the late capitalist era is a constant initiation rite. Everyone must show that he wholly identifies himself with
the power which is belaboring him. . . . The miracle of integration, the permanent act of grace by the authority who receives the defenseless person—once he
has swallowed his rebelliousness—signifies fascism."

The Frankfurt school understood that mass media did not have to clobber
its audience into submission, that people have free will that can be easily, willingly subdued. They understood the comfort that comes with joining a group,
swallowing rebelliousness, integrating oneself into the mass and receiving authority's grace. They saw and noted how easily the popular culture accepted
anti-Semitism, agreed to abstract calls for sacrifice to the fatherland, to the
promises of redemption from a despairing and oppressed life. These demands, along with the offerings of banal entertainment in the form of musicals, melodramas, and comedies made by the ruling powers were hard for
most Germans to resist.

Under Hitler, cultural difference, individual expression, artistic experimentation were not simply discouraged but destroyed. Serious art, modern
and critical art, was declared decadent and was banished. Books were burned.
Artists fled the country. Popular art was molded into the narrow spectrum of
hatred of Jews and communists, adulation of Hitler, and celebration of a
lower-middle-class life of home, family, and fatherland, driven by exhorta-
tions to keep sacrificing in order to perpetuate Nazi ideals. Fascism became a
model for the Frankfurt school's analysis of the culture industry as a conspir-
acy of politics and business to form, out of the most profound and uninformed
aspects of a culture's collective fears and desires, superficial entertainments
that confirmed and reinforced the basest instincts of that culture. The culture
seemed to yield unquestioningly.

The Frankfurt School in America

Unsurprisingly, Frankfurt school scholars tended to look down upon popular
culture from an elitist perspective. Anything that was part of such an abom-
inable political culture could not have any value. They took this elitist position
with them when they came to the United States in the late thirties. Theodor
Adorno particularly disliked the popular and wrote often of the debasement
of jazz and popular music. The worst part of Frankfurt school elitism was

popularized in the United States during the 1950s and became integrated with the general concern over what some people perceived as a decay of the culture and a rise in adolescent misbehavior. The fifties were a period of serious cultural instability, during which post–World War II anxieties were heightened by the Cold War with the Soviet Union. A paranoia about being subverted and infiltrated took over the country during the first half of the decade, and popular culture became a main target of its fears.

Right and Left   The anti–popular culture discourse of the 1950s was carried on by many sides. Attacks by right-wing politicians and journalists were not very sophisticated, though they stirred up many anxieties. They did not present the Frankfurt school's complex portrait of a culture industry that was an interrelated process of the government and the producers of entertainment crafting their products to manipulate the willing masses. Indeed, some Cold War writers and politicians put the argument of the Frankfurt school on its head. Where the Frankfurt school analyzed a top-down control of media and the population, fifties critics of the media argued that the media—especially film and television—were elitist and left wing. Rather than controlling the belief system of the people, the media subverted it, destroying their values.

Less virulent ideologues, indeed many fifties intellectuals on the left, argued that popular culture was simply too debased and shallow. If people were entertained by mass media, they were already diminished in intellectual and emotional response by contact with films, pop music, and television, or soon would be. Some critics of popular culture saw it—and some still do—as a promoter of violence and sexuality. Comic books, movies aimed at teenagers, and, near the end of the decade, rock and roll music were deemed the worst offenders. Congressional hearings investigated their influence. And, of course, the explosive growth of television in the fifties was looked on with dismay. While its manufacturers, producers, and promoters saw it as a miracle that would placate bored housewives and keep families together, its detractors saw it as a further degradation of cultural standards. Television was yet another sign that the culture was being reduced to a featureless, homogenized mass.

Masscult and Midcult

The social and cultural complexities of mass media were not as important to fifties critics as were pronouncements of decay and corruption. In the fifties and early sixties, elitist categories maintained a strict segregation of the arts and their audience based on matters as vague as taste. The film reviewer and cultural critic Dwight MacDonald categorized fifties culture into three parts. Creating a less ethnically and racially biased metaphor than the old "low brow, middle brow, and high brow" classification, he spoke about high culture—the complex, resonant art for the elite—but concentrated his attention on what he called Masscult and Midcult. By splitting popular culture into two groups, MacDonald could address a decade that was entertained by a new range of entertainment from Elvis Presley records and movies to plays and films written by Tennessee Williams and live television drama.

These new categories began to introduce an element of complexity into the American discussion of popular culture. They were still derogatory and judgmental: Masscult, MacDonald says, "is bad in a new way: it doesn't even have the theoretical possibility of being good." Midcult only reproduces the bad in a better light: "it pretends to respect the standards of High Culture while in fact it waters them down and vulgarizes them." However derogatory, these classifications at least began to recognize or point to the fact that popular culture was not monolithic, that issues of class and taste could be used to achieve a finer definition. But, without the Frankfurt school's complex ideological analysis and with the conservative bias so many of them held, the mass media critics of the fifties and early sixties mainly railed and raised alarms. These were the views from above. Meanwhile, the culture of the popular expanded.

By the late fifties, rock and roll, which began as African American rhythm and blues that was then integrated with country and western formats, became an important component of a revived, activist youth culture that began to have purchasing power to match young people's desire for a unique entertainment. In cinema, the influence of foreign films began nudging movies in the direction of high culture. At the same time, because of population shifts to the suburbs, movie attendance began to fall off and television viewing went up. In response, American cinema changed and began targeting specific age groups with specific kinds of movies, trying to pinpoint an ever-changing audience with both Low and Midcult films. Popular culture—both its products and its audience—grew more complex and needed new theories to deal with it.

Benjamin and Aura

New theories began to converge from many directions. The growth of film studies in the 1960s and the development of feminist theories in the early 1970s laid the ground for a growing interest in serious analysis of popular culture. Some of the new theories grew out of an essay by an associate of the Frankfurt school, originally written in 1936. It helped form the basis of a nonjudgmental, appropriately political, speculative, and complex meditation on popular art and its relation to the larger matrix of cultural practice. Walter Benjamin's "The Work of Art in the Age of Mechanical Reproduction" takes as its starting point the new elements of reproduction, storage and distribution that made film and other forms of popular cultural practice possible. For Benjamin, the difference between the old art of the elite classes and the new popular art of the masses is that popular or mass art is readily available outside the usual sites of museums and libraries. The image (film is Benjamin's main object of study, though his ideas can usefully be applied to recorded music, photography, television, and now to digital media) is not a unique, one-of-a-kind event, kept in one place, and viewed with awe and reverence. The image is now infinitely reproducible and available. It has lost that which makes it special, even worthy of worship, what Benjamin calls its aura.

Aura can be thought of as the uniqueness of a work of traditional high art. An original painting has aura. It is one of its kind, visible in its originality only where it is hung, looked at with the privileged relationship of viewer and the work itself. The autographed first edition of a novel might have an aura, as would the live performance of a play or symphony. Aura is the nonreproducible, the authentic, the original production from the hand of an artist or ensemble. Popular, mass-produced art is without aura. The compact disc by a rock group that you own is the same as thousands—hundreds of thousands—that were cut from the same master. The print of a film viewed in a mall multiplex in Cleveland is the same as a print viewed in a multiplex in West Palm Beach, or (except for the redubbing of the soundtrack) in Frankfurt, Germany. There is nothing unique about it. In fact, there is nothing about it. Nothing is there but digital, electronic, or optical data; no human presence but the beholding eyes and ears of the viewer, who the producers hope will respond in the same way as every other viewer anywhere—by paying for access.

Benjamin, unlike most of his Frankfurt school associates, did not look at this development with alarm. He looked at it as historical fact—something going on despite what social and cultural critics might think about it. He thought about the growth of popular culture as something to be understood not as an oppressive reality, but as a potentially liberating one. Loss of aura and ease of access meant two things. Everyone could come into contact with works of the imagination and everyone would be free to make of the auraless work what she could. Curiously, the loss of aura could lead to a greater intimacy with the work. The ritual and awe that surround the work of original genius might be replaced by the intimate interpretation of each viewer. "The progressive reaction," Benjamin writes, "is characterized by the direct, intimate fusion of visual and emotional enjoyment with the orientation of the expert." Every person becomes a critic, able to make sense and make judgments. Every person's perception becomes enlarged. "By close-ups of the things around us, by focusing on hidden details of familiar objects, by exploring common place milieus under the ingenious guidance of the camera, the film, on the one hand, extends our comprehension of the necessities which rule our lives; on the other hand, it manages to assure us of an immense and unexpected field of action."

Film and other mass media offer a place of entry and participation in the imaginative representations of the world. Certainly, Benjamin was not out of touch with the realities of mass media and politics, especially in his own country. He knew that the larger an audience, the more difficult it would be for mass art to present progressive ideas. He knew as well what the Nazis were doing with mass media and to the culture as a whole. He experienced it directly. Forced out of his country in 1940, this Jewish, mystic, Marxist intellectual, who wrote about angels as well as the mass media, would take his life on the Spanish border. He understood that Fascism attempted to reintroduce a false aura into the mass-produced art, turning it into spectacle and putting it into the service of political ritual and, inevitably, of war. Communism, he believed, might work the other way, by liberating the viewer and the work of art into a politics of communal action. While such a view is out of fashion at the moment, it reflects an understanding that an art of the masses can mean a participation of the masses in the political work of the culture.

The Aura of State Intervention   There have been important examples of governments working with artists to promote a popular art that involved many people on many levels, including the political. The artistic activity that followed the Russian revolution—and formed the model for Benjamin's idea of a communal, politicized art—is one successful example. The work of Eisenstein, Dziga Vertov, and other filmmakers, writers, and visual artists in the twenties exhibited an energy and a desire to reach their audience and actively engage the audience's intellect and emotions unparalleled in the century. Stalin put a stop to all that. Elsewhere, throughout the century, there have been many attempts at state intervention in the arts. Germany revived its film industry in the 1970s through state subsidies to television. Films were made for television and also exhibited in theaters. Popular response was mixed, but most of the films made under the subsidies were excellent. By and large, public funding has helped to foster a serious and engaged, personal and political cinema. But public funding has been less successful in forging a large-scale interaction of audience, work, and culture at large that Benjamin hoped might occur in the age of mechanical reproduction.

Mechanical Reproduction Online   Only recently has such an interaction occurred, and not in the cinema. The government, university, corporate-supported Internet is proving to be the one arena in which individuals form large communities of interaction and communication, where mechanical (in this case, digital) reproduction offers groups of people who have access to the appropriate equipment the ability to penetrate beyond the restrictions of personal and national borders, dissolving both into a large communal space. Nothing is so entirely without aura as the digital; there is nothing that allows such direct participation of one and many imaginations.

Nothing is as elitist, however, as the digital. Restricted to a middle class who can afford access, cyberspace is quite different from the movies, which, for Benjamin, offered access to everyone. For Benjamin, the age of mechanical reproduction offered the utopian possibility of integrating everyone into the work of the culture. To use a current cliché, it would be empowering. Benjamin's analysis also introduced a new way of thinking about the popular, a way of seeing culture as multifaceted, as having dimension and difference. Rearticulated, brought up to date, many of Benjamin's ideas—along with those of a contemporary of Benjamin's, the left-wing Italian intellectual, Antonio Gramsci—have formed the foundation of new approaches to culture and media. These approaches do not condemn the popular as vulgar and unredeemable, but attempt to understand its attraction, and its interactions. Benjamin insisted that popular culture was a culture of involvement in which viewers actively engaged the work, where everyone was an interpreter, molding the popular to our needs. The critical approaches that emerged from these ideas go under the heading of cultural studies.

CULTURAL STUDIES

Cultural studies is less a movement than a loose affiliation of intellectual agreements about how to think of culture and its productions. Influenced by the British cultural theorist Raymond Williams, and given its name by the British Birmingham Centre for Contemporary Cultural Studies, this wide-ranging discipline has some important foundational principles: the study of culture is interdisciplinary and broad. All events are seen in the context of cultural practice, and that practice is determined not only by the elite culture industry, but by the activities and interventions of many subcultures, which are determined by class, race, and gender. Cultural practice involves both the production of works and their reception by an audience. Culture and all its various components can be understood as coherent, legible, interactive "texts."

These texts can be briefly isolated for the purpose of study and then placed back in their cultural context. I can analyze Alfred Hitchcock's *Psycho* or James Cameron's *The Terminator* (1984) as unique texts, as I might a novel. I can examine their formal structure, their images and narrative form. But I must also integrate them within the culture of the late fifties and the economics of the end of the studio system (in the case of *Psycho*), or the apocalyptic consciousness of the 1980s and the melding of the superhero into the science fiction genre (in the instance of *The Terminator*). I can read parts of these films as cultural texts: the way the automobile in *Psycho* reflects an ambiguous response to mobility and security, and how the old dark house recapitulates familiar images from gothic literature and Hollywood horror movies. I can look at the way robotics in *The Terminator* is a sign of the culture's long-term attraction to and repulsion from the image of the automated human. *Psycho* and *The Terminator* can be analyzed as another entry into the popular imagination of Freud's story of Oedipus: *Psycho* talks about a child destroyed by his mother; *The Terminator* addresses the unending and impossible search for patriarchal figures who destroy and are destroyed. *The Terminator* can be figured as a response to the end of the Cold War and the unknown terrors that occur when we discover that the enemy is really us and not them. Both films can be seen as ways in which the culture continues to come to terms with the modern world, with despair, emptiness, and terrors of the unknown, how it deals with issues of the feminine and masculine, with its attraction to and repulsion by sexuality, with its fascination with and fear of otherness and difference.

Text and Context

Text and context—in their usual senses of the work of art and its cultural and historical surroundings—are reconfigured in cultural studies. The individual work, the work of culture, our acts of looking, understanding, and participating can all be read as interacting texts. Form and meaning make sense only when we examine their intersections in all their complexity. The key is *legibility*, the ability to read culture and its work, to understand, dissect, and then reassemble what we have read into a coherent analysis. No one element can be taken for granted. The whole is made of its parts.

Negotiation

Reading Benjamin, we introduced another principle of cultural studies which opposes many of the ideas of the Frankfurt school and almost all of the ideas of mass media studies of the fifties and early sixties. Instead of positing a "culture industry"—a conglomeration of governmental, political, and business forces that determines the commodities of popular culture and conforms the culture from the top down—cultural studies sees a complex interaction of production and response and reception. The consumers of popular media are not a dumb, cowed, undifferentiated mass, repressed and oppressed by the banal homogeneity of what they see and hear. People consume in many different ways, and with varying degrees of comprehension and ability to make interpretations. Individuals, as well as small and large groups, determined by their economic and social classes, make up subcultures who negotiate (a key word for the Birmingham school of cultural studies) meanings with popular texts, much like readers of high cultural products do. People have different backgrounds and different needs, which they put to use in negotiating with the text meanings that are most useful or pleasurable. People are capable of comprehension and of articulation, of struggling against the desire of the producers of the popular to inundate them with sounds and images. Everyone interprets, everyone responds. What the Frankfurt school sees as a monolith, cultural studies sees as a complex group of class-, race-, and gender-marked individuals, with desires and with intelligence. We don't merely accept what the culture industry hands down, we deal with it and use it.

Along with the process of negotiating with the text comes the work of unpacking. Earlier I spoke about the economy of the image. Films made in the classical style—as well as television, advertising, and other popular forms—pack a great deal of information into a small space. Much narrative detail is stored in a glance, a gesture, a nod, a camera movement, a cut. We understand films because we know the conventions, we know how to read and interpret. I suggested earlier that we interpret only what we have been trained to interpret through the repetition of banal conventions. Cultural studies holds that we can move through the conventions and unpack more subtle meanings, that we decode according to what we want or need to understand about a film or a song or a television program. We open the text, pick, choose, and interpret. What we interpret might not necessarily be what the producers intended. Women fans of *Star Trek* and *X-Files,* for example, write highly erotic, homosexual stories—"slash fiction"—about the heroes of their favorite programs and publish them on the web. Freddy Krueger, the evil dream figure of the *Nightmare on Elm Street* films, becomes a figure of fearful admiration for adolescents. Weekend soldiers in Serbia dress up like Rambo. Madonna is taken by teenagers as an icon of sexual liberation. Rap music and its lyrics provide the rhythms and narratives of African American street life. The Terminator moves, by means of subtle negotiation between filmmaker and audience and movie star, from destructive monster to substitute father. Forrest Gump becomes a role model. The class-crossed lovers of *Titanic* (James Cameron, 1997) become objects of adoration and a confirmation of teenage despair.

Judgment and Values

Not all the negotiations, unpacking of codes, and rereadings of cultural texts are for the good (Serbian nationalists playing Rambo only means that real people get killed; Forrest Gump is a role model only for dumbness); rarely are they ennobling in ways that we expect works of high art to be. But the idea of "ennoblement" may be as much a cultural cliché as is the notion that popular culture is a debasement. That some individuals or groups use culture badly is not unique or new. The Nazis made Jewish prisoners who were musicians play Mozart in the concentration camps. The point is that cultural studies attempts to be nonjudgmental while, we can only hope, maintaining a moral center. It seeks to describe and analyze and broaden. Judgment comes after comprehension.

But judgment must come. The interplay of perception and analysis, guided by methodology, that makes up critical thought must lead any critic to abstract what she finds about the culture into broad, general patterns and then analyze those patterns for subtle meaning. The description and evaluation of these patterns will be subjective, based upon the values and moral beliefs held by the critic. Some aspects of popular culture will be found wanting, even intellectually or morally degrading, but this judgment will not then become an all-embracing condemnation. Perhaps the key element of cultural studies is its ability to analyze broadly and make judgments discriminatingly.

Intertextuality and the Postmodern

The works of popular culture, however, make discrimination difficult because they feed upon themselves, interact, and absorb one another to a remarkable extent. Films refer to other films; musical styles are filled with quotations from one another—sampling, for example, is a popular formal element of rap; news gets confused with sensationalism; sexuality and violence constitute the major elements of almost all mass media, substituting themselves for more rational explorations of the world. The culture seems to be enthralled with images and sounds rapidly edited together. Fragmentation rules. In rock videos, the unifying elements of the classical style in film are sacrificed to the sensation of rapidity. The classical style made fragments look like wholes, and while that style still predominates in narrative films, in other forms—music videos, television commercials, news reports—fragments are presented as fragments while at the same time moving in a flow that is almost undifferentiated. Commerce, imagination, culture, news, intermingle and move us along in a process that makes analysis difficult.

This is the style of the postmodern, where hierarchies, definitions, and separations are broken down, and the quickly seen is substituted for the deeply understood. Cultural studies discovered the postmodern and, as if by necessity, adopted it. No one can look at popular culture for long and not recognize—with delight or with horror—the often indiscriminate flow of images and ideas. In film and television, images of extraordinary violence become as commonplace as the sentimentality of the characters who take part in them; images of the poor and the starving appear on television news, call upon our emotions and as rapidly disappear again. When images disappear so does sympathy. A clothing manufacturer uses images of the dead and dying to sell his goods. Everything seems to be occurring on the same plane of comprehension, or willing incomprehension. Popular culture appears to be in a steady state of assertion and denial, of claiming the importance of what is shown and then denying that it really means anything.

CONTINUITY This has made media historians and critics of all of us. Intertextuality—the interpenetration of various texts, one within the other—keeps reminding us how wise we are to the popular culture we've grown up with. The rapid association of images in film, television, and advertisements forces us to analyze and make sense of the image inundation. Staccato shrieks of violins in a television commercial will make us all think about *Psycho.* A commercial for a local car dealer will play the opening of *Also Spake Zarathustra,* and we will recall *2001: A Space Odyssey.* Any episode of *The Simpsons* will contain references to a dozen movies. Everyone is wise to the sounds and images of the culture, though, perhaps, no one is the wiser.

If you detect overtones of the Frankfurt school as well as fifties critiques of the popular in this argument, it is because of the tension between the open embrace offered by cultural studies and a need to maintain some balance between what may be important and what may not be. Cultural studies insists on accepting all aspects of the popular with an understanding that individuals take from it what they feel is important to them. More traditional criticism asks for value judgment, discrimination, and a preservation of hierarchies. Some practitioners of cultural studies may applaud the undifferentiated flow of the postmodern while other critical schools look in horror at its surrender of judgment and discrimination. As always, an intelligent compromise works best. The concept of negotiation, the recognition that the audience for the popular is not stupid, helps us understand that there may indeed be discrimination at work. A postmodern critic might argue that it is precisely because viewers and listeners are so sophisticated that sounds and images can be used in a rapid-fire, punning, intertextual structure. Perhaps it is because we have seen and heard it all before that no one accepts the old meanings, and the new ones have yet to be invented. At the same time, any critic must be aware of boundaries even as they are being broken down. Making judgments depends upon recognizing boundaries. We may not always want to keep them in place, but we must note their location, their history, and where they might be moved.

CULTURAL CRITICISM APPLIED TO CINEMATIC TEXTS

Cultural Studies and Film

How do we combine a theory of cultural studies with an understanding of the formal structure of film and come up with a reading of cinematic texts that situates them within larger cultural practices and within the culture as a whole? Such a task would involve looking closely at a film and how it is put together—including its form, its narrative structure, the function of the actors and stardom. We would need to address the thematic structure of a film—what it is saying. We would want to place the film in the context of other films of its kind and examine its intertextual structure. We would then need to take all of this and look at the film through the eyes of the period in which it was made, as well as the period in which it is being analyzed. In other words, we would try to see the film as its contemporaries did and then see it again as it looks to us now. We would have to place all of this information in line with larger social issues: politics, questions of gender, race, and class, of ideology and how the film in question fits or contradicts those general ideas and images we hold about our selves and our place in the world. We would want to draw some value judgments about the film. This should not be done mechanically, because the best criticism is written in a comfortable, integrated style, in which ideas are set forth and analyzed, grounded by the film being studied. There will be digressions along the way, but they constitute part of the complex weave of a film and its cultural surround.

Vertigo and *Die Hard*

I would like to attempt such a criticism of two films that could not seem more different and distant from one another. They are *Vertigo*, a film made by Alfred Hitchcock in 1958, and *Die Hard*, the Bruce Willis film directed by John McTiernan, thirty years later, in 1988. *Vertigo* is a film of great complexity and high seriousness, made by one of the few filmmakers in America whose name was as recognizable as that of a movie star. Hitchcock's popular television program, *Alfred Hitchcock Presents*, started airing in 1955, and had made his name a household word. Combined with his appearances in his own films, Hitchcock's weekly introductions to the television show made him among the most recognized filmmakers in the world.

POINT OF VIEW

MISE-EN-SCÈNE

LIGHTING

Vertigo appeared during Hitchcock's most fertile filmmaking period, right after the popular films *Rear Window* (1954), *To Catch a Thief* (1955), *The Man Who Knew Too Much* (1956), the less popular, darker film *The Wrong Man* (1957), and just before *North by Northwest* (1959) and *Psycho* (1960). *Vertigo* bears every sign of a careful, deliberatively crafted film, structured with a master's understanding of his own time and the methods of his art. Hitchcock attended to every last detail of his films and his career. A self-conscious artist, Hitchcock tried to gauge public taste and his own imaginative needs, to make the commercial and the subjective work together.

Die Hard appears to have come out of nowhere, like most Hollywood films. But we know by now that "nowhere" really means the anonymity of studio production. *Die Hard*'s director, John McTiernan, came to film from television commercials, a major breeding ground—along with MTV videos and the University of Southern California film school—of new directors. He had made two feature films before *Die Hard* (*Nomads*, 1986, and *Predator*, 1987). After *Die Hard*, he made two more successful films—*The Hunt for Red October* (1990) and *Die Hard*'s third sequel in 1995. In a business in which "you are no better than your last movie," McTiernan's career tottered with the expensive flop *Last Action Hero* (1993); the success of *Die Hard with a Vengeance* gave him a boost. Hitchcock is an example of a filmmaker who worked and thrived within the Hollywood system, using it to his advantage, stamping his personal mark on the films he made. McTiernan is a figure of the new Hollywood. While not a contract director, as he might have been in the old studio days, he is still typical of a decent commercial director. A better-than-average craftsperson, working as part of a large group of collaborators who are experts in the action/special-effects movie, he is sometimes able to bring together a film that is ultimately greater than its parts. With *Die Hard* he succeeded once in making a film that was successful on all counts.

Die Hard is very much a film of its time. A big-budget, action-adventure, special-effects blockbuster, it is one among a number of eighties' films that owe their lineage to *Raiders of the Lost Ark* (Steven Spielberg, 1982), the James Bond films of the sixties and seventies, and various political thrillers, heist films, and other adventure-based genres. *Die Hard* is a mixture of many kinds of films. Its originality and attraction derive from its consciousness of this mixture. This is a postmodern film that is wise to itself and its audience and that depends upon that audience getting all its jokes. It is ironic, knowing, and even a bit self-effacing.

Vertigo is also ironic, but its irony is dark and full of despair. Like *Die Hard*, it is also a film of its time, a complex time of introspection and anxiety. *Vertigo* is not self-effacing and takes itself very seriously. Where *Die Hard* keeps winking at its audience and inviting them to have a good time, *Vertigo* asks its viewers to examine their most uncomfortable emotions. This is a film in the modernist rather than postmodernist tradition. That means it demands its audience pay attention to its intricate structure—the way, for example, it seems to start its story twice and give away all its plot secrets before it unfolds its more serious, interior secrets near the very end. It asks that attention be paid to its ironies and its themes of an uncomfortable, fragmented world in which individuals always lose. But, because Hitchcock was mindful of conventional necessities, it is also romantic and glamorous. The latter qualities weren't enough to cover the darker qualities, and, unlike *Die Hard*, the film was not a big, commercial success.

The Cultural Mix: Film and Television

Analyzing films in their cultural contexts leads us into interesting, sometimes unexpected byways. The very technologies of film, especially when they are driven by commercial imperatives, become issues needing attention.

Screen Size   Both *Die Hard* and *Vertigo* owe a great deal to television. Hitchcock's fame had blossomed because of his television program. But *Vertigo*'s debt to television is more indirect, more technical, and driven by economics. It has to do, interestingly enough, with screen size, which becomes part of the film's aesthetic.

Film is made to immerse us in the process of its narrative. Part of that immersion is the consequence of the sheer size of the image. Larger than life, the image engulfs the viewer, overwhelms his space. Television, on the contrary, is overwhelmed by the space around it. Small, with poor resolution, its image is not comparable to the large, sharp image projected on the movie screen. So, during the fifties, when audiences left theaters by the hundreds of thousands to stay at home and watch TV, Hollywood responded by making movie screens larger and wider. Hollywood pretended not to get what television was all about—namely visual narratives delivered for free in the comfort of home—and thought their films could conquer the desire for TV by further overwhelming the viewer with the image. Of course, to hedge their bets, they also bought television stations and produced films and series for TV.

MISE-EN-SCÈNE   Various wide-screen processes were developed, invented, and reinvented in the early fifties (actually, Hollywood had been experimenting with wide-screen formats from the early part of the century). Cinerama used three cameras and three projectors to show an enormously wide image. Cinemascope (and, later, Panavision) squeezed the image onto the film—called an anamorphic process—and then unsqueezed it with a special projector lens. The result was that the standard ratio of the movie image, which had remained the same since the early thirties, permanently changed. It had been in a ratio of 1:1.33 or 3 × 4 (three units wide to four units in height). Cinemascope and other anamorphic processes turned it into 1:2.35 (more than twice as wide as it is high). Other processes involved matting the image in the camera or projector—putting a black mask across the top and bottom—to change the image size to 1:1.66 or 1:1.85, creating a wide screen.

A few people came back to the theaters to see the novelty of wide screen, but its legacy has not been a happy one. Cinerama went the way of 3-D, another visual gimmick of the fifties, which demanded glasses be worn to see the 3-D image. Hitchcock actually made a 3-D film in 1954, *Dial M for Murder*, but he never used Cinemascope or Panavision. Both Cinerama and 3-D were too ungainly and not well suited to narratives. Panavision and other wide-screen processes have remained. But because the screens of mall theaters are sized to fit the auditorium and not the film, directors can never be sure what will be seen on the edges of the frame. Therefore everything tends to get composed toward the middle. Television and videocassette have never become comfortable with masking the image top and bottom, presumably because viewers would complain that something is missing, and so they crop the image off at the sides, guaranteeing that something is definitely missing (about one-third of the Panavision or Cinemascope frame). Compositional precision was the victim of Hollywood's attempt to conquer television by drowning the viewer in image size. Viewers were subjected to experiments in the size of the image that resulted, ultimately, in a loss of the image.

Paramount Pictures, Hitchcock's studio during most of the fifties, developed its own wide-screen process called "VistaVision" and used it to compete with Twentieth-Century Fox's Cinemascope. All of Fox's films from 1954 to the end of the decade were filmed in 'scope. All of Paramount's films during the same period were filmed in VistaVision, *Vertigo* included.

Scottie drives around San Francisco in VistaVision. Shot . . .

Reverse shot—which is also a point-of-view shot. Vertigo *(Alfred Hitchcock, 1958).*

Wandering in Wide Screen   Hitchcock turned necessity to advantage. *Vertigo* is, in part, a film about a man wandering and searching. In the first part of the film, Scottie, the central character played by Jimmy Stewart, tails a friend's wife. He falls in love with her and, when she dies, he searches for her replacement. Much of the first half of the film is taken up by shots of Scottie in his car, driving through San Francisco, following the woman, Madeleine, to a museum, a flower shop, Golden Gate Park. While these languid sequences of driving, looking, spying constitute a major narrative expression of Scottie's deeply obsessive personality, they are also a kind of travelogue of San Francisco, presented in VistaVision. Hitchcock was a studio director and paid his debt by filming in the studio's proprietary format. At the same time, he made the wide screen part of the film's narrative structure, using its horizontal frame to show Scottie's wanderings and also his boundaries. The screen opens point of view and limits it as well.

Bruce Willis, TV, and Movies   By the 1980s, the screen-size wars were over. Films were, and continue to be, made in a variety of wide-screen formats. *Die Hard* is in Panavision (the ratio of 1:2.35). It makes excellent use of its broad horizontal scope especially by framing its characters in the corners of large architectural spaces so they seem overwhelmed and diminished by their surroundings. (*Die Hard* looks particularly dreadful on videotape where the sides are cut off: as with *Vertigo*, a letterboxed laserdisc is the best place to see it). *Die Hard*'s connection to television is not via the circuitous route of screen size, but directly through its star, Bruce Willis. He came to the film with an enormous reputation as a character on the popular television series *Moonlighting*, in which he played a snickering, wise-cracking detective—a somewhat overgrown adolescent with some conventional characteristics of self-assurance and an ability not to take himself too seriously. *Die Hard* was only his second film (the first was *Blind Date* in 1987), and it launched the second phase of his career, which followed an unusual track through the culture of American entertainment.

There is, generally, a lack of exchange of actors from one medium to the other. Some movie stars, like Willis, start on television, move to film, and never go back. Most stay in one medium or the other. The reasons have partly to do with old antagonisms between the two forms, despite the fact that those antagonisms are now gone on the economic front as the ownership of the companies that make or distribute television programs and movies converges. One reason has to do with salary: movies pay more. But mostly it has to do with status. Movies, even though they are seen by fewer and fewer people in theaters, retain a higher status than television's.

Bruce Willis versus James Stewart: The Function of the Star

Bruce Willis is a television link in *Die Hard*, where he expanded characterizations already familiar to millions of people. Within his own brief career, Bruce Willis has tried various roles, serious and comic, but keeps returning to the tongue-in-cheek adventure figure he does so well. His range is limited, his expressions restricted mostly to sneer and smirk with a small amount of vulnerability. He is a very physical presence: he uses his body as an expression of effort and turmoil, violence and revenge. Through physical stamina and wiliness, he transmits a sense of smartness, an engaging quality at a time when many people—men in particular—are uncertain how to express themselves in the world and are liable to choose dumb rather than smart.

James Stewart, the star of *Vertigo*, was also familiar to millions, but as a movie actor who had been in films since the 1930s. Stewart's acting range was also limited, but his was a limitation that allowed him, in the course of a very long career, to become something of a cultural barometer. Stewart's on-screen persona embodied, until the fifties, variations of a passive, sweet, vaguely embarrassed and self-effacing character. That very passivity and self-effacement seemed to make him into a kind of rubber stamp, onto which could be impressed not only the characterizations demanded by a particular role, but the responses of the audience as well. The illusion of simplicity and gentleness made him something of a mirror for everyone's best intentions. Until the fifties, he specialized in comedy roles, often assuming a foot-shuffling, head down, aw-shucks characterization, whose simplicity was irresistible. His characters were nonthreatening; a viewer could feel both kindly and superior to him.

It's a Wonderful Life   The role of George Bailey in Frank Capra's *It's a Wonderful Life* (1946) simultaneously summed up and altered this persona that Stewart, his various directors, and the audience had so carefully nurtured. Stewart and Capra added a measure of anxiety and despair to the character of George Bailey. The film's narrative is driven by George's attempt to get out of Bedford Falls and his continual frustrations in realizing this dream. The frustrations and anxieties reflect the lack of clarity about how an individual of ordinary means would make it in the new, unfamiliar world that had formed at the end of World War II, a world where old institutions and accepted ways of life were changing. *It's a Wonderful Life* is a rare Hollywood film that refuses to give its hero his life's dream and forces him instead to accept another role—almost literally forced upon him by the film. Indeed, the frustration George feels at the way his story refuses to come out the way he wants it to leads him to attempt suicide. Only through angelic intervention does he understand that, without him, the town he wants so desperately to leave would be a dark, violent, corrupt place. With this understanding, he takes the more "responsible" path and becomes a family man, a banker, and a protector of his town's interests.

  It's a Wonderful Life is one of the great postwar narratives of uncertainty about the present and the future, a statement of the culture's discomfort and yearning for fantasies of simpler times. It launched Stewart's career in a different acting direction. His roles became more serious, and that aspect of despair and moral confusion that he manifests in *It's a Wonderful Life* is played out through a succession of roles, most notably in the films he made for Hitchcock and in a series of Westerns he made for Anthony Mann, such as *Bend of the River* (1952), *The Naked Spur* (1953), *The Man from Laramie*, and *The Far Country* (both 1955).

POINT OF VIEW   Hitchcock began playing on the changes in Stewart's acting persona in *Rope* (1948), *Rear Window* (1954), and *The Man Who Knew Too Much* (1956). In *Rear Window*, a serio-comic film about the unpleasant consequences of being a voyeur, Hitchcock began to elicit from

Stewart a worried, somewhat obsessive performance. Playing a photographer confined to a wheelchair because of an accident, the character spies on his neighbors and forces his girl friend to investigate a murder he believes occurred in an apartment across the way. Beneath its jokey surface, the film raises serious points about the gaze, about the morality of looking and seeing what you are not supposed to see. It is a virtuoso riff on the technique of shot/reverse shot. In *Vertigo,* Hitchcock plays up further the obsessive characteristics he gave Stewart in *Rear Window,* and the two of them create one of the best portrayals of near-psychosis in contemporary film.

Vertigo and the Culture of the Fifties

To understand *Vertigo* and *Die Hard,* we must pause a moment to understand what happened in the late forties and the fifties to bring about the despair in Hitchcock's film and, ultimately, the various questions about heroism we will find raised in *Die Hard.* The end of World War II did not bring a feeling of victory and power to American culture. Instead it created a churning discomfort, an uncertainty about the future and a lack of clarity about the past. The revelations of Germany's attempted extermination of the Jews and the explosion of two atomic bombs over Japan that ended the war shook the culture and confirmed how easily our myths of civility and order could fall. The revolution in China and the expansion of the U.S.S.R. into Eastern Europe in the late forties further upset a society that thought the second great war of the century might settle things down overseas.

At home, major changes involving economics, race, gender, and class began in the early forties, continued throughout the war years, and generated anxiety for years to come. Labor expressed its unrest through a number of strikes during the war. There was a migration of the African American population to the North, creating economic opportunities for some who had not experienced them before, while disturbing the majority white population. Meanwhile, African American soldiers fought bravely in a segregated army overseas. Other minorities expressed their presence at home. Attacks against Hispanics resulted in the "zoot suit riots" that spread from southern California to Detroit, Philadelphia, and New York. The outbreaks of violence signified not only the willingness of minorities to express themselves, but set the stage for the creation of the myth of the juvenile delinquent after the war.

Women's Roles   The roles of women changed dramatically during the years of World War II. With most young men fighting abroad, women came flooding into the workforce, did quite well, and enjoyed the financial benefits. While few women rose to executive positions, they kept factories and shops operating and discovered a welcome liberation from old domestic routines. The liberation was such that, when the war was over, a massive ideological retooling had to be put into place. Men were returning from battle and wanted their jobs back. Women had to be reinserted back into their former routines.

Movies, magazines, and newspapers once again extolled the importance of motherhood and family, the submissive role of women, the nuclear family in which mother was anchored to home while father was free to move like a satellite out of the home, into the office and back.

An Age of Anxiety   By the early fifties, the culture was wracked with events it could barely understand. Huge internal and external changes continued to occur, such as suburbanization and the flight from the central city, the formation and institutionalization of the multinational corporation, the slow, painful progress of civil rights, the continued redefinition of gender roles. However, the United States sublimated these and many other pressing issues into a struggle against a mostly mythical external enemy, the "communist threat." Almost every issue was absorbed into the Cold War discourse of anticommunism.

Beginning in the late forties, and continuing through the fifties, the House Committee on Un-American Activities, the various committees run by Joseph McCarthy, newspapers, magazines, much of the language of political and popular culture, condemned as communist almost anyone who had once held or continued to hold liberal or left-wing views. People informed on friends and colleagues. Government workers, teachers, screen and television writers, directors, and actors lost jobs. Intellectuals were discredited. The blacklist thrived. American culture and politics underwent a purge.

Gender and the Cold War   Even discussions about gender got caught up in the absurd momentum of the anticommunist discourse. The political and the personal, the power of the state, the workplace, the family, the sexual all became confused and self-contradictory. The larger fears of subversion and conformity, of being taken over and changed by enemies from without were filtered down into the more immediate concerns of the role of men and women in the culture and the way gender determined the structure of power. Fifties culture was as much obsessed with sexuality and gender roles as our own. It tried to assuage obsession through control. The decade's most conservative desire was to maintain a perfect imbalance of male domination and female subservience, male mobility at work and female stability in the domestic space. But at the same time people feared that this desire for control in matters of gender and throughout the entire patriarchal structure would bring about an unwelcome conformity.

People seemed to find security in sameness while fearing that too much conformity would be dangerous. For example, while the growth of corporate culture was recognized as the source of secure jobs for men and a secure consumer economy for the country, it was also seen as something that interfered with the image of the free, unfettered male, who should be making his own way in the world. Voices were raised and books were written about men being unmanned by their new subservience to the corporation and the family.

The Kinsey Reports   The fifties culture of work, family, and community seemed to some to be causing a loss of male individuality and this caused even more confusion. Sexuality could be liberating but it could also be too liberating, and therefore subversive. But if men became too passive, this too could be subversive. Spurring on this confusion was one of the most influential and disquieting cultural events of the fifties: the publication of the Kinsey Reports on male and female sexuality (published in the late forties and mid-fifties, respectively). These scientific analyses, presenting themselves as objective, methodical surveys, frightened people. They claimed that there was no normative sexual behavior, no controllable, conventional way of defining what people do in the bedroom. In a world where moral, cultural, and political safe harbor was becoming increasingly harder to locate, the Kinsey Reports seemed to remove yet another anchor. Somehow, what the Reports seemed to be saying about sex became part of the general concern about subversion. Nothing seemed secure.

The Decline of the Male   Popular literature was more direct and less scientific in its anguish over conformity, the apparent diminishing of male potency, the growth of corporate culture, and communism. Articles in the popular *Look* magazine, gathered in a 1958 book called *The Decline of the American Male*, claimed that women control male behavior, from the early formation of men's psyches, to the kinds of jobs they take, to their competitiveness. Because women now demanded equal or greater satisfaction than the male, they were beginning to control his sexuality. The subjugation to women and the pressures brought by the culture had produced a broken shell of a man, without individuality, without power, overworked, stressed-out, unable "to love and to make moral decisions as an individual." Men were weakened and regimented, made impotent and recessive. "In the free and democratic United States of America, he had been subtly robbed of a heritage that the Communist countries deny by force." As males went, so went the country. Communism by female control.

The Vulnerable Male in Film   To be sure, fears of conformity and the decline of masculinity were not always represented in such bizarre terms. In fact, many films of the decade examined questions of gender with some delicacy and complexity. They were able to put aside the anticommunist hysteria. Many of them created interesting narrative combinations out of the culture's fears of conformity, out of juvenile delinquency (which the culture invented as another way of scaring itself about what was happening to masculinity and another reason to excoriate mass media), out of notions about gender that somewhat altered the old stereotypes of the rugged male hero. Some of these films, such as *A Place in the Sun* (George Stevens, 1951) and *The Man in the Gray Flannel Suit* (Nunnally Johnson, 1956), presented male characters who in their passivity, sensitivity, and vulnerability took on characteristics and attributes usually associated with female characters.

On the face of it, The Wild One *(Laslo Benedek, 1954) is a fifties juvenile delinquent-motorcycle gang movie. But it is also a fifties vulnerable male movie (like its near cousin, Nicholas Ray's* Rebel Without a Cause, *1955). In this close-up, Brando emotes his sensitivity and despair over being misunderstood and mistreated.*

A number of postwar film actors, Montgomery Clift, James Dean, Marlon Brando, and Paul Newman, in films like *A Place in the Sun, Rebel Without a Cause* (Nicholas Ray, 1955), *The Wild One* (Laslo Benedek, 1954), and *The Left-Handed Gun* (Arthur Penn, 1958), expressed a search for new ways of expression under the guise of a withdrawn sensitivity. Their acting styles were a major break with prewar movie conventions; their roles spoke to the repressed anger and sexuality of the culture at large. In *The Wild One*, Marlon Brando plays a biker with a very sensitive soul, who, in one scene, alone with his motorcycle in the night, weeps. Early in the film, a girl asks him, "What are you rebelling against?" "Whaddya got?" he asks. This film, along with *Rebel Without a Cause*, spoke to many people's feelings about the constraints and confusions of the fifties. *The Wild One* was considered subversive enough to be banned in England for many years, but its interest is really not in the rebelliousness of the male character, but in his ambiguous expression of anger and passivity. The film's representation of masculinity plays against conventions of heroism and strength; it is, finally, the feminizing of the male that make this and other films of its kind attractive and curious.

Vertigo and *Die Hard:* Men in Film

Vertigo is not a film about youthful rebellion. Nor is it on any explicit level about fears of conformity or communist subversion. Quite the contrary, it is about a middle-aged man who implodes under the weight of sexual repression and despair, bringing about the death of other people in his wake. It is more closely related to the fifties films of constricted and destroyed businessmen, films like *The Man in the Gray Flannel Suit* and Nicholas Ray's *Bigger Than Life* (1956), than it is to Ray's *Rebel Without a Cause* or to *The Wild One*. But it is of a piece with the decade's concerns with change and betrayal, with power and passivity, domination and servitude, and sexual panic. It quietly addresses all of these concerns and the culture's sense of incompleteness, its sense of business that is not merely unfinished but unfinishable. It touches, obliquely, on the Cold War obsessions of containment, though here it's not communism that is contained, but the emotions of a deeply repressed man, unsure of his place, uneasy with his sexuality.

Die Hard would seem to be *Vertigo*'s opposite. It is a film about getting things done, and its hero is uncontained. The film has evil villains who are taken care of by a strong and resourceful man. *Die Hard*, unlike *Vertigo*, is about male strength and heroism, about action that is not questioned. Yet resourceful and heroic as he is, Bruce Willis's John McClane bears a relationship to the sensitive men who began appearing during the fifties. He carries pain with him. Not the vague cultural anxieties that afflicted characters thirty years earlier. John's is a much more contemporary pain—though its roots lie deep in fifties gender ideology as well as conservative 1980s notions about individual initiative. John's wife has left him, and *Die Hard*'s narrative is set into motion by his traveling from New York to Los Angeles to attempt a reconciliation. John's responses to his wife's newfound independence bear traces of the same sexual anxieties that marked his predecessors. There is even a touch of the fifties fear of corporate strength mixed in. But John McClane is a man of the late eighties. His insecurity is marked by the cultural discourse of women's independence, not male dependence, by the fact that his wife left him to take a corporate job, even to reclaim her last name. Such an event in a fifties movie would be the cause of derision, not anxiety. More accurately perhaps, it would be anxiety turned into derision.

Die Hard's John and *Vertigo*'s Scottie do have a common lineage. Both characters are policemen. John comes from a long line of movie cops, those tough New York Irishmen with soft hearts. These are figures unique to film, yet reassuring in their mythic qualities. Scottie's lineage is more local—he is a San Francisco cop—and more engaged with fifties film images and narratives of damaged men. He cannot live up to the expectations of his job. While John McClane is sick at heart over his separation, Scottie is sick in soul and mind, a sickness that manifests itself as vertigo, a paralytic response to heights. This results in the death of a colleague at the very beginning of the film, when a rooftop chase leaves Scottie dangling, paralyzed, unable to save one of his men. Scottie leaves the force and is made vulnerable to a monstrous plot by a businessman who plays upon his sincerity, insecurity, and self-doubt, and destroys his life and that of a woman with whom he thinks he's fallen in love. Scottie is left at film's end alive but reduced, staring into the void. John McClane, through a series of explosively adventurous acts, saves his wife, develops a profound emotional attachment to an African American policeman, and emerges from a series of apocalyptic events alive, triumphant, but a somewhat conflicted super cop.

Scottie's despair and John's conflicted state are the result of gender confusions specific to the moments of their stories. Scottie Ferguson is the timid fifties male, reduced in stature, capability, and agency in the world. There is little he can *do*. He is, in his small fictional container, a metaphor of the fifties middle-class, middle-aged man, undone by forces over which he has lost control. John McClane is a collective fantasy of exactly the opposite response. By the late eighties, fear of loss of control had turned into the reality of lost control. The succession of blows to the culture's self-esteem and to the power of the individual over anything in the world had taken their toll. While there were some major victories in the sixties and seventies—gains in minority and women's rights, effective mass protests against the Vietnam War—there were greater, more profound defeats. A lingering unhappiness was the result of the Kennedy and King assassinations, the frustrations caused by Vietnam experienced by those who supported and opposed it, the corruption of the Nixon administration, culminating in Watergate, the stagnation of real income, and a more subtle, yet farther reaching realization that America had little power in an increasingly complex and fragmented world, that an individual's power over everything had diminished. Fifties anxiety became the helplessness of the eighties, figured in its quest for suitable heroes, reflected in the election of Ronald Reagan, the movie star hero–president.

The Hero's Role   The role of the hero, intimately tied to issues of masculinity in any cultural period, is always under question. It was being questioned in the fifties, and it was again in the late eighties. The notion of the strong, moral, righteous, and courageous man of action, who would cleanse the entire culture of corrupt and violent forces—by means of greater violence—has never held up very well when tested in reality. After World War II, the premise of heroism was examined in film across the board. The great Western director, John Ford, was exploring the corruption of the Western hero as far back as *Fort Apache* in 1948. In *The Searchers* (1956), Ford was pressing his and America's favorite heroic figure, John Wayne, to give a performance in film that explored the proximity of heroism to psychopathic obsession.

This examination and debunking continued, particularly in the Western, through the early seventies and resumed in the late eighties in other genres. *Die Hard* thinks a lot about the old movie hero, and John Wayne in particular. I pointed out that the Bruce Willis character is related to the movie stereotype of the Irish cop. But there is more. His character is named John McClane. In 1952, John Wayne played the title character in an anticommunist cop film called *Big Jim McLain.* John Wayne as Jim McLain becomes Bruce Willis as John McClane. But this is not a simple substitution or even a complicated reference to the great film hero. It is an attempt to embrace and deny heroism, all at the same time. At one point in *Die Hard,* the terrorist Hans, frustrated by John's clever and heroic efforts to outsmart him, calls to him in desperation, "Who are you, just another American who's seen too many movies . . . ? Do you think you are Rambo or John Wayne?"

Sylvester Stallone's *Rambo* was, just two years before *Die Hard,* one of the last action-adventure films to take its central character with deadly seriousness. Rambo became a right-wing icon. It was not until *The Terminator,* in 1984, that the action film hero began to take on some of the reflective qualities that the Western hero had in the fifties. Arnold Schwarzenegger, ex–muscle man turned actor, moved his career forward by not taking his characters too seriously. There was always something safe and nonthreatening in Schwarzenegger's posturing, and it became even safer after *The Terminator,* when he began actively poking fun at his earlier characters and went on to play comic roles. His presence is invoked by John in *Die Hard,* who says, at one point, "There's enough explosives in here to blow up Arnold Schwarzenegger."

John McClane *is* a hero and would be directly in the John Wayne–Rambo tradition if he would take himself more seriously. He fights manfully; he gets bloody (or "blooded" as some die-hard believers in trial by violence would say); and he demonstrates uncanny recuperative powers, so uncanny that they became a model for action-adventure films that follow. He becomes John Wayne and Rambo and a parody of both. *Die Hard* begins a new phase of movie violence that is now called cartoon violence. The damage being done to human bodies in film is so enormous that "real" people would never survive it. These films, which include the *Die Hard* and *Lethal Weapon* series and Bruce Willis's film *Hudson Hawk* (Michael Lehmann, 1991), as well the Stallone vehicles, *Demolition Man* and *Cliff Hanger* (both in 1993, directed respectively by Marco Brambilla and Renny Harlin), are some of the contemporary popular movies that begin to reveal the fact that the image and the narratives made from them are not of the world, but of film, and that film violence is a visual trick. They can, of course, go only so far. Audiences do not seem to want a full-scale revelation of artifice and self-reflection. *Hudson Hawk* and the Arnold Schwarzenegger film *Last Action Hero* (1993, directed by *Die Hard*'s John McTiernan) failed partly because they did not take themselves seriously enough and revealed a sense of play that went beyond some viewers' desire for a necessary illusion. We want heroes to be self-mocking, but we don't want them mocking us.

Heroically antiheroic might best describe John McClane. He is the confused late-twentieth-century man turned into a courageous, resourceful, and indestructible defender of his wife and her fellow workers. He is always a little befuddled, but always ready for action.

Stories of Modernity

In order to understand more clearly where these two films and their heroes diverge and converge, we need to consider for a moment their narrative approaches, which determine the way they speak to their contemporary experience. *Vertigo,* with its dark, ironic structure, is a modernist narrative. Modernity—the movement of technological advancement, increased urbanization, rapid fragmentation of dependable, cohesive structures such as the family, religion, dominant race or ethnicity, and government, along with the falling away of individual agency—climaxed in the seventies and eighties. The responses to modernity are represented in various ways, including the stories the culture tells itself. Movies and television bring our fears to our attention, sometimes confirming them, sometimes attempting to assuage them with narratives about mastering our destiny, overcoming great odds, and recuperating our emotional losses. In the fifties, science fiction films spoke to our terrors of vulnerability to alien forces—stories which are being retold again today. Melodrama tended to confirm the loss of individual power by insisting that the family, the married couple with children, rather than the individual, was the best bulwark against modernity—all the while confirming the fragility of the family. *Vertigo* is an unusual affirmation of the disintegration of both the family and the self in modernity. It has romantic elements and touches of fantasy. But it is concerned mainly with the coming apart of the modern male.

Scottie is lost, unable to act or to love. His female friend, Midge, has been unable to get him to respond to her sexually. Her simplicity and directness frighten him. So does her sense of humor. She is a designer, currently working on a brassiere ("You know those things. You're a big boy now," she tells him). The brassiere she's designing has "revolutionary uplift," based on the principle of the cantilever bridge, and it parodies the fifties fetishism of the female breast, the formulating of women's bodies into preconceived male fantasies.

Scottie's own fantasies are so powerfully conceived that women are unattainable for him, and he suffers either from impotence or sexual incompetence. Immediately following the banter about the brassiere, Scottie and Midge talk about a moment, years ago, when they were engaged for three weeks. Scottie insists that Midge called it off. She doesn't respond. But Hitchcock does. He cuts twice to a close-up of her, very tight, and high enough to knock the balance of the frame off center. She simply frowns a bit and looks slightly off into the distance. It's a very typical Hitchcockian gesture, exploiting the standard grammar of the reaction shot to expand the viewer's comprehension of the situation. In this case, the reaction shot of Midge indicates to us that Scottie is not only in trouble sexually, but is unaware of it. He is unaware of who he is and what he is capable or incapable of doing.

Scottie is an emotional void, into which a rich businessman pours an incredible plot about his wife who thinks she is inhabited by the spirit of a nineteenth-century woman who committed suicide. (A major best-seller in the early fifties was *The Search for Bridey Murphy*, about a woman who, under hypnosis, revealed a past life. In 1956, Paramount, the studio that produced *Vertigo*, made a VistaVision film of the book. Hitchcock may be consciously parodying the Bridey Murphy story in *Vertigo*.) The businessman asks Scottie to follow his wife (who is not really his wife) and report on her action. She becomes the obsessive core of Scottie's life, which is so lacking a strong center that it barely survives. Scottie is the man of the postwar age, without power, without a sense of self and able only to recreate his desires in other people, who are not who he thinks they are.

Everything is false, a huge ruse created by the businessman—and by Hitchcock, who gives nothing away until much later in the film—to cover up the murder of his wife. But the ruse itself, as is typical in a Hitchcock narrative, is less important than its effects on the characters and the viewer. We are privy to the decay of Scottie Ferguson from someone who is already weak and afflicted, to an obsessive-compulsive, to a sado-masochist, to a shell of man, gazing down at the abyss, having finally caused the death of the woman he has tried to re-create into another's image. If this sounds melodramatic, it is. *Vertigo* is in the tradition of fifties melodramas about repressed desires exploding and then imploding back onto the central character—who is usually a woman. *Vertigo* makes its figure of melodramatic suffering a man. It is unusual too because its narrative plays ironically with Scottie's perception and the viewers'. We must disentangle ourselves from Scottie. In the first part of the film we tend to identify with him; in the second, we are asked to pull away and judge. There is no comfortable closure. Neither the character nor his world is redeemed at the end of the film. Scottie is left utterly, unrecuperably alone and in despair. In short, *Vertigo* has aspects of tragedy about it.

Stories of Postmodernity

Modernity, and its narrative expression, modernism, speak to the loss of a center through an ironic voice with a whisper of tragedy. Postmodernity sees the center—the binding stories and beliefs of culture—as already lost and decides to get on with it through many voices, many images, spoken and shown with irony and cynicism. *Die Hard* builds its structures by borrowing from wherever it can and using or alluding to whatever fits—or doesn't. It is a ping-pong game of pop-cultural memory and contemporary cynicism. It plays havoc with any serious moral structures other than the sentimental affirmation of individual heroism. Like the postmodern in general, *Die Hard* is a roller coaster of images, a feast of the intertextual, the junk food of the indecisive and confused.

As a postmodern work, *Die Hard* tries, and largely succeeds, in being everything to almost everyone: an action-adventure movie, a political thriller, a buddy cop film, a discussion of race, an ironic commentary on movie heroism, and (though it may not be quite serious about doing this) a study of gender conflict in the late 1980s. *Vertigo* is a movie conscious of its seriousness, a slow, thoughtful, and formally acute meditation on gender and male anxiety. *Die Hard* is a big, loud, explosive ball of fire that is built out of one of the oldest narrative structures in cinema, the alternation of scenes of pursuers and pursued, an alternation of action and reaction. It is a captivity narrative, entranced with violent action and a hero who doesn't take himself too seriously and can't be killed, who is compared to John Wayne and Rambo but thinks of himself as Roy Rogers.

Postmodern Villains   If John is confused as a hero, the villains are confused even more. John has flown into Los Angeles from New York to see his estranged wife, Holly, who works for a rich Japanese company, the Tagaki Corporation. He visits her in the middle of the company's Christmas party, which is attacked by a group of terrorists, who kill the boss and take the rest hostage.

The 1980s were a decade of swiftly changing attitudes toward foreigners as well as women. The latter had found their voice, and men were uncomfortable with what that voice was saying. The former were creating other kinds of confusion. The Japanese were particularly frustrating to Americans. We had been victorious over them in World War II. Now their economy was booming and their products, from VCRs to automobiles, were used by almost everyone.

They seemed to be buying up everything in this country from movie studios to golf courses to major tracts of real estate in large cities. They were held up as a model of productivity, yet demonized as a strange, alien culture. Though it was never quite spoken, they remained in memory as our dark-skinned enemies. There were other enemies as well, and *Die Hard* seems to acknowledge them all. If the Japanese seemed to be threatening us with economic takeover, then Europe and the Middle East were threatening us with terrorists: people with less than comprehensible political goals that they attempted to achieve by the most appalling violence. In all cases, we responded with fear and loathing to the cultures that threatened us, that we did not understand, or that provided convenient diversion from the complex economic and social processes occurring at home.

Die Hard plays with these complexities and confusions and turns them inside out. Holly's Japanese company is apparently quite benevolent, and her boss, Mr. Tagaki, is a kindly and paternal man. He talks gently and has the rare quality of dignified self-mockery. "Pearl Harbor didn't work out," he tells John, "so we got you tape decks." In fact, the villain in the company is not the foreign boss, but another paper tiger of the eighties, the yuppie, Ellis. The yuppie was the eighties version of an old cultural stereotype once called "nouveau riche" and yuppies became figures of resentment and ridicule to the working- and lower-middle-class people who were not part of the eighties boom. They were the subject of a number of "yuppies in hell" movies—such as *Fatal Attraction* (Adrian Lyne, 1987) and *Pacific Heights* (John Schlesinger, 1990)—in which yuppie characters had to go through humiliating, often violent, events to redeem themselves.

Die Hard's yuppie is a coke-snorting, sniveling fool, who shows off his Rolex, comes on to John's wife, and betrays both her and John to the terrorists. In return, the terrorists shoot him dead—much to everyone's delight. Mr. Tagaki is also brutally murdered by the terrorists, much to everyone's horror. This kindly, civil man stood in contrast to everyone else but John and Holly, and his murder clearly marks the ruthlessness of the terrorists—who turn out not to be terrorists.

Midway through the film, Hans, their leader, is discovered to be not the politically driven terrorist he pretends, but just a thug whose gang is out to steal from Tagaki's safe. Suddenly the film is stripped of the problematically political and becomes simply a struggle between good and bad. Even when depoliticized, Hans's gang is a strange model of cross-cultural diversity: there is a violent Russian, a number of Asians, and an African American who is both a computer wizard and a heartless murderer. This is an international cross section of the bad and it mirrors the film's unusual treatment of race.

Race in Die Hard   The only references to race in *Vertigo* are in Gavin Elster's fantastic story about his wife, who, he says, is possessed by the spirit of a nineteenth-century Hispanic woman, stereotypically marked as sensual and exotic. Although there were a number of films throughout the fifties that did deal with racial issues, usually in very positive, liberal ways (films like Joseph Mankiewicz's *No Way Out*, 1950, and Martin Ritt's *Edge of the City*, 1957, to name only two), there existed another kind of segregation. In most cases, if race was not a central subject of the film, it was not considered at all. Therefore, in most films, people of color either did not exist or were treated as servants. By the eighties, race was a consciously pursued issue in popular culture, almost always present, though treated with various degrees of sincerity and enlightenment. In good, postmodern fashion, *Die Hard* plays its race card in an indecisive and noncommittal way, giving and taking, leaving us in a quandary. John is picked up at the airport by Mr. Tagaki's driver, a young black man named Argyle, who, throughout the film, sits in his limousine, listening to music, seemingly oblivious to the mayhem going on in the skyscraper above him. He threatens to be another in the long, ugly history of stereotypes of the dopey black man—until he becomes a hero, by driving his limo into the van of the escaping gang.

Early in the film, as John is cornered by the gang in the unfinished floors of the skyscraper, another African American makes an appearance. This is Al, the cop. He is introduced as a bumbling, good-hearted soul, buying junk food for his pregnant wife, driving his car into a ditch when he learns what's going on in the building. However, he quickly emerges as the only representative of authority who has any sense. When the police arrive in force, their leader proves to be a dope. Two FBI men, Johnson and Johnson (one of whom is black), arrive, and are pompous fools. A representative of the media turns out to be a self-serving, dangerous man, whom John's wife, Holly, punches in the mouth. But Al quietly endures, out on the street, in phone contact with John, remaining calm amidst the growing chaos, supporting John in his isolation, providing our point of view from the outside. The cross cutting between the two of them creates their bond and assures us that John will be saved, no matter how perilous his situation seems. Al becomes more than a black cop, and this transcendence is important, because it leaves the race issue unresolved. He becomes—after Tagaki is killed—a paternal figure, John's surrogate father. He also becomes John's surrogate wife and mother, falling into the stereotype of the protective black mammy.

The Buddy Film

Vertigo is one of the most potent investigations of heterosexual panic undertaken in the fifties film. (Hitchcock visits the problem again in *Psycho*, in which he solves it in an especially perverse way, indicating that the male personality can be entirely absorbed by the maternal female.) By the seventies, Hollywood found other ways to deal with the crushing difficulties of men living up to the image of themselves produced by the culture. One was the buddy film, in which two men—most often cops—are paired in a loving union of support and good humor in which everything is possible but sex. Buddy movies always insist that the two male figures are heterosexual. They have wives or

The romance of the buddies. These stills represent the parallel sequences of recognition and embrace in John McTiernan's Die Hard *(1988). In the first sequence (figures 1–4), John greets his estranged wife, Holly. Then, after his adventures in the skyscraper, he greets Al (figures 5–8), the cop and John's new buddy (his new love? note how Holly is marginalized on the edge of the frame). The gestures and the affection are mirrored.*

girlfriends. But the women are peripheral; true nonsexual love and unfettered pleasure are derived from the relationship between the men. It is a narrative construct that avoids the painful introspections of the fifties films of male despair, skirts issues of race by having one buddy white and the other black—providing a weak pretense of racial equality, and avoids more complex investigations of male–female or same sex relationships.

Die Hard is a great riff on the buddy film. Al and John are given a multifaceted relationship. They are father and son, mother and child; they embrace almost like lovers. Near the end of the film, most of the villains having been killed off, John emerges from the skyscraper; he and Al recognize each other through a rapturous exchange of point-of-view shots. Al, once afraid to shoot his gun, redeems his manhood by shooting the last of the bad guys. John walks away from Holly, and embraces Al passionately. Holly is marginalized on the edge of the frame as the two friends express their love.

The sequence echoes one early in the film when John has his first reconciliation with Holly in Tagaki's office. Holly enters the male space where John is talking to Tagaki and Ellis. There is an exchange of glances between John and Holly; they walk over to each other and embrace. In the sequence at the end of the film, the same pattern occurs, but the genders are reversed. John and Holly meet again, but now the exchange of glances and the final embrace is between two men. The bond between the buddies is sealed.

Were the film to end here, interesting questions would be raised and the line between buddies and lovers might be confused. But remember, this is a film that will not allow any statement or idea to stand without presenting its opposite. Al soon yields his embrace. He tells Holly to take good care of John, and the husband and wife are sent out of the picture arm in arm. John is saved, his marriage is saved, Al is redeemed, and the love between two men is strong and protected from a tantalizing suggestion that it might be something more. Al changes from potential lover to protective mother. The domestic, nuclear family is saved. After all, the premise that begins the film is John's coming to Los Angeles to see his estranged wife and save his marriage. After so many trials, he may now assume his place as the heroic head of the family. He has proven himself. But, in the process, he has made a strong male bond with Al, the kind of bond, movies keep telling us, men need to be comfortable and free; to be protected, finally, from those domestic bonds that always seem to be so difficult for men to maintain.

The End of Redemption

Scottie is not saved or protected by anyone. He wants to be the hero who saves the heroine in distress, except that the heroine is not in distress; he is. First he pursues the lie that Elster manufactures for him, then he attempts to re-create the lie by searching for a woman who never existed. In the second part of the film, Scottie discovers Judy—who was the woman who "played" Madeleine in Gavin Elster's hoax. Scottie forces her to remake herself as Madeleine. He denies her personality and tries to suck her into his. They return to the Spanish mission and she falls from the roof of the bell tower. There is not triumph over evil because, unlike *Die Hard, Vertigo* does not externalize it. Where love and friendship are offered to John McClane, Scottie is left only with his own narcissism and madness. *Vertigo,* like its name, is about an unbreakable downward spiral.

There is much falling in both *Die Hard* and *Vertigo.* Hans falls from the skyscraper. John falls down an elevator shaft and swings out a window supported only by a fire hose. But these falls solidify his heroic stature, even as he downplays it. He returns from struggle bloodied but unharmed, saves the captives, and appears reunited with his wife. The film quietly admits it's all too fantastic, as fantastic as Scottie's obsessive attachment to Madeleine/Judy. But *Die Hard* asks us to join in the joke. *Vertigo* asks us to observe Scottie with pity, seriousness, and even with sad awe as he destroys his life. The relationship between viewer and *Vertigo* is as serious as Hollywood ever demands such a relationship be. We are asked to read this film carefully, to understand its subtleties, to stay with it as it reveals to us the secrets that aren't revealed to its central character. There are no secrets in *Die Hard*, only spectacle. Its internal confusions about gender, race, nationality, politics, authority are meant to be taken only as passing jokes, as momentary bits of relevance, or irrelevance.

We could conclude from this that the Frankfurt school and the fifties media critics were correct, that there is an unalterable breach between high and low culture and that, at its best, *Vertigo* falls into Dwight MacDonald's category of Midcult and, at its worst, *Die Hard* is irredeemably Masscult. *Vertigo* attempts to be tragedy, though, at bottom, it is a strong romantic melodrama, well constructed, dark and complex. *Die Hard* makes no such reach and comfortably accepts its Masscult status as a simple entertainment, acceptable as straightforward action film or as a sarcastic, cynical, even ironic, play on serious issues. Its refusal to take seriously any of the issues it raises only emphasizes its lack of commitment to serious intellectual inquiry.

But our reading suggests another path. By noting the different directions the films take, and recognizing that despite their different intentions, they are very serious about using film form expressively, we discover a common base. Then, analyzing their proximity to their cultural contexts and the ways, consciously or not, they address those contexts, we see that it is possible to understand both films as serious imaginative statements that come out of commercial intent. We could argue that *Vertigo* is a less cynical film than *Die Hard* because it is thematically more complex and makes more demands upon the attention and the intellectual and emotional response of the viewer. But ultimately, this is a difference in *address*, in the way the filmmakers and their films decide to talk to us. The address requires a difference in *response*, the ways in which we choose to react to the film.

This brings us back to the cultural studies position. The imagination operates in many different ways and for many different reasons, none of them completely pure or completely corrupt. The imagination of a viewer responds in different ways to different films. I find the racial and gender ambiguities of *Die Hard* extremely interesting and revealing, and the overall structure of the film irresistible in its confidence and engaging in its mixture of humor, action, and absurdity. *Vertigo* impresses me with the fine care and detail of its structure and moves me with the depth of its insight into male vulnerability. Both films are impressive in the ways they deal, subtly but pointedly, with the culture from which they emerge.

On another level, both films, fascinating as they are in their differences and similarities, clarify the ways all films tell their stories, sometimes the same or strangely similar stories, in various guises, various forms. Even two such different films as the ones we have analyzed here converge at sometimes unexpected points. One reason for this is that stories are a limited resource. Another is that what we seem to want our stories to tell us is limited as well; we demand convergence and repetition. We find security by having the same stories told over and over again.

NOTES AND REFERENCES

Definitions of Cultures, The Roots of Cultural Differences Two standard works on the history of melodrama are Peter Brooks, *The Melodramatic Imagination: Balzac, Henry James, Melodrama, and the Mode of Excess* (New Haven: Yale University Press, 1976) and David Grimsted, *Melodrama Unveiled: American Theater and Culture, 1800–1850* (Chicago: University of Chicago Press, 1968).

Theories of Culture There is another branch of media research known as mass communications research. This is mainly statistical and, while it may make analytic judgments about its numbers, rarely addresses the cultural and political ramifications of what the numbers reveal. A book that combines mass media and cultural studies is James W. Carey, *Communication as Culture: Essays on Media and Society* (New York: Routledge, 1992).

Theories of Culture, The Frankfurt School The quotation is from Max Horkheimer and Theodor W. Adorno in *Dialectic of Enlightenment,* trans. John Cumming (New York: Herder & Herder, 1972), pp. 153–54. (Original publication, 1944.)

Theories of Culture, MassCult and MidCult The quotation is from Dwight MacDonald, "Masscult and Midcult," in *Against the American Grain* (New York: Random House, 1962), pp. 4, 37. One writer in the early fifties attempted a somewhat neutral analysis of popular culture. Although much of his work is marked by Cold War rhetoric, Robert Warshow wrote some groundbreaking analyses of the Western and gangster film genres. See his book, *The Immediate Experience* (Garden City, N.Y.: Doubleday, 1962). Another critic, Gilbert Seldes, also wrote against the grain in his book *The Seven Lively Arts*, originally published in 1924, the early, formative period of mass culture. (New York: A. S. Barnes, 1957).

Theories of Culture, Benjamin and Aura The Benjamin quotation is from "The Work of Art in the Age of Mechanical Reproduction," in *Illuminations*, trans. Harry Zohn (New York: Schocken Books, 1968), pp. 234, 236.

Theories of Culture, Mechanical Reproduction Online For a serious discussion of fans and their work, see Henry Jenkins, *Textual Poachers: Television Fans and Participatory Culture* (New York: Routledge, 1992).

Cultural Studies The literature on cultural studies is quite large. Here are a few titles: Stuart Hall, ed., *Culture, Media, Language: Working Papers in Cultural Studies, 1972–79* (London: Hutchinson, 1980); Stuart Hall, *Critical Dialogues in Cultural Studies*, ed. David Morley and Kuan-Hsing Chen (London and New York: Routledge, 1996); Richard Hoggart, *On Culture and Communication* (New York: Oxford University Press, 1972); Lawrence Grossberg, Cary Nelson, Paula A. Treichler, eds., *Cultural Studies* (New York: Routledge, 1992); and John Fiske, *Television Culture* (London and New York: Routledge, 1989).

Cultural Studies, Intertextuality and the Postmodern Raymond Williams first articulated the concept of "flow" when he noticed how various television events moved together without being differentiated. See his *Television: Technology and*

Cultural Form (Middletown, Conn.: Wesleyan University Press, 1992). A sharp, concise summary of postmodernism can be found in Todd Gitlin's essay, "Postmodernism: Roots and Politics," in *Cultural Politics in Contemporary America,* ed., Ian Angus & Sut Jhally (New York: Routledge, 1989).

Cultural Criticism Applied to Cinematic Texts, *Vertigo* and *Die Hard*   For a study of Hitchcock's popularity, see Robert E. Kapsis, *Hitchcock: The Making of a Reputation* (Chicago: University of Chicago Press, 1992).

Cultural Criticism Applied to Cinematic Texts, Screen Size   The best work on screen size is John Belton, *Widescreen Cinema* (Cambridge, Mass.: Harvard University Press, 1992).

Cultural Criticism Applied to Cinematic Texts, Wanderings in Wide Screen   David Parker of the Library of Congress pointed out to me the connections between Scottie's driving around and VistaVision.

Cultural Criticism Applied to Cinematic Texts, *Vertigo* and the Culture of the Fifties   For a good history of the fifties, see James Gilbert, *Another Chance: Postwar America, 1945–1968* (New York: Knopf, 1981). On the zoot-suit riots, see Stuart Cosgrove, "The Zoot-Suit and Style Warfare," in Angela McRobbie, ed., *Zoot Suits and Second-Hand Dresses* (Boston: Unwin-Hyman, 1988), pp. 3–22.

Cultural Criticism Applied to Cinematic Texts, An Age of Anxiety   There is a large literature on the work of House Committee on Un-American Activities in Hollywood. Two excellent sources are Larry Ceplair and Steven Englund, *The Inquisition in Hollywood: Politics and the Film Community, 1930–1960* (Berkeley and Los Angeles: University of California Press, 1983) and Victor S. Navasky, *Naming Names* (New York: Penguin Books, 1981).

Cultural Criticism Applied to Cinematic Texts, Gender and the Cold War   One of the most popular books voicing the fear of conformity in the fifties was William Whyte's *The Organization Man* (New York: Simon and Schuster, 1956).

Cultural Criticism Applied to Cinematic Texts, The Decline of the Male   The quotations about declining masculinity are from J. Robert Moskin, "Why Do Women Dominate Him?" and George B. Leonard, Jr., "Why Is He Afraid to Be Different?" in *The Decline of the American Male,* by the editors of *Look* (New York: Random House, 1958). One of the best new studies of the changing ideas of masculinity in the fifties by a scholar whose work led me to the *Look* articles is Steven Cohan, *Masked Men: Masculinity and the Movies in the Fifties* (Bloomington, Indiana: University Press, 1997).

Cultural Criticism Applied to Cinematic Texts, The Hero's Role   Susan Jefford's *Hard Bodies: Hollywood Masculinity in the Reagan Era* (New Brunswick, N.J.: Rutgers University Press, 1994) offers an interesting political take on contemporary action/adventure films.

4

THE STORIES TOLD BY FILM

MASTER NARRATIVES AND DOMINANT FICTIONS

Internal Tensions

In the previous chapter, we spoke about the tensions that emerge in *It's a Wonderful Life*, a film that pulls its hero and its audience in many directions as it tries to reconcile post–World War II anxieties with a story that wants to be upbeat and morally responsible in a conventional way. In the process, the film tries to make up its mind whether it is a comedy, a fantasy, or a melodrama. It is full of high emotion, but also has plenty of jokes and silly characters; angels guide the main character; and it ends, as comedies do, with a reconciliation, a reaffirmation of harmony and happiness. Everyone forgives, everyone appears ready for long-term happiness. But the film's central character, George Bailey, is not a comic figure. He is wracked with doubts; he fights against the calls of his community, wishes to break from his father, to leave the constraints of the small town of Bedford Falls. During much of the film, he is represented as a man on the verge of a nervous breakdown. He attempts suicide and is saved only because he has a guardian angel, who brings George to his senses by presenting him with a vision of the town as it would have been without him, dark, corrupt, violent—almost like the inside of George's mind.

The film, like George, is a bit schizophrenic, split between various fantasies and nightmares of its own making. Coming at the end of World War II, it tried to create a story that would bring the culture together, remind it of its responsibilities, reinstate the nuclear family headed by the working man, nurtured by the stay-at-home mother. It wanted to be a good populist warning about the need to shift large capital out of the hands of single owners into the community. But it too fully absorbed the uncertainties of the moment and all it can do in the end is breathlessly proclaim a happy ending. Its vision of George's conversion, and the town's sudden unity; its images of the smiling

family and presumption that everyone will live happily ever after, are as great
a fantasy as Clarence the angel's vision of the town without George.

Closure

Despite the tensions within the film that threaten to break it down, it manages
to reach closure, that conventional narrative event in every kind of fiction that
stitches together the loose ends, the broken lives, the ruined love affairs, the
villains still at large, the people physically and emotionally lost, what has
come unwound as a narrative moves along. More than simply ending a story,
the act of closure brings back into harmony and balance lives and events that
have been disrupted. That harmony and balance is always contrived to fit
with what filmmakers believe to be dominant cultural values: victory over
evil, as defined by the film, comfort to the previously afflicted, redemption of
the lost and abused, reassertion of the family as the most valued cultural unit.
    Despite the tensions, *It's a Wonderful Life* manages to position itself within
the framework of the Hollywood master narrative and, by so doing, positions
us within it as amused, intrigued, and delighted spectators. Like *Casablanca*
(Michael Curtiz, 1942) before it, *It's a Wonderful Life* has become even more
popular than when it was first released. Not only because it tells a universal
story, a grand fiction applicable to all people throughout time (keep in mind
that "universal" is a culturally generated idea), but because it generates a large
and inviting fantasy out of a style that carefully and invisibly propels us
through a narrative of desire, sadness, fear, reconciliation, to a final proclama-
tion of self-worth and fulfilled communal need. A master narrative contains
the elements that please us with their ease of access, with the way they raise
our expectations and satisfy them, generate fears and then quiet them, and
conclude by assuring us that all is right with the world.
    Narrative is a general term indicating the construction, development, and
telling of a story. We use it in many contexts. The concept of master narratives
is of large culturally, historically, and economically determined constructions,
many of them formed long before film. Master narratives drive the dominant
fictions—the reigning stories of the culture—that address the most comforting
abstractions of love, family, sin and redemption, life and death, and of our
deepest fears of disruption of order, of violence and despair. *It's a Wonderful
Life*'s story of a man who overcomes his fantasies of independence to settle
down and be the center of his family and community derives from a dominant
fiction of how men should act, and it is driven by a master narrative of disruption and harmonious closure. Master narratives drive the dominant fictions
which are articulated in the particular stories told to us by film. Even the classical Hollywood form that we spoke about in detail in Chapter 2 is, in effect, a
master narrative. It is not only the form that so many films use to tell their stories, but it is a story itself. It offers an invitation to pleasure without work, invites us to see without really having to understand what we see, and gives us

an illusion of continuity and process without asking us to understand the way the links work. The classical Hollywood form enfolds us within a comforting space between the gazes of the characters and constitutes—no matter what other story is being told—a tale of desire for excitement, danger, transgression that is satisfied by film's end. It is the form that embraces the others, the particular stories that eventually make up individual films. These are the large dominant fictions not only of love and hate, fear and desire, but of male heroism, female dependence, the liberal virtues of racial equality, the conservative virtues of demonizing and destroying selected enemies, the imperatives of family, self respect, and all of the other good and bad stereotypes of human behavior that films talk to us about.

Narrative Constraints

Master narratives and dominant fictions do not exist "out there," though many exist outside of film and have been constructed out of the long lineage of our culture and others. They have a history and, most important, they can be varied, told and retold, reworked at different times and for different needs. Film can trace the lineage of its narratives back to Renaissance comedy and nineteenth-century melodrama, stories of love lost and reclaimed, of virtuous women attacked by corrupt men; families and other beloved institutions imperiled by greedy and immoral individuals; the sanctity of home and the order of the nuclear family; the innocence of children; the patience of women; the resolvable confusion of men.

The structure of the master narratives and the fictions that result are based on constraints. Cultural contexts, social norms, dominant beliefs dictate their form and evolution. In a capitalist society, cultural constraints encourage narratives that promote close families and dependent women because this is a manageable structure that urges the woman to stay at home and care for children—future homemakers, workers or managers—while the male is freed to be in the workplace. Socialist countries may generate narratives of communal activity rather than families and celebrate the laborer's and the farmer's work. Socialist narratives are constrained by state ideological necessity—celebration of the revolution or of workers, for example. In a commercial system, constraints are created by the need for a film to make a profit. Story and structure that push too hard against what has already been proven to work are discouraged. There are still other ideological constraints that we will need to examine.

Censorship   In the history of Hollywood film, events occurred in the early thirties that further restricted the contours of the master narratives. Responding to pressures raised by the Catholic Church over what it perceived as licentiousness in film—especially the films of the sexy actress Mae West and the violence of the gangster film—and faced with falling revenues caused by the Great Depression, the film business decided to censor itself before the government stepped in. The studios adopted a "Production Code" written and administered by a Catholic layman, a Jesuit priest, and a Catholic publisher. The Code essentially forbade films from showing anything sexual—even married couples had to be shown sleeping in separate beds—or allowing any crime to go unpunished. Films could not show the details of a crime, or any explicit violence. There was to be no profanity or any other activity suggestive of the ordinary or the extraordinary behavior of flesh and blood individuals, nothing that wasn't conventionalized by the formalized code of cinematic representation and the restricted behavior it portrayed. No one in a film narrative could be allowed to get away with anything that transgressed the culture's most conservative notions of legality and morality. Films had to restrict themselves to the stereotypes of heroism, virtue, and reward that they themselves had imported from the Victorian stage and reworked into their native language.

If the Code had been followed religiously, movies of the thirties, forties, and fifties would have been banal to the point of being unwatchable. But screenwriters and directors created their own codes through images and editing that suggested things rather than stated them. Rain and cigarettes, for example, were often coded to signify sexuality. A look or gesture was loaded with meanings that might not otherwise have to be spelled out in dialogue. Often, screenwriters put in outrageous sequences in early versions of their scripts—a visit to a brothel, perhaps—guaranteed to throw the censors off so that they would not notice more subtle elements elsewhere.

A good argument can be made that the Production Code forced film to be more indirect, more implicit and subtle than it is now in the post-Code period. Today, even with the Code long gone, and with violence, profanity, and sexuality rampant across cinema, the stories films are telling remain largely the same. In the great majority of films, evil is still punished, the complexities of individual, communal, political, economic, and cultural behavior are largely ignored. Redemption stands as the promise offered by every film and demanded by every audience: the promise that lost men will find their way, that a confused and threatened people will find clarity in the action of a male hero; that women desiring more than the culture allows will finally understand that the love of a man and the raising of a family will bring their lives to fruition; that domestic harmonies will be restored; that the right way will be found.

All of this constraint and repetition must be understood within the cultural contexts of film. The ability to repeat the master narratives means that they respond to important individual, social, and cultural needs. We respond to films because we want to; we want to because films show and tell us the things we want them to. Subtleties and variations are continually added to the dominant fictions driven by the master narratives. They have to be rearticulated at different times, for different audiences. The narratives always have to be given the concrete details of a story. They are abstractions which become concrete in individual films. But the concrete stories are themselves structured against the regular patterns, the recurring themes and characters of *genre*, literally the *types* of film narratives that relate the stories we want to see. There are many layers and terms here—master narratives, dominant fictions, genres—and they are useful to help us understand how film gathers its materials and moves from the large fictions of its culture to the concrete, recognizable conventions of form and content that are repeated and varied from film to film to our continued delight.

GENRE

We invoke genre whenever we classify a film narrative. Video stores do it when they arrange their titles by categories such as "Action," "Comedy," "Drama." Like any generic classification, they help prepare viewers for what they will see, though the video store categories are often broad and imprecise. To better understand genre, we need to create categories that are not only inclusive but also more definitive. When we do this, we find there is a moderately stable group of major genres—comedy, melodrama, action-thriller, crime, film noir, war, musical, Western, science fiction, horror—that flesh out and individualize the master narratives and tell us the stories we like, with the variations and invention that keep them interesting.

Subgenres

From within these large groupings, subgenres emerge. The action-thriller genre, for example, spawns such subgenres as spy films, and chase and caper films. Under and around crime film are its satellites, the gangster movie, the detective film, and film noir, which began as a subgenre and quickly emerged into a full-fledged genre of its own. Road movies like *Bonnie and Clyde* (Arthur Penn, 1967), *Thelma and Louise* (Ridley Scott, 1991), and *Natural Born Killers* emerge from the crime genre. Comedy and melodrama often cross. *Forrest Gump* is a melodrama with comedy; *Sleepless in Seattle* (Nora Ephron, 1993) is a comedy with melodrama. Genres are often inflected and changed by gender. The Western, a genre in steep decline since the early seventies, has seen recent attempts to revive it. One attempt, *The Ballad of Little Jo* (Maggie Greenwald, 1993), makes a strong case that a generic narrative can be retold by imagining what would happen were a women in the role usually reserved for a male.

Generic Limits

Genres can be quite supple, stretching and moving with the cultural demands of the moment. They help the viewer negotiate with the film, promising to provide certain narrative structures and character types that the viewer finds satisfying. But they have definite limits. For example, we saw in the last chapter that the action-adventure film can stretch to contain a great deal of self-mockery and exaggerated, cartoon violence. But when the mockery becomes too severe, as it did in *Hudson Hawk* and *Last Action Hero,* audiences rebel. If a film is too self-conscious, the narrative bonds are in danger of being broken. If the audience feels it is not being taken seriously enough, it may not show up.

Genre and Gesture

Genres began to form as soon as films developed a narrative sense, as they moved quickly from merely showing things, such as a train leaving the station or two people kissing, to telling stories. When stories began being told, they quickly fell into recognizable types: romances, melodramas, chases, Westerns, comedies. As we said, much of this was familiar to audiences of the Victorian stage, vaudeville, and popular fiction. Types and stereotypes of villain and hero, bad woman and faithful wife, stories of captivity, heroic action, individuals wronged unjustly and then saved, chases and rescues both comic and serious were constructed, developed, and conventionalized into film from the stage within a matter of years. Acting styles, borrowed from the stage and further exaggerated into the pantomime of silent films, established the conventions of demeanor and gesture that, modified over time, are still used and still specific to particular genres. A man or woman may no longer raise the back of a hand to the forehead to indicate melodramatic distress, but a man will bury his head in both hands and a woman will put both hands up to her mouth to show us she's shocked and frightened. Men still jut out their jaws to represent determination in an action film, and both sexes will look to the floor to show contrition, part their lips and roll their heads upward as a sign of passion in a romantic melodrama.

Generic Origins

Melodrama is an especially interesting case in point. The genre had its origins in the eighteenth century, when the English novel gave a voice to middle-class romantic fantasies aimed at a female audience. In the drama of pre- and postrevolutionary France and America, melodrama at first personalized great political aspirations of a middle class yearning to be free of aristocratic baggage. After the revolutions in both countries, melodrama expressed middle-class moral principles of virtue rewarded and vice punished. In nineteenth-century French and English novels—Dickens and Balzac, for example—melodrama still combined the personal and the political, addressing issues of gender and class, discovery of lost identity, strenuous pursuit of freedom from oppression, and self-sacrifice for the cause of others. These master narrative principles would become embedded in melodrama's transformation to the cinema.

The transformation was made through the Victorian stage, where the passions of melodrama were played out with exaggerated abandon and the clichéd gestures that are now referred to whenever the genre is parodied. These gestures were, in fact, codified, illustrated and written down so that actors would know how and when to use them. Exaggeration was required in the pantomime of silent film. Intertitles, which interrupted the action with printed words, might represent the intended dialogue or summarize narrative events, but emotional continuity needed to be maintained by physical movements and facial expressions. In many countries during the silent period a live speaker might be present at a screening to narrate the events on the screen. Music also provided continuity and emotional support for the images. Melodrama means drama with music. Silent films were rarely shown silent. By the 1910s, orchestral scores were distributed with major film productions and were played by orchestras in urban movie theaters. In smaller theaters, a pianist might play from a score or improvise music to the film. Music provoked the emotions and made connections between what the characters on the screen and the viewers in the audience were supposed to be feeling. It still does this on the soundtrack and remains a major element of film in general and melodrama in particular.

The great dynamics of emotion generated by melodrama were supported by the economic dynamics of an audience willing to pay to see virtue rewarded and vice punished; to be assured that heroic men would save women from disaster, and that the moral balance of the world would be restored. These dynamics were set into motion by writers and producers who worked in concert with what they intuited or analyzed as audience desire. Audience desire and creative supposition were more often in sync than not.

In literature, genres were born out of the complex interactions of form, structure, individual imagination, and social need. Forms of story telling developed and were repeated, rules were constructed, obeyed, and repeated, in acts of collusion. An artist's imaginative needs, the audience's desire (originally, a limited, upper-class audience), and larger cultural events conspired to establish specific forms and formulas that generated specific meanings and maintained them in the social conscience. Tragedy, originally stories of kings and rulers, evoked the social profundity of the cyclical movements of power and pride, authority, self-deceit, and fall from power. The pastoral became the form for discriminating between the simplicities and complexities of a culture by contrasting an innocent, rustic world against the corruptions of the city. The epic told the large, complex story of the origination and formation of the culture and its politics from the perspective of a great hero. In film, genres are also born out of social need and continue as long as the need is there. But while they have literary and theatrical origins, film genres rarely emerge out of the work of individual artists. In fact, many have argued that, in film, individual imagination is the enemy of generic purity. The genre transcends the artist and is therefore the perfect example of the mass production of narratives that constitutes studio filmmaking. A genre film is the result of many imaginations, including the collective imagination of the audience and the dominant fictions that nourish it. And, as in all imaginative issues relating to film production, it is economically determined.

Generic Patterns   Establishing a genre means establishing a pattern—a blueprint—and, as in the making of a car, once the pattern is established, it is easier and cheaper to turn out many versions of the same pattern than reinvent a new one for each unit. During the thirties, when Warner Brothers decided to make a gangster film—a genre that the studio came to specialize in and, with Mervyn Leroy's *Little Caesar* in 1930 and William Wellman's *Public Enemy* in 1931, practically invented—a number of events would occur almost automatically. A basic story line would be at the ready: a young man from the slums would wander into a life of crime. Since this was the period of prohibition against alcohol, the life of crime would usually be illegal trafficking in booze. The young man would collect around him a close male friend and a girlfriend. They would all be seduced by fame and fortune, build a gang, gain riches through violence, reach for more than they could grab. The young man would become entranced by his fame and wealth, fall out with the friend, the girlfriend, or his mob, be betrayed, and finally get gunned down by the cops. This narrative appealed to the Depression audience's desire to break out of the difficult, poor life many of them suffered during the decade and helped them fantasize a life of power, riches, and comfort that ran parallel to the "legal" system. At the same time, it appealed to a dominant fiction which spoke about the moral prohibition against easy money and provided a cautionary restriction on the too easy satisfaction of desire. If wealth came too easily and illegally to someone, he needed to be punished. The gangster film offered the fantasy of wish fulfillment and the reality of cultural restraints all at the same time. The audience was tempted and was redeemed from temptation, though apparently not redeemed enough to keep censors from getting nervous.

Along with the gangster narrative, the apparatus for the gangster film could be easily constructed. The studio would have everything at hand: the city street already built on the back lot, a cutout of a car placed against a rear-screen projection of a city street in motion, guns of all kinds, fedora hats, sharp suits for the men, low-cut gowns for the women. The actors were under contract: Edward G. Robinson, Humphrey Bogart, James Cagney. Writers and directors, also under contract, could be assigned to the latest gangster production. In short, all the elements were there and ready to make a genre film. As long as the audience and the censors remained receptive, the economies for this kind of production were sound and returns on investment guaranteed. Unfortunately, the censors soon cracked down on the studios and so they modified the genre, sometimes turning the actors who played gangsters into FBI agents, repeating the patterns but with the "good guys" in the foreground.

Genre and Narrative Economy

By the thirties, as the studios geared up production, many of them releasing a film a week (six major studios and a number of smaller ones averaged over three hundred narratives a year for almost twenty years), originality in story line was not a practical or affordable quality. Genres, fed by adaptations from existing novels, stories, plays, or other films, allowed this vast production of narratives to go on with ease. The question of originality was rarely raised.

Audiences became habituated to seeing variations on a theme with apparent ease. The studios continued the variations on a theme with obvious ease. Each part of the process—production and reception, filmmaker and audience—remained in contact through genres. The studios negotiated generic form and content with an audience that signified its acceptance of the contract by buying tickets.

In the days of the studios, executives would hold previews in the Los Angeles suburbs. The film's director and producer, perhaps even the studio head himself, would travel to a theater and, from the back of the house, watch the audience watching the film. Afterward, they would collect note cards from the audience. Depending on the audience's reaction during the film and on their written comments after the screening, the executives might order retakes, demand an alternative ending be filmed, ask to have more funny lines added, or have the entire film recut to increase or slow down its rhythm. Based on audience response, the film would be reshaped, the variations on a theme reworked.

Previewing still goes on. Some moviemakers hold focus groups, in which a representative group of people are invited to discuss their attitudes about a particular film or about film in general. But currently the main negotiating power of the audience is mediated through the money they pay in film admissions and videocassette rentals. The main "preview" is a film that makes a great deal of money. If a film is successful, it becomes a model for films to follow. The audience resides mostly inside the gross receipts a film earns. On the basis of those receipts, writers, agents, producers, and directors attempt to guess what variations on the successful genre or story might make them more money still. They guess wrong more often than right. But every right guess usually pays for the wrong ones. Think of how that single variation of the old thirties action-adventure film, *Raiders of the Lost Ark,* led to a string of imitations. When *Batman* (Tim Burton, 1989), a variety of the heroic thriller and the fantasy film, came along, filmmakers seized the opportunity to combine comic book action, heroism, fantasy, and elements of the science fiction film in a variety of ways. There were the sequels of the films themselves (two for *Raiders: Indiana Jones and the Temple of Doom,* 1984; *Indiana Jones and the Last Crusade,* 1989; both directed by Spielberg; and three for *Batman:* Burton's *Batman Returns,* 1992; and Joel Schumacher's *Batman Forever,* 1995; and *Batman and Robin,* 1997), and there were spinoffs from both films like Robert Zemeckis's *Romancing the Stone* (1984), Sam Raimi's *Darkman* (1990), *The Crow* (Alex Proyas, 1994), *The Shadow* (Russell Mulcahy, 1994), and *Stargate* (Roland Emmerich, 1994), to name a few.

But we cannot simply blame the studios for churning out generic clones. In fact, no one is to blame. The key to genre is the circulation of stories, and as long as audiences enjoy the product and pay for it, the circulation continues. As long as the stories keep shifting and changing shape, the studios keep making them applicable and acceptable to a large enough audience, audiences keep reading them and making them applicable to themselves, a large enough generic community will be achieved. The films will be successful and the genre will thrive.

GENRE ANALYSIS

We have, so far, been giving examples from various genres in order to create a general idea of how they are made, how they work, and how they succeed and reproduce themselves. Now we need to examine in more detail an old and a relatively new genre—melodrama and film noir—in order to see in more detail how their structures and themes and variations work. These case studies will allow us to examine a range of structures and meanings across the history of film.

Melodrama can be understood as a genre and a master narrative, an overarching narrative form that controls all films that aren't comedies and that had an existence before film was invented. Film noir, on the other hand, is original to film and is also a kind of hybrid. It developed out of detective fiction, the gangster film, the thriller, and melodrama itself. Film noir occurred at a very specific moment in the history of film as a response to specific cultural events. Its uniqueness has made it one of the most imitated forms in current cinema, and its name is one of the few terms from French criticism that have entered common usage. Curiously, at the time of the creation of noir in the early forties, nobody knew they were inventing what would become one of the most celebrated of genres.

MELODRAMA

As we noted earlier, melodrama is not original to film. Its origins are historically defined, and its evolution is clear and orderly. As a popular form it is even represented by a popular stereotype. Because it is the dominant serious dramatic and narrative form of so many cultures, it contains within it the seeds of its own parody. In popular usage, "melodrama" is often used to describe an exaggerated, emotionally overblown situation. But in this case, parody turns out to be a form of flattery (or self-protection) because melodrama has never lost its power to make grown people cry. It is the central cinematic form that creates empathy and identification. In its most popular guise, as television soap opera, it demands the attention of millions of viewers around the world.

Melodrama is about feeling or, more accurately, about provoking emotions, perhaps more intense than what are called for by the story being told. The desire to provoke emotions, and, for the audience, to have them provoked, was a driving force in the development of American cinema's classical style. Its formation and the development of film melodrama went hand in hand. Knitting the viewers' gaze within the narrative space of a film, emphasizing glances, faces, hands (D. W. Griffith especially liked closeups of women's hands, wringing, twisting), finding ways to mold the viewers' response into a narrative flow of despair, loss, anxiety, hope, and eventual triumph, suffered or instigated mainly by women, helped filmmakers establish a style of visual, narrative, and emotional continuity. Exaggerated as they might seem to us now, the gestures of silent film melodrama were in fact a refinement, even a rethinking, of their stage originals, providing an emotive language of look and gesture that created and maintained a connection with viewers. An intimacy between the audience and the representations of actors on the screen was greater than that achieved when live figures gesticulated on a distant stage. These looks and gestures and the way they were edited together became conventionalized codes that triggered conventionalized responses, predictably, time and time again. In their predictability lay their security. It lies there still. The gestures and looks are less broad now, but still codified. It must be so, because melodrama is about security, about the safe expression of overwhelming passion, safe because confined within the known bounds of cinematic codes. Circumscribed, predictable, closed, the codes of melodrama can permit extravagant stories to be told, stories that articulate deep, subjective passion and terrors, which are always contained within the bounds of the master narrative.

Griffith

D. W. Griffith was a central figure in the development of the contours and contents of film melodrama. He was a man of conservative, populist, Southern character, and his background and ideology colored his films. His racist film *Birth of a Nation* (1915) not only expanded the narrative scope and running time of theatrical film, it also celebrated and managed to revitalize a then dormant Ku Klux Klan. Griffith spent much of the rest of his career attempting to atone for the appalling social-political results of his "masterpiece." His racial attitudes were matched only by his attitudes toward gender (though it should be emphasized that these attitudes were shared with large parts of the contemporary culture). Women, in most of Griffith's films, fulfilled conventional roles of wives and mothers. They were weak and got into trouble, often at the hands of desperate, angry men. They needed saving by good, virile men. One of the essential, primary structures of narrative film, the cross-cutting editing pattern that links a sequence of captivity and a sequence of rescue, is based on this response to gender difference. The pattern was not invented by Griffith, and it was used in comedies as well, but he fully exploited it, made it essential to melodramatic construction, and climaxed it, in fact, in the great rescue scene of *Way Down East* (1920) where the woman—passive, trapped, stranded on rapidly dispersing ice floes—awaits rescue by her man, who is desperate to arrive before she dies.

Broken Blossoms Griffith helped institutionalize this formula—made it a permanent part of the language of melodramatic cinema—and he could also reverse it. In *The Mother and the Law*, a film made right after *Birth of a Nation* and included as one of the stories in *Intolerance* (made in 1916, the first of Griffith's films made in atonement for *Birth of a Nation*), it is the woman who leads the rescue of her son, imprisoned because he is wrongly accused of labor violence (Griffith's populism occurs in other films, like the 1909 short film, *A Corner in Wheat,* where he takes the side of labor against business). Such a reversal in gender expectations is nowhere as startling as it is in *Broken Blossoms* (1919), a melodrama in which gender positions are set askew, and both the male and female characters suffer an enormous amount of repression. *Broken Blossoms* was another film made in atonement for *Birth of a Nation*'s racism, and it sets some basic patterns for the family melodrama that have persisted, with much variation, but little fundamental change, to the present.

POINT OF VIEW

MIS-EN-SCÈNE

Griffith's overt theme for the film is a rather weak-willed wish for "universal brotherhood." What the film crucially investigates is miscegenation (interracial sexual relations) and brutality to women. The central male character is a Chinese man, played by a white actor (Richard Barthelmess), who is referred to in the intertitles as "The Yellow Man." He comes to London—a mythical movie-set London, a place removed from any reality, a perfect mise-en-scène for this fantasy of domestic terror—on a religious mission to calm the savage white man. He lives an isolated life in the East End ghetto. He takes no part in the pursuits of opium smoking, which Griffith portrays in an extraordinary tableau, showing men and women lounging sensually in a smoked-filled opium den, and maintains a spiritual aloofness as a small shop owner. His revulsion from violence, his features and gestures, the very way he holds his body, are strongly marked as female. That is, they are marked by what the culture recognizes as feminine—small, mincing gestures; hands and arms drawn close to the body; a nonaggressive personality.

"The Yellow Man" is doubled by the film's female character, Lucy. In gesture and demeanor she is his mirror image and they are even composed by the camera in similar ways. Though white, Lucy is also an outcast, a poor, withdrawn, helpless creature of a monstrous father, the prize fighter "Battling Burrows," who beats her with ferocious violence. The melodramatic triangle set up by these figures is fascinating in its complexity and in the ways it reveals basic principles of the genre. Lucy is oppressed by a paternal

In Broken Blossoms *(1919) vulnerability and sensitivity are marked by gender and race. The two main characters are drawn to each other in an impossible attraction. They become reflections of each other.*

figure of such violence that she attempts to escape him by turning to the gentle, feminized male—a vulnerable, regressive figure like herself—for comfort. But the comfort she receives is also threatening in its otherness.

CAMERA   Melodrama must create a world of threat, not only to its characters but to its audience, before it resolves itself. Filled with desire of his own, "The Yellow Man" turns Lucy into a fetish object, making her up to look like an Asian doll and placing her on his raised bed. This really frightens her—and us. In one closeup from her point of view, "The Yellow Man's" face moves toward her filled with lust—a shot that will be echoed later when "Battling Burrows' " face moves toward Lucy, filled with violent hatred. But "The Yellow Man" has sublimated his lust and is no threat to her; he worships her. The look on his face actually reflects her own fears. Everything, the erotic in particular, remains repressed. In melodrama, sexuality and desire must be sublimated into something else. In *Broken Blossoms*, their sublimation results from the cultural prohibition against miscegenation and the fact that protection is stronger than the need for sexual satisfaction.

The sublimation turns "The Yellow Man" into a maternal figure, a strangely desexualized, but somehow still erotic maternal figure who both worships and cares for the battered Lucy. But this adoration and care is no match for "Battling Burrows." The tension of the narrative is built when he finds his daughter. The brutality of the crazed patriarch will destroy the apparently innocent pleasures of this odd couple. He drags Lucy back to their hovel and beats her to death after she flees to the confines of a closet. "Battling" breaks down the walls she hopes would protect her, the camera capturing Lucy's entrapment and exposure through a sequence of point-of-view shots that is chilling and unrelenting. It is a scene so grueling and so expertly done that Hitchcock does homage to it in the shower scene in *Psycho*, as does Kubrick in *The Shining* (1980) when Jack breaks down Wendy's door with an axe.

It is typical of melodrama to create an experience of such extremity, a cruelty so enormous, that it seems impossible to correct it. But it must be corrected, because without closure, without recuperating the situation, the internal melodramatic world would be in perpetual disruption. Often, when the situation appears to have no probability of closure, the film will simply kill off its participants, which is what happens at the end of *Broken Blossoms*. Griffith tries to create standard intercut sequence of rescue. But "The Yellow Man" doesn't arrive in time to save Lucy. She is murdered and he shoots "Battling Burrows" and then himself.

Melodrama is structured on the containment and release of desire. It calls for the end of repression and then reimposes it at the end. That is because melodrama is essentially a cautionary form. Yes, it says, people live constricted and hurt lives. They want more; should have more. But too much more will damage the fragile emotional equilibrium, the sets of oppositions, the dominant and regressive states that the culture needs to survive. So melodrama always enacts, at its end, a process of recuperation, bringing its characters back to a kind of cultural health, or, more accurately, a "health" prescribed by the dominant values, and the dominant fictions, of the culture. Melodrama is an expression of the master narrative of equilibrium, of bringing characters and culture into a manageable steady state, and if it cannot recuperate its characters into a steadier state than the one in which they began, or if they cannot be recuperated because they have transgressed too far, it will enforce an equilibrium through their absence and kill them off, usually in the name of their being too good or too bad or too damaged to survive.

As a dynamic genre, depending upon a close interaction with the people who view it, we can almost say that melodrama has a life of its own. "It" can do things to characters and to viewers. All genres can do things, because they are prescriptive mechanisms. Within a genre, certain actions can and *must* be taken by or occur to certain characters, and the narrative that directs their lives must follow a proscribed path.

Broken Blossoms deals with one of the ultimate cultural transgressions, miscegenation. And while the film pretends a tender understanding of how "The Yellow Man" and Lucy find comfort in their bizarre, asexual union, it cannot possibly allow that union to prevail or endure. Melodrama is self-censuring. It always assumes to know how much passion and transgression the audience, within its cultural constraints, will or should manage. In the process of censure, it will also gauge the maximum emotional capital it can cause the audience to use in exchange for the images they are watching. So, while Griffith has his three characters killed off because the triangle was simply more than cultural reality in the late 1910s could bear, he manages to wring from his viewers as much sympathy, or even empathy, as they can muster or commit.

Caution and exploitation are two of melodrama's main attributes. If tragedy—the dramatic form that preceded melodrama—asked of its audience a profound recognition of great human achievement undone by greater human limitation, melodrama asks for a less lofty but more emotional recognition of the necessity to contain all aspirations within comfortable and known boundaries. "Asks" is wrong, though. Melodrama demands. For melodrama to work, an audience must be told what to feel and when to feel it; viewers must be hooked and reeled in. If, at any point, melodrama permits an opening through which the viewer can look and say, "this is ridiculous, such events, such suffering could or should never occur," the structure would fall to pieces. Melodrama demands continuous assent and uses all the force of the continuity style to get that assent. It sutures the viewer into its fabric and makes the viewer's emotional response part of that fabric's pattern.

The pattern is often enough based on very primal stuff. Simple human need for emotional comfort in the face of outrageous brutality is the baseline of *Broken Blossoms*. But elaborated into a narrative of interracial romance, gender diffusion, and a grotesque representation of an abusive father, the baseline is built up just to the point of collapse. Griffith's delicacy and restraint (not qualities he shows in many of his other films) and the constant fascination of his mise-en-scène—the mythic constructions of East End London streets; the conversion of "The Yellow Man's" room into an exotic, erotic temple; the oppressive grunge of "Battling Butler's" room—keep the viewer contained within the narrative. The simple cutting, the connections of gaze and response, ease the viewer into this mise-en-scène of gender hysteria. The sexual ambiguities, the continual threats to Lucy of violence and rape, even her ghastly attempts to smile at her beastly father by pushing up the corners of her mouth with her fingers, fascinate because of their very outrageousness. Melodrama turns the outrageous into the plausible and asks us to believe that plausibility is close to reality.

Now, Voyager   Melodrama throws pain and dissatisfaction in our faces, insists we can do better, and then, in the end, takes it all back, assuring us that we'll be fine if we only modify desire and deflect pain somewhere else—or end it with death. In 1942, Warner Brothers made a rich and complex melodrama called *Now, Voyager*, directed by Irving Rapper. With Bette Davis, one of Warner's major players, as its star, it combines an Oedipal narrative with the story of Cinderella to create the classic structure of melodramatic proposal and denial. A superb example of the classic Hollywood continuity style, *Now, Voyager* knits its pieces together within a narrative of such perfect continuity that the viewer is compelled across its parts into an illusion of a seamless flow of events. *Now, Voyager* substitutes an oppressive, upper-class mother for *Broken Blossoms'* brutal working-class father. Mother is always shown rigid and dominating the frame, even if it is only her fingers, ominously taking up the foreground of a composition, impatiently tapping on a bed post. The subject of her oppression is her daughter, Charlotte Vale, seen early in the film as a mousy, gray, emotionally arrested, neurotic middle-aged woman. The film plays out the introduction of Charlotte as long as it can, in an interesting display of the intimacy filmmakers knew existed between viewer and film. Audiences already knew very well what Bette Davis looked like from her many other films: she was a major star who had gained even wider recognition by unsuccessfully attempting to break her contract with the studio because she did not like the roles she was being given. Viewers could be depended upon to have read stories of her lawsuit and also to have read publicity that stressed how ugly she was made to look early in the film. Therefore, *Now, Voyager* takes its time introducing her, and, when it finally does, shows her legs first, descending the stairs, to further heighten expectation.

The film posits two men who come to Charlotte's rescue, each one a "foreigner," each one offering a different kind of assistance and release. One is a psychiatrist, a figure with a mixed history in American film. The cinematic role of psychiatry and psychiatrist reflects the profession's mixed reputation in the culture at large. Feared and admired, looked to as someone to deliver us from emotional pain, or as a personification of individual defeat and helplessness, or as the embodiment of evil influence, the psychiatrist can help or destroy. In *Now, Voyager* psychiatry is salvation, and its incarnation in Dr. Jaquith, a wise, ironic, and self-contained Britisher, enters Charlotte's mother's house at the very beginning of the film and rescues Charlotte. He is

Cinderella in melodrama. Charlotte, in her ugly, repressed state, with Dr. Jaquith.

Charlotte liberated, beautiful, romantic with Jerry. Now, Voyager *(Irving Rapper, 1942).*

an asexual individual, emotionally potent but no romantic threat. Because the sexual is so foregrounded in melodrama and placed as a primary cause of most of the characters' activities, the genre often needs clean divisions between those for whom sex is a central issue and those for whom it plays no role. These non-threatening figures (very often represented as the woman friend of the central character) are mediating forces. They act a bit as our presence in the film, guiding, threatening nothing, seeing everything, assuring the success of the main character. In *Now, Voyager,* Jaquith figures as a pleasant, though aloof, patriarchal counter to Charlotte's mother—understanding, supportive, curative where she is negative, mean, and destructive. Though the film does not show the details of her cure, Charlotte is indeed transformed by her stay at Dr. Jaquith's sanitarium and emerges, as if from a cocoon, to appear as the glamorous Bette Davis everyone in the theater would have been familiar with—as familiar as now we would be with Julia Roberts.

Jaquith helps execute the Cinderella myth embedded in this particular melodrama. The genre demands, however, more than physical and emotional transformation. Sexual transformation must occur as well. Jaquith provides the paternal guidance. Jerry, an architect with a European accent, provides the sexual awakening. Charlotte meets Jerry on a cruise. This is an important moment in her life. In a flashback to an embarrassing moment in her past, on another cruise, we learned the reason for her repression: her mother caught her making love to one of the ship's crew. The incident is coded to indicate that the mother's oppression of Charlotte's sexual awakening had lasting effects on her sexuality, constricting her, bringing her to that condition so abhorred by melodrama—and the culture that melodrama addresses—of being an old maid.

In melodrama, repressed sexuality is a standard starting point, liberated sexuality its apparent goal, moderated sexuality its favored closure. *Now, Voyager* pursues this path with relentless determination. In Brazil (Latin America being a stereotyped place of the erotic in classic American cinema), Charlotte and Jerry fall in love and make love, in the spaces of a fadeout between a glowing fireplace and its afterglow embers—a lovely substitution for the physical contact the censors forbade showing on the screen. Their affection is signaled by one of those great Hollywood inventions that hooks a film into our imagination. Jerry begins a habit of lighting two cigarettes in his mouth. One is for himself, the other he hands to Charlotte. The gesture is repeated many times in the film and, with the recurring theme music on the sound track, it becomes a correlative of the couple's passion. The critic Thomas Elsaesser points out that in film melodrama, music and mise-en-scène often express the excess of emotion experienced by the characters. The lighting of the two cigarettes in *Now, Voyager* and the swelling sound track that accompanies it, are excellent examples of gesture, movement, and sound that express to us a world of emotion.

Back in Boston, Charlotte's mother feigns illness and a crippling fall in an attempt to reclaim her daughter, who wavers momentarily and, out of touch with Jerry, thinks she will marry a local Bostonian of good family. She also discovers that Jerry is married. This decline and dangerous reversal is an important part of melodramatic structure, which depends upon graphing our emotions in predictable patterns. Having shown Charlotte a way out of her misery, melodrama insists on letting her—and the viewer—know that a return to the darkness is not far out of sight. Suspense and fear for the central character are constructed by means of comparing where she was, how far she has come, and how tentative her liberation remains. The female character of melodrama is always on a precipice, and we are depended upon to agonize over the chances of her falling back to where she was.

So tentative is Charlotte's situation that she winds up back in Dr. Jaquith's sanitarium, where a series of events occurs that is less important as a matter of story than indicative of what melodrama must do to recuperate its characters, even at the expense of strained credulity. The intolerable paradox of melodrama is that the liberation of its characters is also their transgression. To make themselves free they break culture's rules and have to pay. Through Jaquith's intervention and Jerry's intimacy, Charlotte achieves a degree of sexual freedom and emotional maturity. But a narrative and cultural tension is thereby created. As far as our identification with the character in her narrative is concerned, her freedom is a relief and our emotions soar with her. Charlotte has become an independent agent. But in terms of what is culturally allowable, what she has done is impossible.

In film, and perhaps still in the culture at large, a woman cannot express an independent, joyful sexual freedom outside of marriage without paying some price. Certainly, in the early 1940s, when restrictions on the representations of sexuality in film were stronger than they are now, Charlotte could not be permitted to go much further in her explorations of independence. But, in fact, little has changed. In the wake of the feminist movement there have been many films about liberated women. Most of them always compromise their female characters in one way or another. If such a film is a comedy, the strong-willed woman will be convinced that marriage is the only final outlet for her energies. This is not surprising, given the fact that, as a genre going back to Shakespeare and earlier, comedy ends in marriage. Marriage remains the rit-

ual representation of harmony and rebirth in most cultures, the joyous repro-
duction of the family, and the unstated representation of sexual containment.
If the film is a melodrama, the unrepressed woman is as often as not depicted
as crazy or evil, threatening the man and his family. Think about three
Michael Douglas films, *Fatal Attraction* (Adrian Lyne, 1987), *Basic Instinct* (Paul
Verhoeven, 1992), and *Disclosure* (Barry Levinson, 1994).

Crazy if repressed, crazy if unrepressed, melodrama catches women in a
double bind and allows few escapes other than death or a falling back into
some barely tolerable compromise. The latter is what happens to Charlotte in
Now, Voyager. Back in Jaquith's sanitarium, she meets a depressed little girl,
the double of Charlotte in her former state. She nurses the child back to mental
stability and discovers she is Jerry's daughter, product of an unhappy marriage in which Jerry nobly remains because his wife is an invalid. The
metaphor of sickness and health overwhelms the film. Disease is melodrama-
friendly, because it represents people in extreme states. Curing disease, or suc-
cumbing to it, parallels melodrama's accordionlike structure of repression or
restriction, expanding outward to emotional or physical health, and then collapsing again into a more culturally acceptable situation of moderated health
and constrained emotional activity, or death.

As the reigning metaphor of *Now, Voyager*, the cycle of sickness and health
is passed from one character to another—to Charlotte, her mother, to Jerry's
wife, and his daughter. Charlotte gets well. But her cure is entirely local. She's
happy, but her happiness does not satisfy the film's or the culture's melodramatic requirements. Individual happiness is never sufficient for melodrama.
Perhaps because it has never completely shaken off its class origins, perhaps
because audiences find insufficient gratification in a character whose happiness is complete, melodrama must do something to temper events. A selfish
indulgence in sexuality might do well for Charlotte the fictional character, but
it does not satisfy cultural demands for self-sacrifice and moderate behavior,
qualities found if not always in life, then in the ideal representation of life in
melodrama. Melodrama mediates between desire and social probity, what we
want and what the culture thinks it should allow. Its characters must conform
to the impossible demands to be free *and* restricted, liberated *and* domesti-
cated, sexual *and* chaste. For Charlotte, a series of internal mediations is the
only means to salvation. She must bring her desires down to a manageable
level and recontain her passions in a semblance of respectability.

She will not marry Jerry. She will not return to her mother's domination.
She chooses to become a surrogate mother. She will care for Jerry's daughter,
sublimating her passion for him through the child. Sex is out. Marriage is out.
Sacrifice is the key. Liberation from emotional repression is gained by means
of another kind of repression. "Don't let's ask for the moon," Charlotte tells
Jerry, after he lights two cigarettes and asks if she will be happy, "we have the
stars." Why ask for passion, when our ideal love is mediated through the innocence of a child and the perfection of being close and separate at the same
time. This is not happiness, only its perpetual promise. The music swells.

Melodrama's insistence on self-sacrifice or self-denial is a trait even more remarkable than its excessive emotions or piling up of incredible coincidence. It is more remarkable because self-sacrifice is largely an invisible trait. Hysteria and passion can be made visible in the mise-en-scène and audible on the soundtrack. Self-sacrifice is an internal condition, the external manifestation of which is usually *not* doing something rather than taking a visible action. Therefore, unless the act of sacrifice is the ultimate one of dying, melodrama asks us to build our own response to the negative gesture of the character, to Charlotte's withdrawal from adult contact in order to love Jerry through his daughter. Sometimes, if a film is part of a larger social movement, the negative sacrifice can be given positive, even political overtones. Rick gives up his beloved Elsa to Victor Laszlo (played by Paul Henreid, who is Jerry in *Now, Voyager*) and turns to Captain Renault (Claude Rains, who plays Dr. Jaquith) for the greater good of the war effort in *Casablanca* (Michael Curtiz)—the great melodrama Warner Brothers released the same year as *Now, Voyager*.

All That Heaven Allows   An important melodramatist of the fifties, Douglas Sirk (a German-born filmmaker, who made films in that country before coming to the United States in the late thirties) was especially talented at portraying complex attitudes of sacrifice and denial on the part of his male and female characters. Sirk appreciated the power of mise-en-scène to echo their emotional life. He used a lush, sometimes glowing, Technicolor palette, and carefully arranged his characters in compositions that symbolically represented their states of feeling, in shadow, behind partitions, reflected in mirrors, surrounded by spectral light.

Sirk's *All That Heaven Allows* (1955) presents a proper, upper-middle-class, suburban widow, played by Jane Wyman, who falls in love with a nursery man, close to nature, in touch with his feelings. The man, Ron, is played by Rock Hudson, near the peak of his stardom, when the reality of his homosexuality was not permitted to interfere with the obsessive heterosexuality of the roles he played. The complaints and snobbishness of friends and family make the woman falter in her emotional commitment. She understands the rightness of her feelings and goes after him, only to see him fall and get seriously injured. In the last scene of the film, she is seated by his bedside. The doctor assures her that only with her constant care will her man get better. The unseemly sexual passion of an older woman is reduced to the nurture of a mother's protection. Rather than in the bed, the woman is now protectively sitting by its side, looking after her lover turned invalid/child. Outside, a deer, Sirk's sentimental image of innocence and hope in the film, plays by the window.

Written on the Wind   Sirk's *Written on the Wind* (1956) is a complex film of a Texas oil family, seething with sexual intrigue, repression, and anxiety (it was the model for the popular eighties television series *Dallas*). One of its threads concerns the oil patriarch's daughter, who desperately seeks the unwilling affections of her father's close advisor (Rock Hudson, again) and is in constant sexual rebellion. Marylee is in such rebellion that, in one of the great scenes of melodramatic upheaval, she does a boisterous, autoerotic dance around her room as her father has a heart attack and falls to his death down the mansion stairs. The loud music, the intercutting of Marylee's dance and her father's attack and fall create an orgiastic moment of family disintegration. Marylee is doomed by her very boisterousness, her sexual openness. In the end, her father dead, the rest of the family in a state of diminished emotional capacity, she becomes the family heiress and is last seen sitting beneath an enormous portrait of him, as she fingers an obviously phallic model of an oil well.

Marylee is reduced beneath the weight of patriarchy. The last image in *Written on the Wind* is a more obvious, and more obviously ironic, statement of what melodrama does to women. Most female characters are recuperated back into the culture's dominant principle of male domination and female passivity. In *Now, Voyager*, after freeing herself from her mother's domination, Charlotte willingly falls under Jerry's by becoming his daughter's surrogate mother. Women sacrifice their desires for freedom and self-expression by reclaiming a cultural respectability that affirms the gross imbalance of conventional gender behavior.

Douglas Sirk tended to exaggerate melodramatic mise-en-scène. More accurately, he realized that melodrama was already an act of exaggeration and just pushed its envelope further. At the end of Written on the Wind *(1956), the character of Marylee—unfulfilled and still hungry for love—has only her father's oil company. She is oppressed by the patriarch, but fully understands the significance of the oil well.*

Ideological Norms

But what melodrama does on its particular generic turf is what all genres do. They articulate the ideological norms of the culture, which are always, within bounds, shifting. While film's master narratives remain fairly stable, its genres respond to ideological changes slowly, often reluctantly. Ideology is the vast web of socially constructed images, narratives, gestures, or everyday acts of assent—like stopping at a red light or going to college, getting married, holding a job—that permit a culture to act cohesively and stay more or less in one piece. Ideology is made up of the ways we think about or act out sets of beliefs in rights and wrongs, shoulds and should nots. It is the way we interpret reality collectively and individually in ways that satisfy the greatest number of people. Ideology is *not* reality (just as the film image is not reality), but a representation agreed upon by a large number of people. Ideology is not monolithic but, like the culture that adopts and acts upon ideology, always under negotiation and undergoing change or accommodation. It is a complex, shifting array of representations and is given form, expressed in the culture's dominant fictions.

The long struggle over the social, economic, and political imbalance in gender relations that has taken place across the culture has often focussed on issues of ideological representation. That is, discussion of gender is many times a discussion of how gender is seen and spoken about in art, literature, and popular culture. As often as film has attempted to come to terms with this discussion, it has just as often been resistant to presenting images and narratives that break away from the ideological mainstream. The problem is clear in the way film melodrama insists on recuperating its characters, its female characters especially, through acts of self-sacrifice or domestic passivity. Indeed, whether dealing with gender, race, or class, film's master narratives and specific genres render visible the culture's dominant ideologies, and its dominant fictions of imbalance, amelioration, and expediency. For women the imbalance is interpreted through the playing of a supportive or sacrificial role. Gays are interpreted less as individuals than as comic or melodramatic stereotypes. Class difference is almost always stereotyped. The very rich are usually portrayed as villainous while the poor are seen as noble in their suffering and urged to be happy with their lot. The cliché that money can't by happiness and riches bring sadness is offered over and over again—think only of *Citizen Kane* and *The Godfather*, Part II (Coppola, 1974)— films that seem to be complicit with larger ideological notions of stability that urge us not to want more than we have because we will only be unhappy. Only in matters of race—and there only rarely—has film taken something approaching a progressive approach, urging recognition of injustice and a desire for things to be better.

The Western

Film grows out of ideology and feeds back into it. Sometimes, when the ideology shifts radically, a genre can either vanish or go into a recessive state. The Western film is an interesting example of a genre that bent and then snapped under shifting ideological pressures. The Western began almost as narrative film was invented and continued composing our myths of the American frontier and the white man's destiny—the inexorable movement of European civilization westward to the Pacific. The settings of chaparral or desert, of small, dusty frontier towns bordering on vast, open land created the simulacrum of the culture's wilderness fantasies. Narratives of white settlers fighting savages, of heroic gunmen protecting small communities from outlaws, confirmed our belief in the rightness of expansion and in the structuring authority of law and order. Western melodramas of women creating the cultural hearth in a barren land where men broke horses and shot Indians and outlaws and then returned to the domesticity they helped secure reassured us that our contemporary centering of the woman in the house was correct.

Only when historical realities became too overwhelming, when foreign wars put a lie to the notion of manifest destiny, when women fought against the patriarchal center, and the "savages" fought against their demonized images, did the ideologies that supported the Western genre begin to falter. John Ford, the master director of Westerns, began questioning some tenets of the genre as far back as the forties. In the fifties, his film *The Searchers* questioned the battle of the white hero against the savage Indian, though not the community that battle helped to create. Three films of the late sixties and early seventies—Sam Peckinpah's *The Wild Bunch* (1969), Arthur Penn's *Little Big Man* (1970), and Robert Altman's *McCabe and Mrs. Miller* (1971)—shifted the genre's conventional myths of male heroism, the role of Indians, and the place of women on the frontier. They turned tables on the genre. *The Wild Bunch* declared the end of the all-male community of gunfighters propounded by the Western, and showed the violence of gunfighting as a terrible tearing up of the body. *Little Big Man* turned the relationship of Indian and white man on its head, declaring that the "savages" were really the "human beings" and the white men crazy. *McCabe and Mrs. Miller* showed the Western community as a cold place of mutual betrayal, the hero as the joke of his own legend, and women as the marginalized, self-protective maintainers of rationality. Out in the real world, the Vietnam war devalued any lingering notions the culture may still have held that expansionism was good and the destruction of indigenous peoples something that the dominant culture needed to do. With this ideological shift, the Western could no longer provide adequate representation of cultural beliefs in manifest destiny and aspirations to control the social and political rights of others. The Western reached its height of popularity in the fifties, when the culture was busily trying to reaffirm its prewar beliefs and mythologies, and began to show strains even then as the mythologies came under question. It has now all but disappeared. Only the exaggerated, often inverted references to generic principles in the Westerns of Clint Eastwood seem to maintain a hold on viewers. The feminist variations on the Western, mentioned earlier, have served mainly to point up how a genre, once fallen, can become subject to experimentation.

Because the Western mythologized history, it was at risk when the culture's ideas of history changed. Cinematic melodrama avoids history (though there are such things as historical melodramas) and absorbs the external world into the interior. In melodrama, the personal replaces the political. Therefore, it has made itself immune to the forces that have undone the Western. Melodrama offers the pretense of timelessness, even of universality. This allows it to survive, but not unchanged. Douglas Sirk changed melodrama by exaggerating its already exaggerated characters and mise-en-scène. He almost turned melodrama into self-parody, though his good commercial sense prevented him from taking it to the point where the structure might implode. Other changes in the fifties allowed melodrama to focus on the sufferings of sensitive, vulnerable, and repressed men. Again, the structuring principles of the genre weren't changed. If anything, they were reinforced by proving themselves flexible and able to embrace all manner of suffering.

FILM NOIR

In the mid-1940s a new genre developed, though it might be more correct to say that it invented itself. The genre, which was named "film noir" some years after it appeared, changed some elements of melodrama and disrupted some Hollywood stereotypes about gender and the inevitability of sacrifice and suffering. Hollywood didn't know it was making a new genre as the elements of noir were put into place. Neither filmmakers nor film viewers were aware, at least on a conscious, articulate level, that a new story was being told to them in a new visual style. It was the French in the 1950s who finally recognized that something was happening and gave it a name. But this does not mean that film noir was born out of nothing. Like any other genre, it came forth as a response to cultural need and developed out of cinematic elements already in existence.

During the Nazi occupation of France (1940–1944) there was an embargo on American films. *Citizen Kane* wasn't seen in Paris until early in 1946, five years after it was made. At war's end, American films flooded into France, a country that has had a deep and serious love of cinema since its invention. An eager group of young intellectuals—including François Truffaut and Jean-Luc Godard, who would go on to be immensely influential filmmakers—began watching these films with an intense interest. They had a good location in which to do this, the Paris Cinémathèque, run by Henri Langlois, who showed whatever films he could get his hands on, twelve hours a day. They watched everything they could and especially loved American films, the spoken language of which they couldn't understand. They learned what they needed from the visual narrative, the images and their construction. They noted across the films of the mid-forties a darkening of visual style and a darkening of thematic content. After a series of French detective stories called *Série Noir,* one of these critics gave the name "film noir" to this new kind of film. But noir went far beyond the detective genre.

Expressionist Roots of Noir

Three main currents fed into the development of noir: German Expressionism, the hard-boiled detective fiction of the thirties, and the cultural turmoil of World War II. Noir's visual style harks back to the Expressionist movement in German film, literature, theater, and painting that flourished after World War I. Expressionism grew out of the cultural and psychological scars left on the people of Europe by World War I and was fed by a growing interest in psychoanalysis and a desire to make art more responsive to individual and cultural anxieties. A basic premise of Expressionism was that mise-en-scène—the visual space of the film (as well as of fiction, theatrical presentation, and painting)—should express the stressed psychological state of either its main character, or more universally, the culture at large. Edvard Munch's painting

The Scream (1893) best exemplifies this effect, though it actually predates and influenced the Expressionist movement. This painting of a figure on a bridge, standing in front of a violent multicolored sky, hands held up to a face contorted in anxiety and terror, is a dominant image for the twentieth century. It encapsulates the Expressionist desire to make the world a reflection of the interior anguish it has caused.

Carl Mayer and Robert Wiene's *The Cabinet of Dr. Caligari* (1919) is the best-known film of the Expressionist period. A tale of madness, somnambu-

The Expressionist mise-en-scène in Robert Wiene's The Cabinet of Dr. Caligari *(1919). Note how the decor and the shadows are painted on. Perspective is forced, as if this were a painting. Note also how this image (and the film) presages the elements of the horror film.*

lism, and seduction, it takes place in an artificial world of deformed houses, windows out of skew, shadows painted on the floor; a place of the dream: imprecise, hard to locate, distorted and full of darkness. Darkness becomes the key to the cinematic version of Expressionism. Darkness dominates the light, which may only survive as pools punctuating the blackness. Horror, too, is a lasting legacy of the movement. Expressionism's first major appearance in Hollywood was in the great series of horror movies produced by Universal in the early thirties. The first American versions of *Dracula* (directed by Todd Browning) and *Frankenstein* (James Whale) were released in 1931. *Dracula* had already been filmed by F. W. Murnau as *Nosferatu* in Germany in 1922. *Caligari* and *Der Golem* (Paul Wegener, 1914) prefigured *Frankenstein*. The Universal horror films were enormously popular. Nothing like them had been seen by American audiences. These dark visions of mythic European worlds invaded by monstrous figures of destruction had a similar (if belated) effect on American viewers as their predecessors had had on post–World War I European audiences. They articulated the master narrative of a calm and orderly world shattered by an unknown chaos and of nature gone awry through human meddling, and they created a new genre and sequels that go on and on.

The shadowy mise-en-scène of frightening monsters who are deformations of the human form, sexual predators who represent some of our darkest desires to do evil and triumph, brought to America the basic stylistics of German Expressionism. But monster movies were not the only examples of the Expressionist style in thirties Hollywood film. Josef von Sternberg created a heavily shadowed mise-en-scène throughout his thirties work, in films like *Morocco* (1930), *Dishonored* (1931), *Shanghai Express* (1932), *Blonde Venus* (1932), *The Scarlet Empress* (1934), and *The Devil Is a Woman* (1935). Though born in Vienna, Sternberg was American by upbringing. He was deeply influenced by the Expressionist style, and he made his groundbreaking film, *The Blue Angel* (1930), in Germany. Many other filmmakers fled Germany to take up work in Hollywood during this period. One of the great Expressionist cinematographers, Karl Freund, photographed (among many other films) Murnau's *The Last Laugh* in 1924 and Fritz Lang's science fiction film *Metropolis* in 1926. He came to America and was cinematographer for the first *Dracula*. By the end of his career, he was cinematographer for *I Love Lucy*!

MISE-EN-SCENE   But despite the horror films and the work of Sternberg and the German émigrés, dark, shadowy mise-en-scène (a version of chiaroscuro, a term from art history that means painting with light and shadow) was not a dominant mode in the thirties. High-

LIGHTING   keyed lighting—in which the entire set is evenly illuminated— prevailed. Some Depression-era films did express the cultural darkness of the period, but most acted as an important antidote, their images of light and their bright, comic narratives performing a social function that would have been less well-served had they all adopted the brooding, fearful darkness of the Expressionist mode.

Citizen Kane   *Citizen Kane* changed all that. Orson Welles was a man of the theater (and radio) before he came to Hollywood in 1939. He had done many theatrical experiments on the New York stage and came to filmmaking with a desire to translate radical theatrical styles of lighting, sound, and composition to the screen. He was particularly interested in the Expressionist use of shadow, and *Citizen Kane* has a dark mise-en-scène that uses shadow as a thematic device. *Kane* is a film about the impossible attempt to define a complex personality—a definition attempted by five people who think they know Charles Foster Kane and whose stories make up the film's narrative. Kane himself remains often literally in the shadows. The film's mise-en-scène is dark and deep. The combination of chiaroscuro lighting and deep-focus cinematography, in which everything from close foreground to far background is in sharp focus, creates a mysterious world in which space is both inviting and threatening, where everything seems to be visible but little is seen that helps us to understand the central character.

   Citizen Kane was not a commercially successful film. Because its story was too closely modeled on the life of the journalist and millionaire William Randolph Hearst, it was in trouble from the start. At one point, Hearst almost talked another studio, MGM, into buying and destroying the master negative. He was successful in preventing the many newspapers he owned from carrying advertising for the film. But even though its popular appeal took many years to form, its appeal to movie professionals was immediate. Directors, cinematographers, production designers were taken by its radical style, which depended so much on the visual structures of Expressionism. The influence of Welles and his cinematographer, Gregg Toland, on the style of forties cinema was enormous. Darkness descended on Hollywood filmmaking.

Hard-Boiled Fiction   *Citizen Kane* was the main conduit into film noir, fed by the tributary of German Expressionism. Another source of influence came from literature. In the 1930s, a popular school of detective-fiction writers emerged, the most famous of whom were Raymond Chandler and Dashiell Hammett. Their work became known as the hard-boiled school of detective fiction and they were masterful at creating visions of a dark, corrupt under-world of dopers and robbers, of sexual exploiters and an omnipresent im-morality infiltrated by their cynical but morally secure detective characters—Hammett's Sam Spade and Chandler's Philip Marlowe. Their detectives were unheroic but persevering, cunning but flawed and vulnerable, barely surviv-ing their exploits with their moral centers intact.

A third figure connected with this school did not write detective fiction. James M. Cain told stories of sleazy, lower-middle-class families falling apart under the pressures of infidelity, murder, and general moral corruption. Al-most all his novels—*Double Indemnity, Mildred Pierce, The Postman Always Rings Twice*—were made into films in the forties. Cain's work and that of the hard-boiled school did not fit well with the Hollywood of the thirties, how-ever, burdened as it was with its self-imposed censorship code and need to provide ideological uplift for a Depression-ridden culture. But this wasn't for lack of trying. Warner Brothers had acquired rights to Hammett's *The Maltese Falcon* very early on and filmed it twice during the thirties, once as a Bette Davis vehicle. They didn't actually get it right, though, until 1941, when John Huston directed the film with Humphrey Bogart as Sam Spade. During the thirties, MGM was more successful with Hammett's *The Thin Man*, which the studio made as a series of screwball comedies—bright, fast-paced narratives about an upper-class married couple who drink a lot and verbally spar with each other while they do a bit of detective work on the side.

The Maltese Falcon   The 1941 version of *The Maltese Falcon* was not a com-edy, though it did have a more ironic and wry tone than its predecessors. It is also somewhat slower paced and more intensely composed and cut than most films of the thirties. It maintains much of Hammett's tough-guy dialogue and it catches the sense of an infinitely corrupted world that was difficult to do in thirties studio film. Visually, while the film was darker in tone than was usual during the preceding decade, it did not employ the deep chiaroscuro that would occur in films after the appearance of *Citizen Kane*. That darkness began to take over about 1944.

Murder, My Sweet, Double Indemnity, Scarlet Street   The third current that made film noir possible occurred outside of film. The darkness of noir owes much to the darkening mood of the culture during and right after the war. Noir's themes of male isolation and weakness, of female treachery and mur-derousness, grow out of a multitude of insecurities occurring in the American psyche—events we discussed in Chapter 3. These themes settled onto film noir in both form and content. The genre's visual darkness and its obsessive damaged men reflected the culture's anxious postwar state.

Three landmark films solidified the look and the thematics of the new genre in 1944 and 1945. RKO, the studio that made *Citizen Kane*, produced an adaptation of Raymond Chandler's *Farewell My Lovely*, directed by Edward Dmytryk, that they called *Murder, My Sweet*. (Presumably the name was changed because the film was a vehicle for Dick Powell, a lead player in musicals, who was attempting to broaden his acting capacity; the studio feared that audiences would think the original title would be interpreted as another Dick Powell musical.) *Murder, My Sweet* is among the best of the Chandler adaptations. Powell delivers Philip Marlowe's voice-over narration with a grim irony, while the world the characters inhabit is bathed not in thirties light, but in darkness only occasionally relieved by light. "I'm a little man in a dirty job," Marlowe says at one point, a comment that exemplifies the reduced existential circumstances of the noir male in a world he cannot quite see through, cannot accurately detect.

In the same year, 1944, the German director, Billy Wilder, made *Double Indemnity* for Paramount. Based on a James M. Cain novel, with a screenplay by

Domestic noir. The palpable slats of light from the venetian blinds became a visual convention in forties cinema. Double Indemnity *(Billy Wilder, 1944).*

Raymond Chandler, it synthesized noir's essential generic elements—bitterly ironic dialogue, a weak male character who falls prey to a female predator, and a mise-en-scène not quite as dark as *Murder, My Sweet*, but unrelentingly gray and claustrophobic. The film contains some rare (for its time) exterior footage: a nighttime city street is pierced by the headlights of a careening car and the spark of a workman's blow torch; a gray suburban Los Angeles street, its cracks filled with veins of black asphalt, adds to the pervading atmosphere of limited, sleazy lives. Interiors are dusty and gray. The living room of Phyllis Dietrichson—the woman who lures the poor insurance salesman, Walter Neff, to murder her husband and then shoots him and is shot by him in turn—is cut through with light coming from behind venetian blinds. The light makes palpable the swirling dust in the air. The image of the shadowy slits of light from venetian blinds occurs in almost every forties film from this point on.

Double Indemnity can be read two ways. It is either a misogynist film about a terrifying, destroying woman, or it is a film that liberates the female character from the restrictive and oppressed melodramatic situations that render her helpless. Feminist critics are divided in their views of the film and the noir genre as a whole. If it is in fact a film that gives its female character more strength and control, it no longer situates her as the secure center of the family, but its destroyer, it marks a shirt in the dominant fiction that speaks of women's passivity. However, the fact that both she and her doomed, male prey die at the end diminishes its radical potential. What is unambiguous is the film's attitude toward such sacred cultural institutions and generic mainstays as the family and the brave, protective, self-possessed male.

Walter Neff is dying from the very beginning of the film, which is narrated in flashback as, slowly bleeding to death from Phyllis's gunshot, he dictates his sorry tale onto a recording machine in his office. And while Neff is never self-pitying and remains verbally dexterous and self-deprecating in his story, he is also clearly a loser, whose lust for Phyllis undoes his reason and self control. Phyllis, we learn, creates families in order to destroy them. The family into which Walter comes, as an insurance man trying to make a sale, are a bunch of snarling whiners. Phyllis's husband is fully worthy of the death she plans for him. She manipulates first him and then Walter through a morally (and visually) gray world of cheap houses, crowded office buildings, supermarkets, and dark railroad tracks where Walter dumps the husband's body. There is as little sentimentality in this narrative as Hollywood could allow.

The following year, Fritz Lang, another director from Germany, and an important figure in the Expressionist movement, made a film called *Scarlet Street*. Here, a meek, henpecked husband, Christopher Cross (played by Edward G. Robinson, an actor from the early gangster film days, who plays Walter Neff's boss and would-be friend, Keyes, in *Double Indemnity*), becomes sexually in thrall to a young woman named Kitty. His enthrallment is climaxed by the kind of image Hollywood loves to use to indicate male debasement: he paints her toenails. Painting is a major issue in this classic noir film. Chris Cross is a would-be painter, and Kitty has her boyfriend, Johnny, pass off Chris's work as hers. Chris kills Kitty in a rage and Johnny is sentenced for the crime. The meek man is given power only through his reaction to being played a chump, and though Johnny deserves killing for many reasons, his execution is the cause of overwhelming guilt, borne by the ironically named Chris Cross.

This grim little narrative is given considerable substance by Lang's ability to reproduce the desire and paranoia, the failure and miserable triumph of his meek and hopeless main character. The narrative is given existential portent in its climax, as Chris becomes a kind of eternally guilty everyman. He becomes a street person, wandering a city that is empty of other people. He is the only man alive, carrying his despair alone.

Scarlet Street announces a universal anxiety and a reduction of individual agency that is usually associated with great modernist literary fiction. Its point is made over and over again by film noir. The world is dark and corrupt. Women are predators. Men are either violent and brutal or the passive, unwary prey of the violent or the sexual. Any way out is hard to see. As one film noir character says, "I feel all dead inside. I'm backed up in a dark corner and I don't know who's hitting me." All of this is remarkable in a cinema usually devoted to the bright and harmonious or to the safe excesses and reassuring closures of melodrama. While none of the filmmakers had a term for the genre that rapidly took over production across the studios, the darkness reigned, and by the mid-forties, most films from Hollywood that were not comedies shared some noir characteristics, even if only the core image of a room banded by shadows of light coming through venetian blinds.

Noir's Climax

In a Lonely Place   Noir lasted through the early fifties, climaxed by four films that were very self-conscious of what they were doing. Nicholas Ray's *In a Lonely Place* (1950) combines elements of noir with the male melodrama we discussed earlier. Humphrey Bogart, who had helped form the male noir character in *The Maltese Falcon* and *The Big Sleep* (Howard Hawks's 1946 adaptation of Raymond Chandler's novel, the screenplay of which was cowritten by William Faulkner), constructs a figure of repressed rage, a screenwriter who lives in the shadows of his own uncontainable violence. He is recessive and aggressive at the same time, and when he emerges into the light and falls in love, he is undone by his rage. *In a Lonely Place* is as complex and moving an analysis of male angst and the turmoils of gender as exists in the canon of American cinema. This is the rare American film that allows the fact that love may not, actually, conquer all; that differences in gender response may be insuperable; and that the central characters and their narrative may not be resolved.

The Wrong Man   Alfred Hitchcock's *The Wrong Man* (1957) took a "true story" and created a quasi-documentary style to narrate the events of an ordinary family man accused, arrested, and tried for robbery. His wife sinks into madness as a result of the events. Much of the film—visually as dark and claustrophobic as Hitchcock ever made—doggedly follows the process of its central character's incarceration and trial. It has a slow, almost trancelike pace and refuses to mitigate its characters' unrelenting misery. Even more than *Scarlet Street*, made over a decade earlier, it uses the structures of noir to address the loss of individual power and identity in the post–World War II world.

Loss, powerlessness, the inability to pull out of oncoming chaos—the elements of a bad dream drifting from the individual unconscious into the culture at large—had marked noir from its beginning. Now near the end of its first cycle, these noir elements spoke to the fifties with even more immediacy. In a decade characterized by extreme governmental interference into the intellectual freedom of the country, by big corporate growth, by the construction of a myth of a super enemy ready to infiltrate the very fabric of the culture, fifties paranoia was addressed quite profoundly by film noir, as it was addressed somewhat less profoundly by the alien invasion science fiction film, a major fifties genre.

Kiss Me Deadly   Robert Aldrich's *Kiss Me Deadly* (1955) used the private detective version of film noir to address Cold War issues directly. The film is based on a novel by Mickey Spillane, who wrote vulgar, violent, woman-

hating detective fiction that was enormously popular during the fifties. Aldrich's screen version of Spillane's detective, Mike Hammer, removes much of the vulgarity, turns the sexual violence into a peculiar kind of prudery (even sexual reticence), but leaves the physical violence much intact. *Kiss Me Deadly* is about the search for a mysterious box that contains nuclear material. When opened, the box roars, screams, and glows with a deadly light: Quentin Tarantino got the idea for the mysterious suitcase with the golden light in *Pulp Fiction* from the mysterious box in *Kiss Me Deadly*. The box is discovered and opened by a curious woman—the film plays on the Pandora myth with a special fifties misogyny—and it blows up the world.

An example of intertextual allusion. The blinding light of an atomic device hidden in a box in Robert Aldrich's Kiss Me Deadly *(1955).*

Quentin Tarantino is thinking about Aldrich's bomb when he has Jules open the mysterious suitcase in Pulp Fiction *(1994).*

Noir is usually about implosion rather than explosion. But as the poet T. S. Eliot pointed out in the twenties, the end of the world does not have to come with a bang. A whimper is more likely, and a whimper is what's heard in *Scarlet Street* or *The Wrong Man* or *In a Lonely Place*. *Kiss Me Deadly* turns the whimper back into the more conventional bang. When light pierces through the noir darkness, the world comes apart. When the detective finds out the secret he's been looking for, he gets fried. This is the peculiar double-edged paranoia of the fifties. Men will collapse into lonely isolation or, if they really find out the world's secret, they and everything else will be destroyed.

Touch of Evil   Between implosion and external destruction, there is another possibility. Create a world that appears as an ongoing nightmare of dizzying perspectives, long, dark streets, bizarre individuals careening around an unstable landscape of strip joints, hideous motels, oil fields, barren gray intersections, and open sewers. In other words, update the Expressionist vision to address the modern age. This is what Orson Welles does in *Touch of Evil* (1958), the last film noir of the genre's first cycle. It is fitting that this climactic film should be made by the director who originated the genre eighteen years earlier. Welles had been away from the United States for almost eight years, and returned to find a project based on a second-rate novel about corrupt police, starring Charlton Heston as a Mexican. He took the challenge and created the most intriguing and inventive film noir to date. Filming mostly in the streets of Venice in Los Angeles, and inside actual buildings, Welles turned the "real world" into a bad dream of a border town trafficking in corruption, a local cop who plants evidence to catch his man (the cop is played by Welles himself, puffed up, limping, and growling), and a sappy, moral Mexican official out to save his country's name and protect his American bride.

The apotheosis of film noir. The urban landscape; dark, vertiginous, threatening. Touch of Evil *(Orson Welles, 1958).*

Touch of Evil is, in part, an outsider's view of mid-fifties America just coming out of the grip of Joseph McCarthy and the anti-communist witch hunts—a morass of moral and political corruption. It is also an ironist's attempt to play sympathy for the devil. Welles's Hank Quinlan, the corrupt cop—a Joseph McCarthy surrogate—is, in fact, weak and spiteful, out for revenge against "my dirty job." The world Welles creates for these characters, on the other hand, is of Welles's imagination only, insinuated by his camera, which tracks, cranes, cants, sinks far below eye level and then rapidly cranes high above the characters. The long opening shot of *Touch of Evil* tracks a car moving through the dark labyrinth of an Mexican-American border crossing. The shot lasts for almost four minutes and is one of the most famous long takes in contemporary cinema. The camera articulates the characters and the audience's perceptions of them by means of dizzying, off-center compositions, and enfolds them in its dark, nightmare world. It is the definition of how mise-en-scène can be created.

Noir's Rebirth

There was not very much farther one could go past *Touch of Evil* in creating a dark, decaying, Expressionist mise-en-scène. The genre was spent, and films were beginning to respond to television in ways that made noir obsolete. The deeply shadowed black and white of the forties was giving way to a more evenly graded spectrum of gray tones in the fifties. Then in the sixties, black and white gave way to color. Since film noir was so essentially dependent on the dark end of the black and white spectrum, a move to color would seem to mark the end of its visual life, despite at least one notable noir color experiment, Henry Hathaway's *Niagra* (1953). But color turned out to be a very flexible medium. To understand why, a short history of color film is necessary.

LIGHTING Film had always been tinted and toned in the silent period, with a red tint signifying passion, blue standing for night, gold for day. Experiments with a more "realistic" color stock began in the early twenties, and the three-color Technicolor process was introduced in the early thirties. Color remained a specialty process until the early sixties, used mainly for musicals and fantasy films (that's why the Oz portions of the *Wizard of Oz*, 1939, are in Technicolor). Realism required black and white. We have been discussing all along how conventionalized film is, how it is based on repeated patterns and recognizable structures. This is nowhere more apparent than in the fact that "reality" for film before the sixties meant black and white cinematography. Of course there is nothing inherently "realistic" in either color or black and white. The latter was considered "real" only because it was the dominant mode and color wasn't. But that changed in the sixties. By the early sixties, television began to broadcast in color and, because the final distribution point for any film is the television screen, by the end of the decade, all films had to be made in color.

The influence of film noir was powerful, and young filmmakers, many coming out of film school in the late sixties and early seventies, felt a response similar to that felt by those French intellectuals in the early fifties: the discovery of something extraordinary in the style and content of American film from the forties and early fifties. They began to revive noir, rethink it in color, and to use noir as a way to make color cinematography responsive to their imaginative needs. Arthur Penn made a key film in the noir revival in *Night Moves* (1975), and Martin Scorsese was at the center of the revival. *Taxi Driver* (1976) captures the dark Expressionism of original film noir, with its creation of an urban landscape that reflects the paranoia of its main character more thoroughly than any film since *Touch of Evil*. The genre named by the French became, by the seventies, a genre recognized by many filmgoers. By the eighties, *TV Guide* was referring to film noir in its listings. In 1984, there was a nightclub sequence in *The Terminator*. The club was named "Tech Noir."

Genre Resilience

A peculiar circle is drawn. Genre is a shared experience. Filmmakers create their films within the generic boundaries in which audiences find comfort and affirmation. Noir does not create comfort, yet quickly became a recognizable pattern—of gloom and despair. What's more, noir was not created in the usual generic sense. Rather it grew, almost unconsciously, from a variety of factors that were not directly under filmmakers' intellectual control. Noir, even more than the Western, the romantic melodrama, the science fiction film, or most conventional generic structures, was formed by viewer response and recognition, and was defined by critics rather than filmmakers, first in France, then in America. Once noir was defined—that is, once critics discovered that it existed and young filmmakers understood its vitality as a visual and narrative form—it was revived, restructed, and once again began to infiltrate other genres. Films as various as Alan J. Pakula's *Klute* (1971), the first two *Godfather* films (1972, 1974), Roman Polanski's *Chinatown* (1974), Pakula's *All the President's Men* (1976), Ridley Scott's *Blade Runner* (1982), and *Alien 3* (David Fincher, 1992)—to name only a very few—rethought the form and structure of film noir and reworked if for contemporary needs. Noir continues today in films ranging from Oliver Stone's *U-Turn* (1997), Curtis Hanson's *L. A. Confidential* (1997), to Alex Proyas's *Dark City* (1998), a science fiction film whose title comes from a 1950 film noir.

The key to genre is its ability to be reworked. This may appear to be a contradiction. Earlier I said that the key to genre is the way it maintains itself through a variety of variations over a long period of time. Indeed, there is a point beyond which generic boundaries cannot be stretched, or they will break and the genre will fall apart. But genres are malleable and can infiltrate one another. The Western, along with the war film, was refigured in *Star Wars*, for example. Sometimes, as in film noir, genres can stretch the boundaries of the master narratives and revise its dominant fictions. For some filmmakers, testing the boundaries and even pushing them beyond the breaking point are ways to define a subjective approach to filmmaking, to move beyond the classical American style. By working from a generic base, filmmakers can find their voice, change viewer perceptions, change the genre, and, perhaps, change cinema.

EUROPEAN AND OTHER CINEMAS

Italian Neorealism

We have noted that American cinema is the dominant form across the world. It should not be surprising then to find that when filmmakers in other countries seek their own style, their own methods of seeing the world in cinematic terms, they begin by thinking about American film and how their work can be different. We saw this happening among the post-Revolutionary filmmakers of Russia, and see it again in post-World War II Italy, where a new style of filmmaking emerged that changed cinema the world over for many years. Italian neorealism was born of many economic, social, and political factors—not the least of which was the fact that the Italian economy and the very physical structure of the country were in ruins in 1945. Filmmaking as usual was neither possible or desired. Italy was destroyed by the Fascist regime, a dictatorial structure of corporate state control that managed and brutalized all facets of life, including filmmaking. (Italy's main studio, Cinecittà, was inaugurated by dictator Benito Mussolini.) After the war, Italian filmmakers linked the commercial cinema of prewar Italy with all that was bad about the Fascists. They also saw a link to Hollywood film in those Fascist comedies and melodramas about romance among members of the upper middle class—called "white-telephone" movies because of their overdone decor. They knew that all of this production, with its reliance on elaborate sets, stars that were removed from the life of ordinary people, stories that addressed the lives of people who could not possibly exist in the day-to-day world—the whole artifice of middle-class fantasy—had to be overthrown. In its place would be a new genre of film that addressed poor people in their daily lives, peasants in the countryside, workers in the streets and in their apartments and meeting halls.

Stars and studios, sets, and the elaborate tricks Hollywood used to fabricate complex, unreal images would be jettisoned. Gone too would be stories about doomed love affairs among the rich and the indulged emotions of bored women and heartless men. Instead of the studio, films would be made on the street, on location, amid the traffic and the people of the cities, or in the countryside. Instead of movie stars, ordinary people or semiprofessional performers would be used. Their faces would not be familiar or associated with other films. Hollywood cinema, and the cinema of Fascist Italy, were altogether an act of evasion. People went to movies to see movie life, not the life of the world. Do away with these conventions, strip generic formulae and generic responses, get to the people, and film would in turn communicate back to the people images of life as it is.

It's important to note that the neorealists were not interested in making documentaries. They wanted to continue using fiction as a means to structure an ordered narrative. But for them, the narrative and the mise-en-scène would appear to grow out of the present circumstances of history and place. Many of the films they made had an immediacy and texture quite unlike anything ever seen before. Roberto Rossellini's great war trilogy, *Rome, Open City* (1945), *Paisan* (1946), and *Germany, Year Zero* (1947); De Sica's *Bicycle Thieves* (1948), *Miracle in Milan* (1950), and *Umberto D.* (1951); and Luchino Visconti's *La Terra Trema* (1948) were raw, even unpolished films of great power and clarity. They spoke about Italian life during and after the war. *La Terra Trema* was one of the few films ever made that addressed the poverty and hopelessness of disenfranchised rural life. All of the films have a roughness and directness that move the viewer beyond the form of the film to the movement of its story and its characters. But unlike Hollywood films, which also take us beyond their form and into their content, neorealism addresses poverty and desperation, the social life of the poor, and the difficulties of forming supportive communities in a way Hollywood genres rarely permit. Unlike the classical Hollywood style, these films demand our visual attention. By filling the screen with images of a shattered and destructive world, they ask us to observe what we have never seen in film before.

Bicycle Thieves   And yet Italian neorealism is, basically, melodrama. Hollywood melodrama is about the politics of subjective suffering—individuals oppressed by gender, domesticity, unrealizable desires to escape. Italian neorealism is about the suffering brought on by political and economic events, as well as the lives affected by them. The characters of neorealism are deeply oppressed, not by domesticity or gender but by war and poverty. *Bicycle Thieves*, for example, has a simple premise: a very poor man gets a job putting

up advertising posters. In a key sequence, he pastes up a poster of the very famous late-forties movie star Rita Hayworth. It is a kind of symbolic act that
demonstrates his distance, and the film's, from the world of Hollywood glam-
our. In order to do his job, he needs a bicycle to get from street to street. To get
the bicycle, he hocks the family's linens. He is happy at his new job. Then his
bicycle is stolen by someone in even worse economic shape than he is. The rest
of the film follows his search around Rome in a hopeless attempt to find the
bike and restore his life.

Ricci, the main character (played not by an actor, but by a laborer), is seen
amidst family and comrades in the houses and streets of Rome. The camera
will often move away from him to observe passersby and the life going on
around him. At one point, when he is putting up his posters, two beggar children wander by and the camera casually stops looking at Ricci to follow these
two along the street. The American continuity style insists that narrative and
visual focus remain at all times on the central figures of the story. The world
around them is often only suggested or caught in quick cutaways. In neorealism, the world that surrounds the characters is given equal space with the
characters themselves. Neorealism's mise-en-scène is created by the interplay
of city or countryside, people, and the central characters who emerge from the
community. Ricci is one story among others. But his story, finally, is about anguish and hope, which are irresistible. De Sica, no matter how he tries to link
Ricci with his surroundings, still finds that he must focus on his character's
emotional state, though he never lets us forget that it is tied to the class and
economy in which the character lives. He communicates these emotions and
creates empathy in his audience by one of the most standard of melodramatic
means, triangulating the viewer between the main character and his little son,
Bruno. The child clings to Ricci's hand throughout his search for the stolen bicycle. His misery and tears echo his father's despair and amplify it. They finally entrap the audience as much as any other melodramatic device like
death or a dog, both of which De Sica uses in his later film, *Umberto D* (1952).

Neorealism in America   This is not to undercut the power of the neorealist
movement or the extent of its influence, which was enormous. It is important,
though, to stress how powerful genres are, especially melodrama—so powerful that melodrama maintained its hold on a filmmaking movement whose
original aim was to overthrow the structure and ideology of cinema's past.
Neorealism was absorbed into American filmmaking very quickly because of
its melodrama and because its style of exterior shooting was so novel. It influenced—of all things—the gangster genre. By the late forties, some films were
being promoted as shot "on location," where the action "actually takes place."
The Naked City, filmed in 1948 by Jules Dassin, was not a neorealist film by any
means. Neither was it filmed entirely on location. There was still the need to
manufacture images in the Hollywood style. But it used exterior sequences to
a somewhat greater degree than many previous films, and it led the way for
gangster films and films noir to use the streets more than the back lots, to gen-

erate images out of the material of the world rather than putting them together in an optical printer.

The exterior shooting influenced by neorealism also reflected some economic realities. Italian neorealism emerged from the wreckage of the postwar economy and political culture. More subtle wreckages occurred to the United States after the war. What Hollywood faced was a decline in movie attendance (and therefore a fall-off in revenues), the end of many binding contracts between studios and their personnel, accompanied by the blacklisting of many key creative personnel—including Jules Dassin, who directed *The Naked City*, and Albert Maltz, who wrote it. The power of the studio, manifested in its total control of the filmmaking process, was waning. Filmmakers began to form independent production companies and to shoot their films outside the studio. One of the results was a movement out onto the streets. Shooting on location in the United States was not only a matter of aesthetics, and probably never, as it was in Italy, a question of ideology.

The French New Wave

Exterior shooting was the closest American filmmaking came to the neorealist movement. The young French critics—the same ones who discovered film noir after seeing many American films from the late forties—looked also at *Rome, Open City, Bicycle Thieves*, and the other neorealist films coming from Italy. They recognized in both forms a departure from the classical Hollywood style and new ways to imagine cinematic space. When they made the move from film viewers and film critics to filmmakers, they found that, by combining the gangster/noir style with neorealism, they could shake up the very foundations of genre and the way we think of film. They shot on the streets, using new, little-known actors. While they did not make their films about the working class, like the neorealists, they did look at the lives of the dispossessed and the marginal.

Jean-Luc Godard   Most of these young directors started their careers by making interesting variations on the American gangster film. Jean-Luc Godard—who became the most influential filmmaker since Orson Welles—made his first full-length film a celebration of the gangster genre called *Breathless* (1959). Godard would go even further—Godard was always going further—and in 1965 made *Alphaville*, a film that places the noir detective inside the science fiction genre, and had his tough-guy hero travel the universe in his Ford Galaxy. (This should not give the impression that Godard was idle between 1959 and 1965. After *Breathless* and before *Alphaville* he made seven feature films and a number of short ones. Every one, and all that followed, experimented with genre, narrative form, and all the basic conceptions and preconceptions of cinema.) François Truffaut, the best known of this group of innovators, made his second film an homage to noir called *Shoot the Piano Player* (1960).

These films were neither imitations nor parodies. They were homages, energetic celebrations of the American films that nourished their directors' imaginations, and they were vehicles for rethinking how genres work and how audiences respond to them. Their films interrogate the ways genres operate and, further, the ways in which films told their stories and developed mise-en-scène. For Godard, the gangster or the private eye became a figure of existential anxiety (not that far from Chandler's Philip Marlowe), who seeks out identity and speaks philosophically about who he is and how he is to be known. The latter becomes the key question for Godard: how do we *know* what we see in a film and learn about characters? What is the nature of the cinematic image and the genre-driven cinematic narrative? When we see the same characters in roughly the same story, with basically the same outcome in film after film, are we lulled into a sense of acceptance, of ideological complicity with the filmmakers and their work, both of which request our uniform response? Can genres be altered in a way to make us ask questions rather than respond with the same feelings?

Godard's answer to these questions was to take genres, the cinematic image, and the narrative apart, in order to make us look and understand that what we were seeing was just an image ("this is not a just image," Godard would say, "this is just an image") and that these images were freighted with ideological and cultural baggage. His films break all the rules: they give up straightforward continuity editing, avoid over-the-shoulder-shots, gaze at length from a position directly in front of the characters, who talk not only to one another, but to the audience. His narratives shift mood and direction, closure is not promised and loose ends, popping out all over the narrative, need not be tied up at the end.

Michelangelo Antonioni   Other filmmakers followed suit in the sixties and seventies, continuing to ask questions about the Hollywood style and Hollywood genres and answer them in their films. If they didn't use the gangster film as their object of interrogation, they turned to melodrama. In Italy, following the neorealist movement, filmmakers examined the world inhabited by their characters, now more often middle rather than working class. They articulated the spaces around the figures, the architectural structures they lived in that defined their social and emotional life. Michelangelo Antonioni, for example, investigated the melodramatic mise-en-scène so that the world surrounding his characters not only expressed their anxieties, but manifested the repressions that caused them, in a strange and powerful combination of Expressionism and neorealism. Antonioni was the great modernist poet of urban space in which architectural geometry delineated the barriers of the spirit. His quiet, oppressed women and jumpy, unfocused men wander through architectural landscapes that don't so much dwarf them as carry on a visual dialogue with them. Unlike the classic American cinema, Antonioni does not privilege the figure in the frame. He insists that composition be about the relationship between the human figure and her surroundings and that emotion emerge from that interaction. His camera is a distant, sometimes disembodied observer, whose movements make us wonder who authorizes the gaze in a film. Who is looking at whom, and why? His films rely on the eloquence and articulateness of the image more than almost any other filmmakers. They are the poetry of the figure in the urban landscape.

Antonioni—in films such as *Il Grido* (1957), *L'Avventura* (1960), *La Notte* (1961), *The Eclipse* (1962), *Red Desert* (1964), and *Blow-Up* (1966)—broke many rules. He substitutes the composition for the cut, forcing the viewer to look *at* the frame rather than across it from one action to the next. He changes the internal dynamics of melodrama. Instead of transposing excess emotion from the individual to mise-en-scène and back again, he makes the individual part of the mise-en-scène and asks the viewer to inspect both very carefully. Emotional excess is replaced by a shifting visual dynamic. Emotion emerges from our comprehension of these dynamics and is never removed from intellectual awareness. The cinema reclaims its obligations to the visible and melodrama is restrained by an active engagement of the viewer's eye and mind.

Yasujiro Ozu   Antonioni is not the only filmmaker to force the viewer's eye to observe composition and make the human figure only one aspect of a complex mise-en-scène. Orson Welles and Stanley Kubrick do the same. Hitchcock does it and, subtly, often without showing his hand, so does the great director of Westerns, John Ford. In Japan, Yasujiro Ozu made many domestic melodramas that addressed the quiet change of culture in that country after the war. Films as moving and beautiful as their titles—*Late Spring* (1949), *The Flavor of Green Tea over Rice* (1952), *Tokyo Story* (1953), *Early Spring* (1956), *Late Autumn* (1960)—examined the Japanese middle-class family from an ironic, quiet distance. Ozu places his camera in the "tatami" position, low on the floor, emulating the traditional seating of a Japanese at home on a tatami mat. But this emulation does not define the point of view of a particular individual in the frame. It is, rather,

The middle-class Japanese family, seen from the tatami *position—that is from a mat placed on the floor.* Tokyo Story *(Yasujiro Ozu, 1953).*

a cultural gesture, looking at the world from a Japanese perspective. That perspective includes a respect for space, an interest in rooms and surroundings that is not confined to the narrative of a particular film, but speaks the narrative of the culture as a whole. As I indicated earlier, American films rarely maintain interest in or focus on spaces that have no human figures in them. Ozu loves these spaces, because, even though no figure is present, they were humanized, made by people to live in, and therefore they retain and define human presence, even in their absence. His camera gazes at a room before someone enters it and after she leaves. He cuts away from the main narrative line to create a montage of the city, a train passing, a rock garden, clothes hanging on a line. Ozu's world is defined by its particular cultural articulations.

But there is no mistaking the melodramatic base of Ozu's films. They are about families in turmoil. Parents die, daughters marry, fathers get drunk, sisters are mean, the domestic center does not hold. None of these situations is addressed with the hysteria and overstatement beloved of American melodrama, nor is the viewer asked to deliver emotion on the basis of a character's death or the redemption of a misguided soul. The viewer is asked only to observe and put things together and to recognize within Ozu's mise-en-scène a harmony that transcends the particular upheavals of the domestic.

Rainer Werner Fassbinder   If Ozu sought a greater cultural harmony out of local family melodrama, the German filmmaker Rainer Werner Fassbinder looked for melodrama to deliver insight into history and politics and to discover in the family a microcosm of large power structures in the culture. Fassbinder was one of the more remarkable figures to appear in European cinema during the 1970s. He started making films in 1969 and directed thirty-nine films—including multipart series for television—before his premature death in 1982. A large, punk, openly gay man, Fassbinder brought together a remarkably talented stock company of cast and crew, who set out to rethink American film melodrama as a mode of addressing the politics of the family and the state.

Fassbinder's idol was Douglas Sirk. Sirk's over-the-top, bigger-than-life melodramas pushed the genre to its limits, made the viewer aware of how the excesses of emotion, and the spilling over of those excesses into the mise-en-scène, were the marks of the genre's artifices rather than imitations of life. Sirk pushed the melodramatic boundaries. Fassbinder attempted to reflect them back in on themselves and exploit them not as reflections of the personal but as statements about the political. In Sirk's *All That Heaven Allows*, an upper-middle-class, suburban widow defies family and friends to marry a much younger, down-to-earth nursery man. Fassbinder remade the film in 1973. *Fear Eats the Soul: Ali* takes the essential banality of Sirk's premise and turns it into political and social allegory. Sirk had tried to transcend the banality of his film's story by creating a complex mise-en-scène and by turning the film into a commentary on sexual repressiveness and the fifties' concerns over conformity. Fassbinder goes further, creating instead of an upper-middle-class matron as the central female character, an old German washerwoman, a widow whose husband was a member of the Nazi party; instead of a handsome young nursery man, a homely, bumbling Moroccan, an immigrant worker, suffering the indignities, scorn, and oppression faced by people of color who are brought in by a rich culture to do the dirty work.

The old German woman and the young, black immigrant fall in love and marry. Fassbinder makes this all so touching that we have to shake ourselves to realize how perfectly absurd it is. It simply couldn't happen. But then, the conventional absurdities of ordinary melodrama could never happen either. The narrative structure of *Fear Eats the Soul* only points up these absurdities and makes us examine our assumptions about them. The film invites us to come to understand how much we take for granted in melodrama, and how much goes unexamined. Emmi and Ali—the unlikely couple—are visited by a string of humiliations. Emmi's neighbors scorn her; her family reviles her. They take out their anger on her possessions. In *All That Heaven Allows*, Carrie's children buy her a television set to keep her mind off her lover; in *Fear Eats the Soul*, Emmi's son kicks in the television set to show his anger at her impending marriage. The local grocer won't sell his food to Ali. And people stare. Fassbinder makes the staring almost comic and absolutely unbearable. He will show people frozen in a stare; he will create tableaux of staring, staged, artificial, and obvious, to make his point. This couple is so transgressive, all anyone can do is stare at them.

Then he reverses the situation. Suddenly, Emmi's children realize that mother is a good resource for babysitting; the neighbors want Ali to help them move furniture; the grocer, realizing that his business is being hurt by supermarkets, welcomes Ali at his shop. But as outsiders change their tune to fit their own needs, Ali and Emmi go through a reverse change and become their own exploiters. Emmi shows off Ali's muscles to her neighbors and refuses to allow his friends to visit the apartment. He, in turn, flees to the arms of the woman who runs the local Moroccan bar. Earlier Emmi was cast out by her co-workers. Now she joins them in taunting and isolating a foreigner who has joined her cleaning crew at the office. Fassbinder makes a special point of this by literally rhyming a shot. Earlier in the film, his camera looks at Emmi sitting alone on the stairs, eating her lunch, as her co-workers group together making fun of her. She is composed between the spokes of the banister, as if

Visual rhyming. Rainer Werner Fassibinder observes his character trapped within the oppressive gaze of other people. Here, Emmi, who has married a Moroccan migrant worker, is badly treated and isolated by her co-workers.

Later, when another worker arrives on the scene, Emmi and her friends isolate her and the shot composition is the same. Ali: Fear Eats the Soul *(1974).*

imprisoned. Later, when Emmi joins her co-workers taunting the newcomer, this poor soul is framed by the camera in exactly the same way Emmi was. Oppression returns like rhyme.

For Fassbinder, oppression is not something internalized. Repression is not only sexual. Unhappiness is not always the result of a bad romance or a failing marriage. Repression and unhappiness are social and political phenomena; they are about power and one-upsmanship—about how someone with a little power exercises it by oppressing someone with even less. This cycle of oppression and hurt is itself contained within a larger cycle of power and repression exercised by the state. Emmi and Ali have a reconciliation. They meet at the bar for Middle-Eastern immigrant workers where they first found each other, and they dance. A happy ending threatens until, suddenly, Ali collapses on the floor. In *All That Heaven Allows*, Cary, realizing that Rock Hudson is indeed her only love and key to happiness (a doctor has told her that her headaches and depression are a result of repressing her desires), pursues him in the snowy countryside. Before he hears her calling to him, he falls off a cliff. The film ends with her assuming a maternal position at his bedside, while a doe plays in the snow outside. Ali's collapse has nothing to do with despair over losing Emmi. He is suffering from an ulcer. The doctor at the end of *Fear Eats the Soul* offers no hope and tells Emmi that Ali will never get well. His condition is a common physical response of immigrants to the terrible conditions and humiliations they face in their host country. The humiliations and the ulcers will keep occurring until he dies. The film ends with the image of Ali in his hospital bed. There is no deer at the window, only the hard Munich skyline.

The Influence of Brecht

Fassbinder does not merely invert melodramatic principles and structures or turn them inside out; he shows how they can be made to work. Instead of absorbing the political into the personal, he shows how personal suffering and emotional repression can be understood as political events on the micro and macro levels. He also shows how melodrama can be made to work on an intellectual level by inviting the viewer to step back a bit and look with some detachment. Fassbinder does this by borrowing principles from the influential left-wing playwright Bertolt Brecht, who said that the work of art should not mystify or make itself invisible, but rather open itself up to interrogation. For Brecht, the more invisible the style, the more the viewer is fooled into believing the illusion. The more fooled, the more he is taken advantage of. The more visible, the more the viewer understands how form and ideology operate, and the work of art becomes a tool for understanding larger structures of power in the culture. Brecht would have the playwright (and, by extension, the filmmaker) build into his work effects that create distance between it and the viewer. Fassbinder does this by creating outrageous narratives with characters who are quite unattractive by Hollywood standards. Then he employs an unusual visual style. His lighting is often very low, so figures don't stand out with the presence we expect in a Hollywood film. He frames his characters in doorways and within rooms so that we become conscious of the framing of the camera and how that framing comments upon the characters and their situation. He will stop dramatic action and have his characters look up and stare at the camera, forcing us to recognize the artificiality of the scene. He will repeat actions and compositions, as when he rhymes the shot of Emmi isolated on the stairs. He will exaggerate actions and make melodramatic coincidences obvious. He is unafraid to make the melodramatic structure totter and even fall, so that he can rebuild it from a new perspective, a public and political as opposed to a private and personal perspective.

The Brechtian influence on Fassbinder (and earlier on Jean-Luc Godard) was important in the reconceptualizing of genre and the continuity style. Since the main function of the classical Hollywood style is to make viewers unconscious of there being any style at all, the Brechtian reworking of the style serves the opposite function. The result is a consciousness of film and its stories as something *made,* not something natural, given, and present. The viewer, forced to come to terms with form, will then be willing to think through why the form is so constructed, why she is asked to look a certain way, at certain things—why she is asked to look at all.

Visual Pleasure

This coming to terms with form is nowhere more important than when we consider how movies make us look at gender. One of American cinema's master narratives is, as we have seen, the confirmation of woman's male-dependent, passive role. It forms the basic pattern of melodrama and it drives comedy. Laura Mulvey, who wrote an influential essay called "Visual Pleasure and the Narrative Cinema," pointed out that the classic Hollywood style is structured through the way the gaze of the camera, of the male characters in the film, and of the viewers watching the projected image in front of them are directed at the female character. She is, as it were, fixed by the male gaze that drives the narrative. She is objectified, her subjectivity transferred to the male gaze.

In melodrama, the woman is fixed by the process of the narrative itself, hurt, kept down, offered a possibility of release, and then returned to the domestic fold, wiser but still kept down. "Don't let's ask for the moon . . . , we have the stars." The melodramatic narrative does not permit her to ask, "Why not ask for everything?" She is there only to be looked at with pity or compassion, admired for her beauty, worried over if she is too demanding or energetic, and then recouped or killed off. More often than not, she is simply the mechanism of the melodrama's sexual economy, its parceling out of desire, sacrifice, and redemption around the fulcrum of the female character. She is the object of the gaze: it gives her value and takes it away.

Jeanne Dielman   Many women filmmakers have attempted to disrupt this mechanism, to see if the gaze can be altered and women given another place in the visual field of cinema. In the United States, filmmakers as diverse in their approach as Susan Seidelman (in *Desperately Seeking Susan*, 1985, and *Making Mr. Right*, 1987), Donna Deitch (*Desert Hearts*, 1985), Barbra Steisand (particularly in films such as *Yentl*, 1983, and *The Prince of Tides*, 1991), Nancy Savoca (in, for example, *Household Saints*, 1993), and Kathryn Bigelow (especially *Strange Days*, 1995, co-written and co-produced by James Cameron) try to alter the direction of the male gaze and resituate the way women are seen in film. They don't move too far from melodrama, but their attempts demonstrate that there are other directions for the genre to take.

One of the most successful attempts to question the gaze and the genre was made by a Belgian director, Chantal Akerman, in a 1975 film, *Jeanne Dielman, 23 Quai du Commerce, 1080 Bruxelles*. Akerman transforms the male gaze at the female character. She makes us look, but removes the pleasure. Our gaze is at a woman, but what we see is not desirable and certainly not erotic. For over three hours, her camera spends much of its time simply watching the central character, a lower-middle-class Belgian housewife, who lives in a tiny apartment with her teenage son and practices prostitution in the afternoons to supplement her pension. The camera looks, unmoving, slightly below eye level, at a distance that prevents intimacy, as this woman goes about her obsessive tasks, cooking, shining her son's shoes, making up the rooms, going to the store, looking after a neighbor's child, talking to her son, entertaining her clients. The camera looks and looks. There is rarely a cut unless there is a change of place, and the change of place is usually to another space in the apartment. Everything is slow, deliberate. The camera looks, relentlessly, but coolly.

The act of looking demystifies everything. The woman and her work, the woman and her sexuality are reduced to the routine of gazing at them. She and her life become objects, just as so many women characters in film have always been. The excesses of melodrama, the assumed intimacy of our gaze, and the forward propulsion of the continuity style allow us to identify with the character. We look at her, we look with her. We want her, we want her to succeed, to be punished. Melodrama transfers desire back and forth. But in *Jeanne Dielman* there are no distractions, no excess—except the excess created by the camera's gaze. Desire is diverted from the character back to our own looking. We either want to keep looking to see if anything will happen or we want not to look. In fact, nothing happens to the woman until late in the film, when her obsessive actions begin to unravel. She forgets part of her routine, does some things over again. Then she sits in a chair for a very long time, the camera gazing at her without a cut. Later, a client arrives. The woman experiences an orgasm with him—perhaps her first—takes a pair of scissors, and stabs him. Her order disrupted, her emotions brought to the surface, she has no recourse but to destroy in an attempt to get the order restored.

Jeanne Dielman is certainly not another postfeminist film about a sexually liberated woman who is really crazy and murderous in the *Fatal Attraction* or *Single White Female* (Barbet Schroeder, 1992) or *Basic Instinct* mode. Rather it is a commentary on melodrama and its attempts to sexualize and then redeem from sexuality the central female character. *Jeanne Dielman* thinks about what melodrama might look like if we were allowed to look at it without embellishment, given the distance that the classical Hollywood style forbids. *Jeanne Dielman* explores how women are represented in film and how that representation turns them into automatons. It also explores the conditions of our own watching of melodrama and, by draining that watching of all spectacle, of all excess, music, elaborate mise-en-scène, camera movement, and cutting, takes us to the bare level of the gaze and makes us very, very uncomfortable.

The last time I showed *Jeanne Dielman* to a class, they began yelling at the screen: "Cut," they yelled, "cut, already." There was nobody to hear them; it was only a film; and the shot went on and on. The melodrama had been transferred to the audience.

Master narratives, dominant fictions, and the genres that are made from them are never immutable. They remain in force through a kind of inertia, which is broken when an energetic, curious cinematic intelligence comes to examine them closely. Which leads us to a question. Who are the intelligences who perpetuate the narratives and who are the ones who change them? Who are the individuals who make films in the classical style, and who explore new, alternative styles? If a genre has a kind of life of its own, what is the role of the individual artist? Can a romantic concept like "genius" and "originality" even have a place in the discussion of the mass art of cinema? These are the questions that concern us next.

NOTES AND REFERENCES

Master Narratives and Dominant Fictions   The term "dominant fiction" is suggested by Kaja Silverman in *Male Subjectivity at the Margins* (New York and London: Routledge: 1992). For a theory of the *end* of master narratives in the postmodern age, see Jean-François Lyotard, *The Postmodern Condition: a Report on Knowledge,* trans. Geoff Bennington and Brian Massumi (Minneapolis: University of Minnesota Press, 1984).

Master Narratives, Censorship   David Cook presents an excellent history of Hollywood censorship in *A History of Narrative Film,* 3d ed. (New York: W. W. Norton, 1996), pp. 280–84.

Genre, Generic Origins   François Delsarte was a nineteenth-century Frenchman who codified dramatic facial expressions and gestures in the nineteenth century.

There is some interesting discussion about the tension between genre and individual expression in Leo Braudy's *The World in a Frame,* which has been previously cited in Chapter 2, and by Robert Warshow in his essay "Movie Chronicle: The Western" in his book *The Immediate Experience* (cited Chapter 3) and the collection *Film Theory and Criticism* (cited Chapter 2).

Genre, Generic Patterns   A lively history of the Warner Brothers gangster film and biography of its stars is in Robert Stam, *City Boys* (Princeton: Princeton University Press, 1992).

Genre Analysis   A good theoretical discussion of film genre is done by Steven Neale, *Genre* (London: British Film Institute, 1983). See also Robin Wood's "Ideology, Genre, Auteur," in *Film Theory and Criticism.*

Melodrama   There are two excellent anthologies of essays on melodrama and film: Marcia Landy, ed., *Imitations of Life: A Reader of Film and Television Melodrama* (Detroit: Wayne State University Press, 1991) and Christine Gledhill, ed., *Home Is Where the Heart Is* (London: BFI Publishing, 1987). The standard essay is Thomas Elsaessar's "Tales of Sound and Fury: Observations on the Family Melodrama," reprinted in the 1992 edition of *Film Theory and Criticism* and in *Home Is Where the Heart Is.*

Ideological Norms   Ideology is a complex topic and so is much of the writing on it. One place to start would be Terry Lovell, *Pictures of Reality: Aesthetics, Politics, and Pleasure* (London: BFI Publishing, 1980).

Film Noir   So much has been written on noir, but the best remains an essay by the screenwriter (of *Taxi Driver,* among others) and director Paul Schrader, "Notes on Film Noir," *Film Comment* 8 (Spring 1972). A good visual analysis is offered by J. A. Place and L. S. Peterson, "Some Visual Notes on Film Noir," in Bill Nichols, ed., *Movies and Methods,* vol. 1 (Berkeley and Los Angeles: University of California Press, 1976), pp. 325–38. See also Frank Krutnik, *In a Lonely Street: Film Noir, Genre, Masculinity* (London and New York: Routledge, 1991). For a feminist reading, see E. Ann Kaplan, ed., *Women In Film Noir* (London: BFI Publishing, 1980).

Expressionist Roots of Noir   The best work on German Expressionism is Lotte Eisner's *The Haunted Screen,* trans. Roger Greaves (Berkeley and Los Angeles: University of California Press, 1973). An interesting cultural study of the thirties horror film is in David Skal, *The Monster Show* (New York: Penguin Books, 1994).

Double Indemnity   Walter Neff is played by Fred MacMurray, until this time an actor in light comedy. Like Dick Powell, he used a noir film to change his style. Phyllis is played by Barbara Stanwyck. For discussion of whether noir elaborates a destruction of the women-based family or merely recuperates it, see Claire Johnston, "Double Indemnity," in the previously cited *Women in Film Noir,* pp. 100–11, and Joyce Nelson, "Mildred Pierce Reconsidered," in Bill Nichols, ed., *Movies and Methods,* vol. 2 (Berkeley and Los Angeles: University of California Press, 1985). The quotation "I feel all dead inside . . ." is from Henry Hathaway's *Dark Corner* (1946) and is quoted in Frank Krutnik's *In a Lonely Street: Film Noir, Genre, Masculinity,* p. 101.

Touch of Evil   There is a wonderful sequence in Tim Burton's film *Ed Wood* (1994) in which the momentarily dispirited director of very bad films goes into a dark bar in the middle of a bright Hollywood day. He finds Orson Welles sitting in a corner working on a script. "Tell me about it," Orson tells Ed Wood. "I'm supposed to do a thriller at Universal, but they want Charlton Heston to play a Mexican!"

The long take at the beginning of *Touch of Evil* is lovingly parodied in the opening of Robert Altman's film *The Player.* Altman makes his shot even longer and the characters who move around in it keep referring to Welles's film.

Noir's Rebirth   Original Technicolor used three black and white negatives which were filtered to respond respectively to the primary colors, red, green, and blue. These negatives were then pressed with dyes during the printing process and, in combination, laid down a full color image on the positive film. By the early fifties, Eastman Kodak developed a single-strip color process. This became the standard and three-color Technicolor disappeared. This was a shame. The original Technicolor was very stable. Eastman color is not, and most films made between the late fifties and the mid-eighties fade if not properly protected.

European and Other Cinemas   A good survey of postwar European and International cinema is in Robert Phillip Kolker, *The Altering Eye* (New York: Oxford University Press, 1983).

Italian Neorealism   On Mussolini, Cinecittà, the history of neorealism, see Peter Bondanella, *Italian Cinema: From Neorealism to the Present* (New York: Frederick Ungar, 1983).

The French New Wave   The best discussion of the movement remains James Monaco's *The New Wave: Truffaut, Godard, Chabrol, Rohmer, Rivette* (New York: Oxford University Press, 1976).

Fassbinder   Some of Fassbinder's crew is now active in America. His cinematographer, Michael Ballhaus, now works for Martin Scorsese and has filmed such diverse projects as *Goodfellas* and *The Age of Innocence.*

The Influence of Brecht   Brecht's theoretical writing is collected in *Brecht on Theatre,* trans. John Willett (New York: Hill and Wang, 1979).

Visual Pleasure   Laura Mulvey's essay is widely reprinted and can be found in *Film Theory and Criticism.*

5

THE STORY TELLERS
OF FILM

WHO MAKES MOVIES?

We've spoken at length about films as economic and cultural productions, dependent upon studios, audiences, market forces, the desire to create emotions and make money from them, and the large cultural forces that play through the entire filmmaking and film viewing experience. We've seen how films operate as commodities in the flow of capital and generic expectations. We've looked at some individual filmmakers who have made special contributions and alterations to cinematic style and, throughout the book, I have used the film studies convention of listing the director with the film's title. But our concentration has been on the larger, cultural aspects of film, and now we have to ask who exactly the individuals are who do the work, have the ideas, and execute them. We need to confront some complicated philosophical issues, too. Can we apply nineteenth-century notions of original artistic genius to a form of popular culture? Where exactly do we locate the individual in mass art? If the popular and commercial must be examined in terms of negotiations between producers and audience, how do we account for singularity or originality?

Individuals and Creativity

The very concept of the individual has come under examination in recent years. Some theorists hold that the notion of human individuality is just that, a notion: individuality isn't a thing every person automatically has, hard-wired into the brain, but an idea that a culture creates and maintains about itself and its members. One of the dominant fictions of movies and the culture at large is the importance of the individual and "individual freedom." Films are always telling us stories about the process of discovering and "being true" to ourselves, to the individuality we each have. But recent thinking holds that this is just part of a story we have been telling ourselves over the past six centuries. What we think of as individuality is really a complicated set of social relation-

144

ships, in which "I" and "you," "we," "them," and "it" are continually shifting arrangements or positions that we all take up from moment to moment according to where we are, to whom we're speaking, or about whom we're speaking. The self, in other words, is neither innate nor permanent. On a large scale, the "self" is a cultural invention that began in the Renaissance when many social, economic, and philosophical forces converged to produce the notion of an individual. Most political ideologies of the West were then founded on this notion of the individual and his freedoms.

The individual really is a shifting thing. The "I" writing this book is not exactly the same "I" watching a Rodney Dangerfield movie, teaching a class, or being silly with a friend. In fact, all the "I's" I am are constructed over a long life of being in the world, a "you" to the person talking to me, "he" to someone talking about me. Individuality is a function of the moment and the place.

Individuality is not a simple given, but is formed by our upbringing, education, class, race, gender, ideology, culture. It grows from a shared belief that each person is a unique and special consciousness: a moral, ethical, imaginative agent, free and self-contained. This shared belief drives our daily lives and determines many of the stories we enjoy having told to us (stories that reproduce the belief that we are unique and have power). The real world often makes it difficult for us to believe in individual consciousness and agency especially when gender or race are involved, which may be why we like the stories. What is not true in reality can be made true in the representation of reality, in film, in novels, legends, folk tales; though, as we have seen, they often represent the very prejudices and stereotypes we may be trying to escape.

The Ideal Viewer

POINT OF VIEW

We can understand this complex argument about individuality if we think about what happens to us when we watch a movie. Our subjective state is changed and manipulated; we assume other points of view as they are shifted throughout the film. We look through the eyes of others and may become a kind of ideal viewer, seeing what the film chooses to show us and, along with everyone else, feeling what the film wants us to feel. In fact, the more a film transforms its audience into an ideal viewer, responding with the precise emotions the film demands, the more successful the film is likely to be. This idea may seem to run counter to the notion we examined earlier, that individuals negotiate the meaning of a work of popular culture, take the meanings they need, reject what they find unacceptable, reinterpret the work to suit their cultural positions. But, in fact, these events happen simultaneously, or even dialectically, when we watch a film or a television program. We are positioned as subjects of the narrative, given points of view to assume. We may also negotiate ourselves in and out of those points of view, accept and reject, agree and reconsider, dialectically moving with the film and against it, accepting and creating meanings as the film moves us along. Those filmmakers who work against the Hollywood style give us even more room for negotiation, by providing space for us to withdraw and look at the film at some distance.

Film and the Individual Talent

The theories that tell us that individuality and subjectivity are cultural formations rather than objective realities are powerful and persuasive precisely because they take culture and history into consideration. They counter individuality with larger forces in which the individual is one particle, always being altered. But even if individuality in the abstract is a cultural and ideological construction, we still believe in its existence and have proof of it whenever we or others act. After all, we do feel, think, and create. Therefore, we can consider various ideas about the individual: Individuality is a shared, cultural belief. Acts, including creative acts, performed by an individual are always formed by many forces, internal and external. A creative work—including the creative work of filmmaking—has in fact many authors, including the audience and the culture that surrounds us all. Individual contributions are finally determined by their manifestation in the work, rather than beforehand. The author is, in a sense, created backward from the work to the person.

So, having investigated the larger cultural forces that make up a film, we can now work backward to discover what some individuals do in making a film possible on the production side. This will be useful because, if we understand the individual contributions to a film, we can continue to understand that a film does not come out of nothing but is the result of craft, calculation, and—sometimes—art, all of which is the result of human activity. We can understand as well that creative imagination need not be thought of in the romantic sense, as the unique working of an inspired individual, creating alone and calling upon the forces of solitary emotions. We can understand imagination as a collective event, the result of a collaborative project.

Collaboration as Creativity

Collaboration is the core of cinematic creativity. From the most independent filmmaker to the largest studio production, people work together, divide the labor, contribute their particular expertise. There may be one single, guiding intelligence that integrates or orchestrates all the collaborations, or there may be many. There may even be an external, abstract force that is doing the orchestration on the economic level: the force of the box office, which is the representative of the audience and its willingness to pay. We must understand, once again, that the Hollywood imagination is an economic system, an economics of the imagination. And this system now works across the world, infiltrating the filmmaking of other countries where individual creativity used to be more easily identified.

Filmmaking began as the work of rugged individualists. We discussed how the Edison factory in the United States, the Lumière brothers and Georges Méliès in France worked to invent the apparatus of filmmaking and film exhibition and develop some of the basic narrative structures that survive to this day. Early in the twentieth century, other individuals battled (sometimes physically) with the goons that Edison sent out to protect his equipment patents and finally set up shop in Los Angeles. For a while, production in Hollywood and New York was the work of individual filmmakers working with small companies, developing their craft. D. W. Griffith was one of them. In collaboration with his cinematographer, Billy Bitzer, and working for five years for the Biograph Company, he made major contributions to the development of the continuity style. He then struck out on his own in the mid-1910s to create *Birth of a Nation* and *Intolerance*, two films that solidified the position of film as a social and cultural form.

But such independence was short-lived. Even Griffith understood the economic advantage of incorporation, of joining his work to that of a larger economic entity. In 1919, along with Charlie Chaplin and two other enormously popular actors, Douglas Fairbanks and Mary Pickford, he formed United Artists, a studio whose main purpose was to distribute the independent productions of various filmmakers. The arrangement never worked to Griffith's economic advantage, but it is indicative of what was happening to filmmaking at the time. The economics of production absorbed the imagination of individuals. The studio system evolved as a means of industrializing the imagination—making it economically viable—and turning individual activity into collaborative effort.

As in any manufacturing effort, speed and efficiency, established with the least cost, are essential in the mass production of film. We've spoken about how these efficiencies worked. The studios became self-contained entities, with facilities, technical staff, producers, actors, writers, composers, directors, all within the physical bounds of the studio, all the personnel under contract. Some of these workers, from electricians to writers, formed unions, and, as a result, clear divisions of labor were marked out. In short, every job had on-site personnel to carry it out, and every staff member knew his or her job. There is a temptation to reduce the outcome of this work—the films that the studios produced—to the anonymity of its production. Indeed, the fifties criticism of popular culture did just that, implying that work of the imagination produced in a factory, for mass consumption and economic gain, could not attain the complexity and status of art. But an opposing argument would be more valid, that a new kind of art, created out of collaboration, emerged from the studio system. We can also argue that there are indeed important individuals involved in cinema's creative process, individuals who develop and use their talents in a collaborative effort in which individual skill becomes absorbed in group effort and assumes anonymity in the resulting films.

MOVIEMAKERS

Craftspeople

On the level of the physical apparatus itself, a number of people plied their skills and talent in the studios (and still do, though more often as independent suppliers): electricians, camera operators, sound recorders, set designers, painters, greens people, film lab technicians, assistant editors. These people rig the lights, set up the camera (as well as turn it on and off and keep it focused on the scene being shot), dress and paint the sets, put up greenery, create the special effects that synthesize actors, backdrops, painted scenery, and models into a single image, develop the film, mix the sound, assist in the complex process of editing the shots, and then match the edits on the master negative that will be used to strike exhibition prints.

Production Designer

Others work on a more conceptual level, closer to our conventional notions of artists, developing the words, the design, and the images that make the film. The production designer (usually called "art director" during the studio period), for example, conceives and elaborates the settings, rooms, and exteriors that together give a film its physical texture, its spatial and temporal orientation, and that mark its setting in the past or present as recognizable, even authentic. If the film takes place in a particular historical era, the work of the production designer takes on a special importance. During the studio period, each company had a head production designer—Cedric Gibbons at MGM, Lyle Wheeler at Twentieth-Century Fox, Hans Dreier (who began his career in the late 1910s at Germany's UFA studios) at Paramount—who had great responsibility for creating the general style of a particular studio.

In this deceptively simple image from Coppolla's The Godfather, Part II *(1974), we can see the art of the production designer and cinematographer (Dean Tavoularis and Gordon Willis for this film). Every item— telephone, books, chair—is precisely placed to evoke a well-to-do interior of the late fifties/early sixties. Lighting emanates from the lamp and dominates the scene, which is composed to emphasize the figure on the right looking into the empty spaces of the room.*

In the post–studio period, production designers have developed individual styles and can sometimes be linked with the work of certain directors. There is the careful re-creation of forties and fifties spaces and objects that Dean Tavoularis develops in Arthur Penn's *Bonnie and Clyde* (1967) and Francis Ford Coppola's *Godfather* films. Cars and dusty midwestern towns in the former film, tables, chairs, carpets, wall hangings in the latter films are chosen and placed to evoke and represent the domestic space of a certain class and time. In *Godfather I,* a newsstand on the street is arrayed with period papers and magazines, which are laid out as they might have been in the fifties. A room in *Godfather II* is laid out to reflect the decorative style of the fifties and sixties. In *Apocalypse Now* (1979), Tavoularis creates for Coppola the nightmare jungle of Vietnam (in the Philippines).

Recall the dark, fantastic urban future designed by the late Anton Furst for *Batman.* Those sets—consisting mostly of hand-painted mattes that were processed into the shots of the film to give them a physical presence—help create the atmosphere of despair and unspoken terror that supplies much of the subtext for director Tim Burton's film. In Europe, the production designer Alexandre Trauner began work in the twenties and helped develop the "look" of French cinema, especially the thirties school of "poetic realism" that climaxed with Marcel Carné's *Children of Paradise* (1945). He went on to work with Orson Welles on his film of *Othello* (1952) and with the German émigré Billy Wilder. Like the work of any good production designer, his design can be detailed and crafted to catch the viewer's attention, or made invisible—depending upon how the film's director crafts his mise-en-scène, which is based partly on the production design.

Production designers combine the talents of graphic artist, interior decorator, architect, art historian, or futurist to create ideas that—once executed in wood, paint, and spatial organization by the set designer, matte painter, carpenter, greens person, and special effects people—fashion a world that the camera can photograph, or the computer generate, and the editor can assemble into a coherent representation of time and place. The production designer readies the space for the actors to inhabit and for the cinematographer, or director of photography, to film.

Cinematographer

The cinematographer is among the most important creative people in the production of a film. He (in a notoriously male-centric industry, there have been few women cinematographers, though recently their numbers are growing) handles the lighting, chooses the appropriate lenses and film stock, decides on all the elements that determine the size of the image, its spatial qualities, density, color values or greyscale that will result in an image appearing, first on the film stock, and finally on the screen when the light of the projector is focused through it.

At his best, the cinematographer is a close collaborator with, and an advisor and consultant to, the film's director. In the days of the studios, some major stars had their own cinematographers assigned to them in film after film. William H. Daniels, for example, worked consistently with Greta Garbo, MGM's glamorous and mysterious star of the thirties, because Garbo and the studio felt he could light her to best advantage. This was not an act of mere vanity but of the studio's and the audience's desire to have a consistent image of its star, which the cinematographer could best provide.

In some instances, a cinematographer exercises extraordinary creative license, expanding upon what the producer or director wants to see on film. This was the case in Gregg Toland's collaboration with Orson Welles on *Citizen Kane*. Toland signed on to the project because he felt that working with a new, young, imaginative director would give him the opportunity to experiment, which it did. He ground and coated new lenses, experimented with lighting, and figured out ways to create the deep field compositions and expressionist style that both he and Welles envisioned. The way *Citizen Kane* looks, its dynamic articulation of space, light, and composition, had more influence on filmmaking than anything since *Birth of a Nation*. That articulation is the result of the Welles and Toland collaboration, which Welles credited. *Citizen Kane* is perhaps the only American studio film in which both cinematographer's and director's names appear together at the end of the film. Many would argue that on many films the cinematographer should get similar or even greater credit as the originator and developer of a film's visual style.

In many instances, directors and cinematographers remain together as a team. This is more usual in Europe and in the post–studio period in American filmmaking, where it is less likely that individuals will be assigned to a film and more likely that writer, director, and producer will choose whom they want to work with. Among the most famous director-cinematographer teams in film history was that of Swedish director Ingmar Bergman and cinematographer Sven Nykvist. When Bergman quit his filmmaking career—after he had become the most widely known European director of the sixties and seventies—Nykvist began working in the United States. He lends his rich style, in which he sculpts fine details of interiors in carefully modulated light and shadow, to an unlikely film, the popular *Sleepless in Seattle*.

Alfred Hitchcock worked with one cinematographer, Robert Burks, on twelve films. Hitchcock, who predetermined the structure of every shot before filming ever began, needed a cinematographer he could depend upon to accurately interpret his instructions. Carlo Di Palma, who photographed two of the Italian director Michelangelo Antonioni's extraordinary color films, *Red Desert* (1964) and *Blow-Up* (1966), has worked with Woody Allen on most of his films since the late eighties.

Editor

CONTINUITY   The cinematographer is the individual with great responsibility for the overall character of a film's visual style, working closely with the production designer and director. He is present throughout preproduction and shooting. After shooting, the editor assembles the pieces of footage into a coherent whole. Editing has been one of the few major roles in filmmaking open to women, a fact that is all the more significant be-

cause the editor is the person who gives a film its final shape, makes it conform to the will of the producer (during the studio period) or the director
(who, in the post–studio period, oversees the editing process). A cynical view
might hold that, because the editor takes orders, producers felt quite comfortable having a woman in a passive role. But the primary talents of an editor are
far more important than passivity and patience. A film editor needs great dex-
terity, a sharp eye for detail and rhythm, a prodigious visual memory. In the
studio days, the editor was the one who managed to structure pieces of exposed film into the patterns of the continuity style. Under the producer's eye,
she made the film the audience would see—and often remade it if previews
went badly. Few directors shot with the precision and economy that could dictate and control the final shape of their material. Many directors shot and still
shoot a great deal of footage, thereby giving the editor much to work with,
much to put into comprehensible shape, and much to throw away.

Many films are still saved in the editing process. Bad acting can be cov-
ered up by cutting away from a talentless actor to something or someone else
in the scene, with newly recorded lines dubbed in to create a better performance. Many films are invented during editing. The violent stunts of action
films are constructed by editing. Sequences in which people knock each other
down, fall off buildings, bash their cars into each other are constructed out of
shots—themselves manufactured out of various image elements—carefully
cut together to create the illusion of fists meeting faces and bodies falling
through glass doors. But this needs to be put in the larger perspective of the
continuity style, in which all motion, progression, movement, and unity are illusions built out of the ways small fragments of exposed film are cut together—and that is the editor's task.

In American cinema especially, editors have had major responsibilities for
executing the cutting style of the studio, and some important editorial names
are attached to their respective companies: Viola Lawrence at Columbia,
George Amy at Warner Brothers. Dorothy Spencer worked at a number of studios, on films as different as *Stagecoach* (1939), *The Snake Pit* (1948), *Cleopatra*
(1963), and *Earthquake* (1974). Like cinematographers, some editors have
worked consistently with particular directors, George Tomasini with Hitchcock, Dede Allen with Arthur Penn, Thelma Schoonmaker with Martin
Scorsese, Michael Kahn with Steven Spielberg. Some of these are creative collaborations. In others, the editor helps the director keep his film coherent, and
in all cases they provide the structure the audience sees.

Composer

MUSIC   The composer of a film's musical sound track is only peripherally
involved with the actual production of the film. He may not necessarily spend a great deal of time on the set. He is not directly
connected with the construction of the film's visual elements, as are the production designer and cinematographer. Like the editor, he is more involved

with fragments than wholes. The composer may confer with a film's producer and director, read the script, and make some melodies in advance. But his main work occurs during the editing process, when producer, director, and editor get a sense of the film's shape and begin organizing its final narrative and emotional direction.

Only the title score and music for the final credits are written as complete, if miniature, musical compositions. The rest of the music is written as "music cues," brief snatches of melody, sometimes only seconds long, that are composed to fit sequences or transitions between sequences, to distract from editing effects (or even bad acting the editing can't hide), and in general used to create emotional responses from the audience, sometimes greater than the narrative, the mise-en-scène, or the acting can.

The history of music in film marks some of the major trends in moviemaking and the cultural forces that influence it. During the studio period, composers, like all creative people and craftspersons, were under contract to individual studios. They, like writers, cinematographers, editors, production designers, and directors, were paid labor, who worked under orders from the producer of the film, who, in turn, worked under the studio bosses. Many composers, like Erich Wolfgang Korngold, Max Steiner, and Miklos Rozsa, had distinguished composing and conducting careers in Europe before moving to Hollywood and becoming contract composers with various studios. Along with others, like Franz Waxman and Dimitri Tiomkin, they made their fame and fortune writing for movies. Some worked closely with a single director. Bernard Herrmann, who started his broadcast and theatrical work in New York with Orson Welles's Mercury Players, came to Hollywood with Welles and composed the score for *Citizen Kane*. He continued working with various directors and in 1956 began an eight-year collaboration with Alfred Hitchcock. His music for Hitchcock is so intensely involved with the narrative images Hitchcock creates that you can listen to a recording of Bernard Herrmann's music and experience the emotions of the film it comes from.

Herrmann's work with Hitchcock coincided with the end of the first era of the symphonic score and a period of change in the constitution of the studios. As movie attendance fell during the late forties and throughout the following decades, and as contracts with staff and players ran out, the studios changed from complete in-house manufacturers of narratives, with a ready, salaried staff always on hand, to less centralized production facilities and distributors. These days, the studios may assist in initiating a project, provide financing, and distribute the completed product to theaters, but leave the details and the staffing to the individual production group formed for the particular film. By the 1960s, an in-house composer and a studio orchestra were among those dependable, off-the-shelf services studios could no longer afford. The same period saw a rise in popular music—rock and roll especially—and a change in film marketing procedures.

Movie audiences had always been segmented to some degree. Studios produced "women's pictures," more accurately known as domestic melodramas, to appeal to the female audience, and action films and Westerns to appeal to women or men. But, at least until 1946, the studios had an audience they could depend upon—an audience eager for their products. By the sixties, the studios had to seek out their audience and discovered that the most attractive group was those between their late teens and mid-thirties. Since this group proved to be a lucrative market, and because pop and rock music were very popular among this group, the symphonic score lost favor. Many films since the sixties use existing pop or rock music as background. Robert Altman's great Western, *McCabe and Mrs. Miller,* uses the music of Leonard Cohen in ways that make it so integral to the images that it might as well have been written for the film. Martin Scorsese creates such complex scores out of old rock and roll (especially for *Mean Streets,* and *Goodfellas*) that some have referred to the films as visual jukeboxes. At the same time, Scorsese is sensitive to the power of the symphonic score. He commissioned Bernard Herrmann to create the music for *Taxi Driver.* It turned out to be that composer's last, and, except for the music he wrote for Welles and Hitchcock, his greatest score.

By the sixties, more and more American films began using some version of rock or pop music and the large studio symphony orchestra all but disappeared, as did the great names of film music composition. In Europe during the same period, some directors still collaborated with individual composers and carried on a sense of textual coherence between image, narrative, and score. Frederico Fellini and Nino Rota, Michelangelo Antonioni and Giovanni Fusco, Sergio Leone and Ennio Morricone are some examples from Italy. Ennio Morricone, who wrote the scores for Sergio Leone's great spaghetti westerns, such as *The Good, the Bad, and the Ugly* (1966), also composes for American film.

One film score convention remained. Almost from the introduction of sound, music associated with a film was turned into a commodity that could be marketed separately from the film. A song or score might become popular and be sold as a record, or a film's producer might specifically commission a song for a film with plans to sell it as a single after the film's release. Fifties songs like "The Tender Trap" and "Three Coins in the Fountain" are examples of this practice, which is now extended to various tie-ins like MTV videos. The video will plug the song and show sequences from the film. If a film score is made up of a collection of songs, the producers will certainly have them packaged as a CD for separate sale and extra income and advertise the music on the trailers—the coming attractions—for the film.

In America, the cycle shifted back to the symphonic score in the late seventies, partly because of nostalgia, partly because young filmmakers, who had been studying film history, were intrigued by the use of music during the studio period, and mainly because of the successful collaboration of Steven Spielberg and John Williams in *Jaws, Close Encounters of the Third Kind* (1977), *E.T.* (1981), and *Raiders of the Lost Ark.* Today, whether an elaborate score is prepared specifically for a film or a series of rock tunes is selected for the sound track, music remains an important part of a film's narrative flow, part of its emotional dynamic, and, in clever hands, an integral part of the film's structure. A film composer can become known for work in many fields, like Henry Mancini, and can also do wildly different kinds of scoring in different media. Danny Elfman wrote the music for the two *Batman* films and the theme for television's *The Simpsons.* John Williams continues to compose for Spielberg and spent time as conductor of the Boston Pops. The end of the studio period seems to have released the composer into activity in many fields.

The role of the composer is oddly secure, because he can remain somewhat aloof from the production. The composer knows his role, knows that he must write to order. Little is left to speculation or temperament. (There is a funny, perhaps apocryphal, story of a conference between the famous Russian émigré composer Igor Stravinsky and the studio executive Samuel Goldwyn about the composer's working for films. There was some mutual accord until the studio executive asked Stravinsky how long it would take him to deliver a score. "A year," he responded. The meeting and the collaboration were over.) For the composer, like the cinematographer, "individual genius" is subordinated to collaborative imagination. Art is put into the service of the manufactured narrative.

Screenwriter

It has not been so clear or easy for the screenwriter. He (and sometimes she) is the one figure in the talent pool of filmmaking wracked with doubts, ambiguities, uncertainties, self-hatred, and mistrust. There is no great mystery as to why the screenwriter has been such a tormented figure or why we, as viewers, can have so little confidence about how much the person we see listed in the credits as writer was actually responsible for the film. American and European culture maintain the nineteenth-century image of the writer working in splendid isolation, with complete control over his or her work. Even when subsidiary myths are bracketed off—the Hemingway myth of the brawling, hard-drinking, adventurous writer—we still think of the process of writing itself as being carried out in a sacred isolation, where the creator is the controller of his or her production. Most writers believe this story, too, even though, like all cultural myths, it is only somewhat true. While much writing is, indeed, done alone, not all of it is (think of coauthorship, even in fiction). And there are few writers who are free of editorial intervention—few whose work gets into the bookstores exactly as was written, almost as few as there are film directors who see their own version of a film on the screen. There is, finally, nothing very romantic about writing: only people attempting to put good words on paper. These words are then sent out to an agent, who looks for a publisher, who will suggest revisions. If the manuscript is accepted, it will go to an editor, who will suggest more revisions still. If writers and their culture needed to maintain their myths of isolated inviolability, film executives knew better.

Writers had always worked in film, but in the late twenties and early thirties, when actors began speaking dialogue, the studios needed writers to do more and write the actual dialogue the actors would speak. Studios had few places to turn. Hollywood, at that moment, was not a great literary Mecca and the studios began importing often well-known writers from New York—novelists, playwrights, essayists—at high salaries. When these writers arrived in L.A., the studio bosses put them in offices and told them to make words from nine to five. The writers found themselves used as common labor. The studio executives loved it, because, semiliterate as some of them were, they felt delighted to have intellectuals under their control. Besides, they were offering a lot of money and expected their control to be heeded. To add insult to injury, the executives rarely allowed one writer to produce all the words for a given film. The studio bosses enforced the collaborative nature of film on all levels, whether the writers were willing or not. Studio executives put scripts through many hands, some of them specializing in very particular kinds of writing: comedy dialogue, romantic interludes, dramatic exchanges, mid-script plot and character complications ("back stories" in current Hollywood parlance). Some scriptwriters, then and now, are known to be good "script doctors." They don't originate material, they fix the words others have written that a producer or director thinks aren't working or won't transfer well when filmed. The names of any of these writers may or may not appear in the credits. In fact, the writing credits are the least dependable of all, because so many hands may go into the creating of a shootable script.

In the studio days, executives took all of this for granted, but the writers did not. An unpleasant culture was created for them, and many felt they were working in bad faith. But two good things emerged from this. One was the Screen Writers Guild, a powerful and, in its early days, a left-of-center union that the writers formed in the thirties to help protect their interests, as best they could be protected. In many instances, the job of the SWG was and is to arbitrate what writer gets credit on a film. During the thirties, it provided a base where writers could discuss the political and intellectual matters they couldn't deal with in their films.

The other good thing to emerge was the great studio films created between the early thirties and the mid-fifties, films that prove the old cultural myths wrong, that it is possible to get good writing and strong narrative structure through a group effort. While few films have shining dialogue, many of them have good dialogue. Some of it captures the rhythms of the language of the day (even though, because of the Production Code and a general fear of offense, profanity was not heard in film until the sixties). Much of it delineates character and propels story and expresses emotions. Like the continuity style of which it is an essential part, dialogue becomes integrated within the seamless web of story and action. If a film coheres, the viewer cannot recognize the fragments of writing that come from various hands. Like the editing, like the music, it becomes unified and coherent, part of the story's presence.

There is somewhat less resentment and self-hatred among screenwriters these days. One reason is that there is little innocence left about the process. Most writers who go into the business know that it will be a collaborative event and that egos and romantic myths about independence and control won't work. Perhaps more important, a screenwriter stands to make a great deal of money. A quarter-million dollars is not unheard of for a first effort, millions for an established screenwriter, someone like Robert Towne (the writer of *Chinatown*) or Joe Eszterhas, who was paid three million dollars for his script for *Basic Instinct.*

The cynical view would be that sanctimony disappears in the face of profit; a kinder view is that more and more writers, who consciously choose what kind of work they want to do, understand what movie writing is all about. This was occasionally true even during the studio years. Some major authors, like F. Scott Fitzgerald, couldn't quite manage it. The few who could, did it on a grand scale. William Faulkner contracted with Warner Brothers and worked with director Howard Hawks on such fine films as *Air Force* (1943), for which he did not receive screen credit, and *The Big Sleep* (1946), for which he did. He asked Jack Warner, head of the studio, if he couldn't receive a special dispensation and work at home. Warner agreed, and Faulkner promptly left Hollywood for his home in Oxford, Mississippi. He wrote scripts for "them"; he wrote novels for himself and his public, and everyone, including himself, profited in many ways from both. This was a rare freedom, but it was not based on Faulkner's fame alone. Rather, it was a demonstration of a rare amount of good faith, understanding, and self-possession on everyone's part.

Moviemaking, like any large business enterprise, is not usually based on self-possession and understanding. Power is the motivating force, and power depends upon generating insecurity, resentment, and fear in order to work. That's why writers often felt miserable under the studio system. Some found that they could not write under the circumstances. The other individuals in the collaborative mix we've been discussing essentially did their jobs, with few fantasies about individual creativity. They *were* creative, but in ways that don't usually fit in with our preconceptions. Which means that we've not quite yet answered the question, "Who makes movies?" We haven't answered it if we are still looking for filmmaking to fit the tradition of the creative individual. Even if we can comprehend the idea of collective creativity, that ideological relay switch almost always trips on, forcing us to say that anything made by a group can't be very creative. So we keep looking for answers even though the answers that come along never quite satisfy our longing for the romantic myths of creativity.

Actors

Early in the history of film, both filmmakers and audiences found a way to evade the entire issue of the creative individual behind the camera by focusing on the visible figures in front of them, the movie actors. Actors are, after all, the most recognizable, most promotable, sometimes the most memorable elements of a film. They create an illusion of embodiment, of giving story flesh and bone. They are turned into simulacra of our desire—representations of what we think we want to be and know we want to see. They are our collective imaginary, the cultural repository of images of beauty, sexuality, romance, strength, and power. Filmmakers, who at first (long ago, at the turn of the century) tried to keep their players anonymous so they wouldn't have to pay them a lot of money, soon had to yield to public curiosity—public *desire*—and actively promote the people who turned out to be their most valuable commodity.

A strong argument can be made that film as we know it, with all its attendant apparatus of publicity, fandom, expectation, identification, and desire, was born when public recognition and admiration of stars forced filmmakers to acknowledge that they could extend their profits by extending the stories they told about the people in front of the camera beyond the films themselves. The film narrative became only one in a larger constellation of stories. The star system became a great attraction and convenience for everyone. Audiences could live out fantasy and desire through their favorite players both on and off the screen. Sexual promise, so much at the core of what movies are about, could be expanded from film narrative to publicity narrative, and journalism became one more extension of the studio system. They could all feed one another. A studio's filmmaking and publicity machines meshed gears with newspapers, magazines, radio, and television to author a supernarrative of sex, wealth, and fantastic irresponsibility. This narrative continues today through radio and television movie reviews, through *Entertainment Tonight, People Magazine, Access Hollywood,* the tabloids, and the tourists' drive through Bel Air.

But what is the reality of the actor's role as creative individual? Film acting, and the very bodies who do the acting, should be understood as part of a film's mise-en-scène. A player is one element of the film's narrative space. How an actor looks, gestures, talks, moves, gazes can be understood in relation to everything else that's going on in the shot or from one shot to another, and becomes an important element of the film's total design. If the actor is well known and his or her gestures are part of a career-long development from film to film, an interplay of recollection is added to this mix. Coherence and continuity are the keys. A good actor can maintain, within one film and across a number of films, an intensity of style. She can create a performance that grows out of the particular film and is marked by a style that can be recognized from one film to another. Gesture, response, and delivery of dialogue propel the narrative of any one film and propel the actor through a number of films.

This may seem obvious, until one considers exactly what film acting is, which is precisely the reverse of stage acting or any other idea we hold about a performance. Acting in film doesn't involve a coherent, ongoing, developing representation of narrative-driven emotion, at least not on the actor's part. A performance is created *by* the film, by the mise-en-scène and editing. The actor actually "performs" in short spurts and in multiple takes of relatively short pieces of business, usually shot out of sequence. The actual process of film act-ing is part of the continuity style, composed out of fragments in the editing room. In reality, the producer, the director, and the editor create the perfor-mance, if we define performance as a process in which a character and situa-tion are developed. They emphasize what they want and hide what they don't, sometimes by no more complicated means than cutting away to something or someone else when a particular character is talking, or mixing parts of various takes of a scene, or cutting a reaction shot into one scene that might have been filmed for another. The filmmaker can provide accents to a scene by lighting, camera angle, and movement when the scene is being filmed and by music and editing rhythm when the film is being assembled. The actor must be able to call upon his or her tricks or talents for emotional delivery on demand and without a real sense of connection to what was going on before or may go on after, when the final cut is assembled. Like the writer and composer, the actor creates on demand and in disconnected bits—a look, a gesture, a piece of dialogue. The continuity style creates the illusion of physical and emotional presence and continuity. The actor's body is given, if not flesh, the immediacy of appearance and it expresses the illusion of emotions deeply felt.

I noted that very good film actors and actresses have the talent to create a role within a film and a style that is carried from one film to another. These are the ones whose presence and style may either transcend the subservience to directorial and editorial manipulation or allow it to be used to everyone's best advantage. We saw an example of this in Jimmy Stewart. Some screen players create personae, versions of themselves that are made up of attitudes, ges-tures, facial expressions so coherent and maintainable that they become in-stantly recognizable and sometimes more interesting than the particular film they are in. When this is combined with the elaboration of a cultural myth about the actor's persona, a story built up in the collective popular conscious-ness from the actor's roles and publicity, a figure is created that transcends his or her individual films. John Wayne is more than the character in this or that film; he is, even dead, an evolving idea of a hero. Marilyn Monroe transcends *The Seven Year Itch* (1955) or *Some Like it Hot* (1959, both directed by Billy Wilder), becoming part of the culture's collective sexual insecurity and its mythologies of the sexually active, self-destructive woman. Others take up somewhat less cultural space, but demand our attention in and out of their films nonetheless: Humphrey Bogart, Henry Fonda, Katharine Hepburn, and Robert De Niro are actors with a reputation for intensity, grace, a peculiarity of gesture and gaze that draws us to them from film to film. So also the great comedians, old and recent: Chaplin, Keaton, the Marx Brothers, Laurel and Hardy, Jerry Lewis, Alan Arkin, Rodney Dangerfield, John Candy.

Some actors can both transcend and inhabit a role. Marlon Brando has a recognizable class of attributes, subtle ways in which he moves a hand, tilts his head, inflects his despair. In *A Streetcar Named Desire* (Elia Kazan, 1951), *On the Waterfront* (Elia Kazan, 1954), *The Wild One, Godfather I,* and *Last Tango in Paris* (Bernardo Bertolucci, 1973), the camera-riveting presence of Brando, the way he is able to focus the viewer's gaze on the character he is making and the processes he's using to make the character foreground his presence as the central point of the film's mise-en-scène. The cliché about "taking up a lot of space" is quite appropriate to Brando. He is, with the help of a good director, able to put his resources in the service of the narrative. He can develop a role and allow the viewer to observe how he develops it. He anchors the narrative and then moves with it. But, while doing all of this, he focuses every action within the film and every perception of the viewer on his presence.

Some current film actors—Kevin Spacey, Bridget Fonda, Samuel L. Jackson, William H. Macy, Glenn Close, Parker Posey, for example—can change their styles, shifting, chameleonlike, into different personae in different films. And there has always been a huge store of character and bit players, anonymous people with instantly recognizable faces who populate television and film and act as anchors. They are like human props, filling out the scene, transmitting important narrative information, securing our gaze. They give us comfort.

A talented player, who can sustain an illusion of performance and build a coherent character across the film's narrative, can be thought of as a creative figure *in* a film rather than a creator *of* the film. The actor whose persona transcends a film can be considered the cocreator of another narrative: her or his mythic life, articulated in films, by the studio's public relations people, newspapers, and television. The strong supporting or bit player works for hire, does her job, helps fill the screen and the narrative, and moves quietly on to the next role. All of this demands an act of recognition by another creative figure, the viewer who enjoys the actor's work in a film and who observes and responds to celebrity, taking part in a story of desire, fulfillment, eventual loss, and sometimes pathetic death of the figure who is partly real human being and mostly illusory construct, the imaginary figure of the movie star.

Collaboration Reconsidered

Let's take stock. There is the group of creative people involved in various stages of film production, from writers to composer, from production designer to cinematographer. There is the creative presence of the actor in front of the camera. It is clear that filmmaking is collaborative work in which each individual contributes a part of the imaginative component that goes to construct the whole. Collaborative, however, is not quite the same as communal. Decisions about how the imaginative pieces are going to fit are rarely made by committee and never through full consensus among the participants. Someone is always in charge during a film's production, pulling things together, giving orders, keeping the hierarchy working—exercising power. We are left with two figures who might still be counted as the major creative forces of a film, and who fit the roles of head of the hierarchy: the producer and the director. Between these two figures, the power, creativity, and the myths of creativity are held in contention.

Producer

Orson Welles once said that no one can figure out exactly what a producer does. At the Academy Awards, the "Best Film" award is given in the name of the winning film's producer. In the credits of a film, the producer's title is prominent, though often sub-divided among many individuals: executive producer, coproducer, associate producer, line producer. What do these people actually do? Depending upon a number of factors, a producer is an initiator of projects, a fund raiser, a deal maker, an administrator. The producer is also a cajoler, a protector of egos, sometimes a tyrant. The producer gets the money and represents it. She or he oversees the writing, casting, design, and direction. More often than not, the producer is on the set during shooting and in the editing room when the film is being assembled. All this control bestows a right on the producer to leave an aesthetic mark on the film itself. Even if it's just suggesting a camera angle or an actor's reading, or cutting a few frames, or entire sequences, during editing, the producer likes to think that administrative creativity should also extend to the artistic.

The amount of power that a producer has cannot be underestimated and never is in Hollywood. From the time that Irving Thalberg was appointed executive producer at MGM by Louis B. Mayer in 1923 and reorganized the film production process, the producer has been the focal point of the American filmmaking system. Mayer and Thalberg were the ones who established the film studio as an artistic version of the factory assembly line. The studio head, through his executive in charge of production, oversaw production in Hollywood. In New York, the studio owners (sometimes relatives of the studio head) controlled the finances. At the studio, the executive producer worked with the studio head in choosing stories and stars and assigning producers to individual films. Staffing for each production was done according to which writers, stars, director, and cinematographer best suited the project, were available, or whose contracts and schedules indicated that they were in line for some work. The executive producer assigned a producer to each film, and that producer oversaw the day-to-day operations of the film, ran interference for the cast and crew to and from the executive producer and the studio head. His word was law. His creativity lay in the marshaling of forces, getting them to work according to plan and schedule, and conforming the film to the studio's style and standards.

The producer system created a perfect hierarchy for order and control. It put someone in charge whose main obligation was to get things done the way management wanted it done. The system mediated and moderated creativity, because the studio's representative was always there to make sure the film was made the studio's way. If this system repressed great flights of imagination, it permitted small ones and, by creating something of a uniform style for each studio, allowed room for variations. From volume came much mediocrity, but also a certain leeway for experimentation. When Orson Welles was invited to Hollywood by RKO in 1939, he was offered a multipicture deal with the right to final cut. The film he made would be the film RKO released. It was the kind of contract few directors have received before or since. It was one of the things that made Welles disliked in Hollywood from the start. But, as a recent biography of Welles has pointed out, the studio never gave up its control. They insisted on consultation at all times and held the right to cut the films for censorship purposes. Though Welles produced and directed *Citizen Kane*, RKO never gave up anything. The fact that RKO threw Welles out when management changed and promoted a new slogan for the studio, "Showmanship in place of genius at RKO," indicates that experimentation was never safe in the studio system; it only had its moments. Welles was fired after beginning work on a documentary, *It's All True*, that he was filming in Brazil. The editing of his second film for RKO, *The Magnificent Ambersons*, along with the reshooting of its final sequence, was returned to the studio.

In the post–studio period, the producer's role has changed only slightly. While some producers still work for studios and sometimes run them, many are freelancers. The studios themselves are no longer self-contained factories but part of large, often multinational corporations that have nothing to do with filmmaking, except that one of their holdings happens to be a film studio. Although a producer may no longer have one boss to whom she must answer, she still remains the mediator between the money and the production, which the producer often puts together (though not always: a film can now be organized by an agent, a director, or a star, who will then hire a producer). Unlike the old studio days, few things are "off the shelf" and few personnel are available down the hall. An array of service businesses has grown around the filmmaking process: equipment renters, sound recording studios, casting agencies, special effects people, caterers, and powerful talent agencies, who represent all those people—writers, cinematographers, composers, production designers, etc.—who used to be under contract. The business of putting together the pieces has become complex, and the producer has to work his way through the complexity and turn out a product that will turn a profit.

In the end as in the beginning, the producer's creativity is that of a manager. He has to know how to initiate, negotiate, mediate. He must believe that he possesses an excellent intuition of what constitutes popular success and impose that intuition upon the entire production, with the control of a stern administrator. He has to believe that he knows "what the public wants" and get a film made that delivers it along with what the studio or the distributor wants, in the only form his bosses understand: box office receipts, cable deals, and videotape rentals. If not, Sony, or Rupert Murdoch, or Time-Warner, or Viacom (owners of Columbia Pictures, Twentieth-Century Fox, Warner Bros, and Paramount, respectively) may not want him to produce any more films for them.

So we need to repeat our question again: Who is the creative individual responsible for a film? The answer may be a bit clearer now, even if we haven't located an individual who fits the traditional stereotype of creative genius. But the cultural desire to find the creative person dwelling inside of and existing as an aura around a work of imagination is very strong, so strong that, without it, a work is in danger of getting no respect. As long as film remains a product of "them," instead of her or him, it is unmanageable by the critical mind; a handle can't be put on it. For film and the study of film to be taken seriously, a single, identifiable author (who is not a manager, a figure held in little respect in intellectual and academic circles) has to be identified. And, indeed, such a person has been identified, or perhaps imagined, in a curious, roundabout fashion.

THE AUTEUR

European Origins

European cinema had always been more individualized than American cinema. Production never occurred on the scale of the Hollywood studios, even though major outfits existed, such as Shepperton and Ealing Studios in England, Gaumont and Pathé in France, and UFA (largely supported by American studios) in pre–World War II Germany. In Europe, small crews and independence were much the style. A film's director often wrote or cowrote the script and guided the editing process. The producer was just another functionary, rarely the overriding force he is in American production. Films made abroad—especially those made for an international audience—were often more intimate and sometimes less dependent on the master narratives and stereotypes beloved of American filmmakers. It is important not to fall into a romantic overvaluation of European cinema. Some of it was different, a few filmmakers took chances, a number of its films are more intense and complex than all but a few American films. The prewar work of Jean Renoir and Marcel Carné in France, Fritz Lang and F.W. Murnau in Germany (to name only a few), and the great explosion of cinema across Europe after World War II attest to a strong, independent filmic intelligence. But two issues must be remembered. Films made for *internal* consumption in other countries are as grounded in clichés, in narrative patterns beloved of the particular culture, and banal execution as anything made in the United States. And cinema in Europe or anywhere else in the world never achieved the variety, the sheer energy, or—and this is a key issue in our search for the creative individual in a mass art—the popularity of American cinema.

The Birth of the Auteur

The myth of the individual creator in film grew, indirectly, from political and economic issues between the United States and France after World War II, and it developed directly from the attempts of a group of post–World-War II French intellectuals to account for American film and react to what they did not like in the films of their own country. We spoke about this group, the French New Wave, when discussing the development of film noir. The political and economic issues were of the kind that develop from time to time in all

countries where the popularity of American film threatens the economic viability of the country's own cinema. France tried to solve the problem by creating a policy about how many American films could be shown in relation to the
number of French films. During the Nazi occupation of France, from 1940 to
1944, no American film was permitted on French screens. In the late forties
and early fifties, a flood of previously unseen movies came into the country,
and filmgoers were overwhelmed and delighted. French filmmakers hoped to
compete against the welcome deluge of American movies and meet their
quota of French films by making a "high-class" product. They wound up producing rather stodgy, sometimes stagy films, often based on popular fiction or
on big literary works, like Claude Autant-Lara's film of Stendahl's *The Red and
the Black* (1954). That young group of film lovers, who were quickly becoming
film critics and who, by the late fifties, became the most influential filmmakers
of their generation, railed against their country's movies and held American
films up as a model. François Truffaut, Jean-Luc Godard, Jacques Rivette, Eric
Rohmer, and Claude Chabrol wrote in disgust about the filmmakers of their
country. Jean-Luc Godard said of them, "Your camera movements are ugly
because your subjects are bad, your casts act badly because your dialogue is
worthless; in a word, you don't know how to create cinema because you no
longer even know what it is. . . ."

Who did know? According to these Frenchmen, some European filmmakers, such as Jean Renoir and the neorealist Roberto Rossellini, knew. But most
important, as far as they were concerned, a handful of American filmmakers
knew best. Orson Welles and Alfred Hitchcock; John Ford and Howard
Hawks and Otto Preminger; Nicholas Ray, Raoul Walsh, Samuel Fuller—
indeed names that many American filmgoers didn't know, then or now, were
placed in the pantheon of great directors. For Godard, Truffaut, and their colleagues, these American filmmakers developed and maintained that very
quality we've been searching for in this chapter: personal style. These French
film critics imagined something so important about American cinema that it
not only enabled them to launch their own careers in France and then interna-
tionally, but to launch film studies as a serious undertaking in the United
States. That's because what they figured out gave respectability to the movies.
They decided that, despite the anonymity and mass production of the studio
system; despite who may have produced, written, photographed, or starred in
a film; despite the studio and despite the amount of money a film may or may
not have made, continuity could be discovered across a group of films linked
by one name: the director's.

The Auteur Theory

The principles of stylistic continuity were suggested by the French critics and
then codified in the mid-sixties by the American film critic, Andrew Sarris,
who imported them to the United States under the name of the auteur theory
("auteur" is the French word for "author"). The principles of the auteur theory

are based on the given that the director is the controlling force in the structure of a film. For Sarris, that control includes three basic attributes. The first is a technical competence that marks a director's ability to understand and practice the techniques of filmmaking in an expressive way. The second is a coherent personal style, a set of visual and narrative attributes that are recognizable in film after film. Examples would be John Ford's use of Monument Valley as the landscape for his imaginary West; Hitchcock's use of "cross tracking," his variation of shot/reverse shot in which a character, walking and looking at a threatening object is intercut with that object, drawing closer, ominously; his use of a high angle shot to show a character in a vulnerable state. The Swedish director Ingmar Bergman's intense close-ups of a character in a profound state of existential despair; the German Rainer Werner Fassbinder's framing of characters in doorways or behind doors; his colleague, Wim Wenders' images of men driving the road from city to city in Germany or America are all ways of perceiving the world, of making images that mark the directors as having special ways of seeing. It is important to understand that these stylistic attributes are formal expressions of ideas and perceptions. Monument Valley is for Ford a representation of the West and all the myths of the frontier that it represents from film to film. Hitchcock's camera strategies express ways of thinking about his characters and showing them in difficult, often threatening situations. They are expressive of his notions of a precarious and randomly violent universe. Style is not decoration, but the visible creation and expression of emotion and thought. This leads to the third, and for Sarris, the most important, element of the auteur: a consistent view of the world, a coherent set of attitudes and ideas. Sarris calls it "interior meaning" or vision, but it might also be called a world view, a philosophy, a kind of personal master narrative that is either unique to the specific director or a major and consistent variation of larger narrative conventions.

The French director, Jean Renoir, once said that a filmmaker needs to learn everything about technique, and then forget it. The ability to think cinematically, to know just the right place to put the camera, to create stillness or motion in the frame, to understand exactly where an edit should occur—these are the initial marks of the auteur. Technique that is learned and forgotten becomes style, because style is technique put to imaginative use. Anyone with good cinematic training can create a low-angle shot, in which the camera gazes up at a character looming above it. But only cinematic intelligence can turn this technique into a stylistic trait, and only true cinematic imagination can make it state a view of the world. Orson Welles loved to use the low-angle shot. In his hands, and through his eyes, it became a way of expanding the horizon and distorting the world around a character. He used it to comment ironically on the strength of a character or to predict the fall of a character who may still believe in his own power. It becomes a part of Welles's vision of a labyrinthine world in which the human figure dominates only momentarily. It is matched by Hitchcock's use of the high-angle shot, used to observe a character in a vulnerable moment or a point of moral crisis.

John Ford's figures in the Western landscape transcend compositional stylistics. They articulate a changing vision of the Western myths of settlement and domesticity, of Indians as a force of the land, and outlaws as impediments to lonely heroes in the inevitable movement of east to west. Ford's visual style fixed individuals in the landscape of a symbolic West; fixed women in the center of the domestic landscape, with men riding out to the peripheries, making them secure. The dynamic conservatism of Ford's cinematic inquiry into our memories of the West developed through a variety of films, written by different hands and made for different studios. He was persistent, silent about his work, recessive; a good movie worker who developed his style and his ongoing narrative without fanfare. His concept of the West kept developing and turned to critique. His later films, such as *The Searchers* and *The Man Who Shot Liberty Valance* (1962), began questioning the very notions of frontier heroism he had originally established.

We spoke earlier of Robert Altman, the director of the original film of *MASH* (1970); *McCabe and Mrs. Miller* (1971); *The Long Goodbye* (1973); *Nashville* (1975); *Popeye* (1980); *Come Back to the Five and Dime, Jimmy Dean, Jimmy Dean* (1982); *The Player* (1992); *Short Cuts* (1993); to name a few. We pointed out that he uses a zoom lens almost obsessively. It has become an expected part of his visual style. He uses it as a probe, a way to move to and beyond his characters, and a way to let us, as viewers, understand that watching a movie is, in part, a desire to come close to the image of a face, which is always slipping away from us. Altman's use of the zoom, especially when he combines it with a telephoto lens and wide-screen composition—a combination that flattens the image and makes space claustrophobic—keeps denying our desire. He plays with what we want to see, getting close, sliding away, and finally isolating our look at the characters and the connection of the characters to each other.

The zoom, along with other compositional and editing techniques, become part of Altman's style not merely because he uses them all the time (in which case they would just be repetitious), but because they are essential to the way he thinks about the world cinematically. They mediate, represent, and generate to the viewer his particular notions about power, the relationship of people to each other and their surroundings, the way stories get to or miss the truth; the way movies reveal and hide personal and global history. They all prove a central point about auteurism: once you see a few films by an auteur and learn her or his stylistic traits, view of people in the world, ideas about politics, history, social order, psychology, sexuality, and power, you should then be able to identify those elements as the work of that particular director in any other of his films. The British critic, Peter Wollen, puts it in structural terms, suggesting that, if we take the body of work by an auteur and strip away the narrative variations that are part of each individual film, we will discover a structure of basic thematic and stylistic traits, a kind of abstract pattern of ways of seeing and understanding the world cinematically. This pattern then becomes a template that we can see generating the form and content of each film the auteur makes. Jean Renoir put it more directly. He said that a director really makes just one film in the course of his career.

At its most fruitful, studying the work of an auteur, like studying the work of a novelist, poet, painter, or composer, becomes a way of discovering thematic and formal patterns, the way similar ideas cohere or oppose each other, how images are constructed in similar ways, how a coherent idea of history and human behavior develops across the artist's work. It is a comfortable kind of discovery, because it breeds familiarity on a personal level. We can get close to a filmmaker by recognizing his or her mark; we can find, as we do in literature, painting, or music, a creative personality. Because of this, the development of the auteur theory made film studies possible as an academic discipline. When we study the novel, we never think about anonymous creativity or a collaboration, unless the novel was coauthored. The author and the work are linked. We study Melville or Flaubert and never refer to the author of a novel as "they." Positing, even inventing, the director as auteur, put film in the same league as other humanities disciplines. We could now connect individuals with their work and analyze structures of style and meaning developed by a single imagination. Connecting a singular imagination to a group of films also allowed film scholars to recuperate film from its debased state as an anonymous commercial form to the imaginative expression of a serious artist. Finally, because the French discovered auteurs within Hollywood production, establishing style and vision within the studio system, American film was redeemed from anonymity.

The success of the auteur theory was enormous. Films were rediscovered, reputations were made, methods of analysis were developed, and a whole new discipline of study developed. Filmmakers themselves were now able to celebrate their medium. The originators of the theory—Godard, Truffaut, Chabrol, and the rest of the filmmakers of the French New Wave—began making films in homage to the Hollywood auteurs they had created. They alluded to American films in their own films—recalling a camera move from a Fritz Lang movie, a composition from a Douglas Sirk melodrama, a character gesture from Vincente Minnelli, a narrative line from Howard Hawks, a snatch of dialogue from Nicholas Ray's *Johnny Guitar* (1954). The New Wave created and honored a universe of cinema and implicitly understood what the poet T. S. Eliot said in his famous essay "Tradition and the Individual Talent." For Eliot, poems coexist and influence each other. So do films. A new filmmaker, like a new poet, responds to, is influenced by, and adds to the existing universe of films; new films absorb the old and then become part of the total film universe.

Many American filmmakers who came to artistic maturity after the auteur theory were influenced by its call to individual expression. Unlike their Hollywood predecessors, who learned their trade by coming up the ranks in the studios, these new directors went to film school and learned filmmaking by learning film history. Like the directors of the French New Wave, they celebrated their knowledge and their medium by referring to other films within their own work and, often, by taking filmmaking as one of the subjects of their films. Unlike their predecessors, who adapted the classical Hollywood style and its invisible access to story, many contemporary filmmakers are less likely to hide style and make us forget we're watching a film. They are more likely to foreground the presence of cinema and its methods and invite us to see the story and understand what allows us to see it.

Martin Scorsese   Martin Scorsese is a perfect example of this new kind of film-maker. A graduate of and part-time instructor at N.Y.U. film school during the mid-sixties, he has since become one of the best-known and most self-conscious filmmakers in the United States. He has worked across a number of genres and for many studios. He has developed a consistent and recognizable style. He has spun off a number of imitators, including Quentin Tarantino and many young filmmakers who make their first and seconds movies in homage to Scorsese's work (think of *Pulp Fiction, The Usual Suspects,* Bryan Singer, 1995, *Albino Alligator,* Kevin Spacey, 1996). Even more mature filmmakers, such as the British Mike Newell in *Donnie Brasco* (1997), have done Scorsese imitations. More than his equally famous contemporaries, Steven Spielberg, Woody Allen, and Francis Coppola, Scorsese has maintained an unflagging interest in exposing the grammar of film to his viewers. But, at the same time, he understands the nature of working in a popular medium. While he plays and tinkers with the classical style, often exposing its workings, he simultaneously observes the basic rules of narrative and visual construction that allow him to continue to receive financial backing for his films and acceptance from viewers, many of whom do not take kindly to experimentation. Like John Ford and Alfred Hitchcock (among two of his major influences, along with Jean-Luc Godard, François Truffaut, and the British filmmaker, Michael Powell), he is able to work many aspects of the system at once. He maintains commercial viability and explores and experiments. This was the talent that originally defined the auteur, the director who, while working within the studio system, could also quietly subvert it, using its conventions to develop a personal style.

Scorsese began his career by making films of small, but consistent quality, and by varying his output. In the late sixties, he made short films and a feature, *Who's That Knocking On My Door* (1969). In the seventies he made *Boxcar Bertha* (1972), *Mean Streets* (1973), *Alice Doesn't Live Here Anymore* (1974), *Taxi Driver* (1976), *New York, New York* (1977), *The Last Waltz* (1978). In the eighties, Scorsese made *Raging Bull* (1980), *King of Comedy* (1983), *After Hours* (1985), *The Color of Money* (1986), *The Last Temptation of Christ* (1988), and in the nineties he has made *Goodfellas* (1990), *Cape Fear* (1991), *The Age of Innocence* (1993), *Casino* (1995) and *Kundun* (1997). Of these films only *Cape Fear* brought in enormous amounts of money, and he made it exactly for that purpose as an offering to Universal Pictures, who had backed the controversial *The Last Temptation of Christ.* Otherwise, he has built both his style and reputation slowly and consciously, on films that viewers remember and which influence other filmmakers.

His films are made self-consciously and are, in important ways, about self-consciousness. While, on the level of story, Scorsese's films often concern small-time hoods or individuals on the edge or over the edge of psychosis, they are, on a more complex level, about style and reputation, about how it looks and feels to *be* in the world, looking at people and being looked at, seen, recognized, and hurt by the glance of others. His films are existential and very physical. Bodies as well as personalities are always at stake. Characters kill and get killed, beat up others or get beat up, thrive and do themselves in by thriving, or are nobodies trying to be somebodies by doing something to their own or someone else's body. That's what Jake La Motta does in *Raging Bull.* He tries to control his body, which is either damaging other people or getting fat, and he tries to control the world around him by violence and jealous rages—by aggressively imposing his body on others. The film is finally a meditation on the inability to get control, or on always being controlled, just as an actor is controlled by a director and a movie viewer is controlled by a movie. *Raging Bull* focuses on a boxer whose awareness of the outside world and his place in it is dim at best. He is moved by momentary, unthinking whims and responses, and winds up becoming a parody not of himself, but of movie representations of a boxer, which is, after all, what Robert De Niro's Jake *is* in *Raging Bull*—an actor, playing a boxer, in a film that grows out of a fairly substantial subgenre of boxing films. In the last shot of *Raging Bull,* Scorsese appears partially reflected in a mirror, telling an aging, fat Jake, who has gone from champion boxer to a nightclub owner to a performer in strip joints, that it's time to go on stage to do his rendition of the "I could have been a contender" scene from *On the Waterfront.* As the film ends, De Niro, as Jake La Motta, urged on by his director, playing a stage manager, does a parody of Marlon Brando playing a boxer from an older film. Jake La Motta is portrayed as a figure made up of self-contradictory parts, a reflection of a reflection. He is "real" and he is a fictional character in a film, there and not there, like film itself. Like Hitchcock, Scorsese impresses his own image on his film (he makes some kind of appearance in almost all of them). He focuses our attention on the artifice of celebrity, the illusory nature of film, and the fact that the film and our response to it are controlled by someone. The illusion totters, though Scorsese never permits it to collapse.

Illusion and celebrity fascinate Scorsese and his characters. Travis Bickle, in *Taxi Driver,* achieves fame without knowing it. Travis is crazy, an uncontrollable psychotic, who can see the world only as a brutal, devastating place. I've pointed out how *Taxi Driver'*s mise-en-scène is constructed through Travis's point of view: dark, off-centered, violent, and threatening. It is a world of sharp and dark fragments, created by a mind that is both paranoid and aggressive. Travis believes that he is responsible for cleaning up the very world he imagines, first by attempting to assassinate a presidential candidate and, when that fails, by saving a young hooker—who doesn't particularly want saving. In the process, he murders three people in a nightmarish episode of violence and destruction and is turned into a media hero. A number of films later, Travis is reincarnated in the person of Rupert Pupkin in Scorsese's *King of Comedy,* played by De Niro, an actor who has become part of Scorsese's directorial pattern and mise-en-scène. Pupkin is not a crazy paranoid like Travis. He is an ordinary lunatic who can't be embarrassed. His goal in life is to deliver a monologue on a late-night talk show (hosted by Jerry Lewis), which he manages to do by kidnapping the star and threatening his way on stage. He gets his wish, is put in jail, and is turned by the very media he hijacked into a star.

Blundering violently, lost in the normal world, compelled by madness, high spirits, or some obsessive-compulsive drive, Scorsese's characters, from Rupert Pupkin to Jesus Christ, try to fight the world's imposition on them and impose their own will and spirit back on the world. This question of imposition lies at the core of his characters and also at the core of the classical Hollywood style. That's where Scorsese's cinematic contention lies. Like his characters, he wants to impose his will on the structures of cinema, to undermine the impositions of the classical style by imposing his own style, his own way of seeing the world through cinema. Unlike his characters, he succeeds. He insists that we, as viewers, come to terms not only with the characters, but with the way they see and are seen. He asks as well that we question our own ways of seeing movies.

One way is to remind us, even on a subtle level, that his films grow out of other films. In *Cape Fear*—not, by itself, a very subtle film—he constructs sequences that are subtly based upon Alfred Hitchcock's *Strangers on a Train* (1951). You have to be really familiar with Hitchcock to understand what's going on. Both films are concerned with apparently upright characters who become involved with, and are stalked by, figures representing their darker, corrupt natures. In each film, there are sequences in which these characters, these mirror images of dark and light, confront each other. For example, in *Strangers on a Train*, the "hero," a tennis player named Guy, sees his evil other, Bruno, staring at him from the stands as Guy attempts to play a match. All the other spectators except for Bruno turn their heads as the ball flies from side to side. Bruno just stares straight at Guy. In the companion scene in *Cape Fear*, the lawyer, Sam, goes with his family to watch a Fourth of July parade. The crowd watches the procession while in their midst Max Cady, the ex-con out to get Sam, stares straight across the street—the tormentor freezing his victim in his gaze.

Once you see the connections—and there are others—*Cape Fear* becomes an interesting conversation with an earlier filmmaker, as is *Taxi Driver*, which is in many ways a remake of *Psycho* (with allusions to John Ford's *The Searchers*). Sometimes, Scorsese can be downright weird about his obsession with drawing attention to the cinematic roots of his imagery. Early in *The Last Temptation of Christ*, Jesus goes to a tent where Mary Magdalene is performing a sex act. He sits in the audience, and the camera observes him as if he were in a movie theater, looking at a screen. At the end of the film, on the cross, his fantasy of a normal life over, Jesus dies, and Scorsese cuts to a montage of abstract colors and shapes. In the midst of this montage are images of film sprocket holes. Even his meditation on the Christ story is, finally, a meditation on film and the way it represents legend and myth.

In Cape Fear, *the psychotic Max Cady stares out at Sam among the viewers of a Fourth of July parade.*

One director sees his work through another's lens. Martin Scorsese overlays Cape Fear *(1991) onto Hitchcock's* Strangers on a Train *(1951). The first image is from* Strangers on a Train, *where the psychotic Bruno stares out at the tennis player, Guy.*

He can be very playful, too, almost teasing us about our position as viewers of a carefully made-up tale. This is what he does at the end of *Raging Bull,* and it is the main ploy of *Goodfellas.* This latter film is a more energetic and imaginative version of his earlier *Mean Streets.* It is also an examination of just what we, as audience, think we're doing when we go to see yet another film about New York gangsters. Most especially, *Goodfellas* asks us to consider who tells us stories in films, to think about whom we listen to and tend to believe—an important question in the context of a film that asks us to find gangsters amusing. Henry Hill (played by Ray Liotta), narrator and main character of the film, seems to be our guide and our eyes. His voice talks to us throughout, and we see what he sees. Or do we? Let's look more closely at a sequence we discussed in an earlier chapter. Early in the film, Henry introduces us, in voice-over narration, to his gangster pals at a bar. The camera tracks along, pausing to look at each face, each character, who smiles and responds to Henry's off-screen presence. Everything here seems to guarantee that we are looking through Henry's eyes, sharing his point of view—until the very end of the tracking shot. The camera moves to the end of the bar, where Henry is heading to examine some stolen furs. A rack of furs appears, and so does Henry. The camera has been moving from right to left, diagonally into the frame. Henry appears on the left, opposite the direction of the camera.

How is this possible, if we were supposed to be seeing things through Henry's eyes? Well, of course we are not seeing through Henry's eyes. Henry is a character in the fiction, who is constructed to appear as if he were controlling the fiction. As we've seen, Scorsese is continually questioning the reality of people's control over things. It's one of his recurring themes and a major part of the formal construction of his style. Like Hitchcock before him, Scorsese plays with his characters and his audience and their imagined relationship to the characters. In *Taxi Driver*, for example, Scorsese limits point of view, forcing his viewers to see through the eyes of a madman a dark, violent city. Playing on the conventions of German Expressionism and film noir, drawing upon Hitchcock's ability to define character by how that character looks at the world and how the world looks back, *Taxi Driver* restricts our vision to that of a single, deranged sensibility. The prizefight scenes in *Raging Bull* attempt to create a mise-en-scène of noise, distortion, exaggeration of movement and sound that represents Scorsese's idea of what it must be like to be in a boxing ring. *What it might look like to someone* is a driving force in Scorsese's films. Limiting point of view, fooling us with who is seeing what, even playing with film speed, slowing down motion when he cuts to a character's point of view, are some of the ways Scorsese communicates shifting feelings, uncertainties, and changing responses. For Scorsese, perception is a liquid, undependable, and tricky business. He uses a variety of cinematic properties to communicate this and to make us aware that film can teach us about perception, or keep us fooled.

Goodfellas plays counterpoint between Henry, who seems to be in control of the narrative, and another perspective—Scorsese's perhaps, or a more abstract "voice" that speaks about film's ability to manipulate perception—with such intricacy that we are left somewhat unsettled. Henry's "story" is punctuated by freeze frames, moments in which the image is frozen while Henry meditates on what's just happened, or what will happen; by virtuoso camera movement, as in the amazing, almost four-minute-long tracking shot that accompanies Henry and Karen as they walk from the street, into the Copacabana nightclub, downstairs, through the kitchen, up to their table—all to the tune of The Crystals' "Then He Kissed Me."

At times, Henry's voice is taken over by Karen's, so that the woman's voice seems to run the narrative. Sometimes the editing takes over both and mimics the characters' point of view, as when, late in the film, frantic and high on cocaine, Karen and Henry believe they are being followed by a helicopter. The cutting is quick and nervous, time seems to speed up.

Finally, Scorsese himself takes over completely. It's his film, and one of the things he wishes to do with it is comment upon gangster films in general and our attraction and reaction to them in particular. He wants us to think about stories and their tellers. He makes Henry, the petty thug, the man who betrays his friends, a very attractive character, but he knows this is easy to do. Henry continually seems to take us into his confidence and remains aloof from the violence he and his friends commit. He is good looking, funny, and full of high spirits. But this shouldn't be enough to make us like a small-time criminal, and Scorsese needs to put more distance between us and his character. He does this by continually pointing to the tenuousness of Henry's authority, finally diminishing it entirely. Throughout the film, he plays with Henry's point of view and our sharing of it. Late in the film, after the mob has been busted, Henry goes to meet Jimmy (played by Robert De Niro in a relatively minor role in a Scorsese film). Henry is about to betray Jimmy and everybody else to the police. They meet in a diner and sit in front of the window, the camera placed so that it sees both men in profile against it.

CAMERA   Suddenly, perspective and space alter. Scorsese executes a simultaneous zoom and track, in opposing directions, so that the background—what's going on outside the diner window—seems to be moving in on the characters as they sit still. This is a technique that Alfred Hitchcock used to represent Scottie's reaction to heights in *Vertigo*. Steven Spielberg uses it to communicate Sheriff Brody's response to his sighting of the shark in *Jaws*, and it has since shown up in many other films. From a self-conscious device used by young filmmakers to pay homage to Hitchcock, it is rapidly becoming a cinematic cliché. In *Goodfellas* it serves as a kind of outside commentary, a caution that the world created in the film is about to slip away, that the character we have been attached to has lost his moorings. Or never had any. It is an artificial gesture of camera and lens used to emphasize that everything we see through the camera's eye is artificial, in the very best sense of "artfully made."

The coup in which the director undermines the point of view of his character and our dependence on it comes in the trial sequence near the end of the film. Here, Henry simply steps out of the scene, literally walks through the courtroom set and addresses the camera, something forbidden by the Hollywood continuity style. By doing so, he acknowledges that it's all an illusion, all going on in somebody's head—Henry's, the director's, ours. As the film comes to an end and we see Henry in the witness protection program, living in some anonymous suburb, complaining in voiceover that he can't find a decent tomato sauce, he once again looks at the camera and smiles, as if to say, "We know what all this is about, don't we?" And just in case we still don't quite know, Scorsese inserts a shot of Tommy, Henry's hilariously violent friend (played by Joe Pesci), pointing his machine gun and firing at the camera. This shot doesn't come from anywhere else in *Goodfellas*. It alludes to another film, made in 1903, Edwin S. Porter's *The Great Train Robbery*. There, a shot of one of the cowboys firing his gun at the camera was put either at the beginning or the end of the film, at the discretion of the exhibitor, to excite the audience.

So, with a wink at the audience and a nod to the history of film, Scorsese lets us know what we like about gangsters and violence. We like to watch. We like to be safe. We like to desire. And we like the delicate balance of control and fear. We also like a wiseguy. In *Goodfellas*, Scorsese attaches us to a desirable character who seems to own the world, only to find that he is owned by the film we're watching, as are we ourselves. The director toys with his character and with us, allowing us in on the joke, or allowing us to go off in a state of being deceived. It's only a movie, and the choice is ours.

Scorsese's desire to reflect the structures of film back at his audience, to attempt to peel away some of the illusion, is a common trait among modern auteurs. Unlike their predecessors, they want not merely to repeat the old strategies of the classical continuity style but to explore and expand them. American filmmakers like Stanley Kubrick, Robert Altman, Steven Spielberg, Paul Schrader, Spike Lee, and Woody Allen look to their European, Asian, and Latin American forbears and contemporaries, Jean Renoir, Robert Bresson, Luis Buñuel, Jean-Luc Godard, François Truffaut, Michelangelo Antonioni, Joseph Losey, Bernardo Bertolucci (in his Italian period), Federico Fellini, Rainer Werner Fassbinder, Akira Kurosawa, Yasojiru Ozu, Humberto Solàs, and Andrei Tarkovsky (to name just a few), who explored and experimented. These filmmakers ask audiences not to look *through* the medium of cinema, as if it were a pane of glass, but *at* it. They never sacrifice emotion and narrative, but attempt to ask us to work for emotion by understanding how cinema itself works. Contemporary American auteurs, in various ways, attempt to communicate this approach.

One of them, Stanley Kubrick, whose *Dr. Strangelove* (1962), *2001: A Space Odyssey* (1968), and *A Clockwork Orange* (1971) have become cinematic prophecies of social and political behavior, attempts to avoid completely the public life of a film director. Kubrick lives and works in London, never travels, and only deals with large numbers of people during the actual filming process. He is the one filmmaker who has tried to emulate the life of a novelist, painstakingly creating his projects—cool films, filled with strong images and tracking camera shots, weaving complex themes about the cultures of violence and politics and the absolute loss of human agency—which are completed every seven or eight years, in isolation and without any publicity.

Others do not strain against the system so thoroughly, and all of them know that their experimentation has to be delivered in a palatable package. But the truth is that even a little experimentation makes producers nervous. Briefly, in the seventies, when films like Coppola's two *Godfathers* and Spielberg's *Jaws* and *E.T.* made a lot of money, some directors were given a good deal of control. Some of them went overboard, like Michael Cimino, whose Vietnam film *The Deer Hunter* (1978) was enormously popular. United Artists then gave him a great deal of leeway and money for a somewhat left-of-center Western, *Heaven's Gate* (1980). The film went over budget, over schedule, and flopped. Its failure helped bring down the studio and pretty much put an end to widespread directorial power in Hollywood. These days, even in Europe, where most films must now fit an American blueprint in order to get made, the director is not likely to be a controlling figure, exercising the creative drive that many were able to do up through the seventies. And this should provoke us to a reassess the auteur theory.

Auteurism Today

The auteur theory was always a theory, a way of talking and thinking about films, much more than it was an accurate description of how films are actually made. There is no question that in Europe, at least until recently, many directors did exercise an enormous amount of control, and usually wrote the films they directed. This has rarely been true in the United States, at least not since the early twenties when the studio system placed the director as one among many craftspeople working on a film. Film can never really be reduced to the imagination of a single individual. It is too much a part of the cultural churn, of the thoughts, acts, artifacts, beliefs, and politics of the society in which it is made. It is too controlled by economics and audience response to be left to one person. But the convenience and implied intimacy of auteurism are so seductive. So are the analytical tools it offers, permitting us to understand the structure of film as the clearly coherent stylistic and thematic operation of a singular imagination. We may often need to sacrifice this clarity to the messier realities of film as part of a complex cultural mix. It is perfectly possible to mix various kinds of analysis—auteur, genre, and cultural.

The actual practice of filmmaking—despite the existence of a few directorial stars, like Spielberg and Coppola, and some who have more control over their work than others, like Scorsese and Kubrick—has pretty much reverted back to the control of the producer and the studio chief, or simply to the current versions of the classical style. The director has become a self-censor. There is little "personal" style and innovation is tightly controlled. But at the same time, there are opportunities for directors that never existed before. This may be the greatest legacy of auteurism: the recognition on the part of studio executives that directors, after all, can have some imaginative say in the creation of films, even if it is limited. Women and African Americans, though still badly underrepresented, are finding opportunities to make movies, to find a voice within the contemporary versions of the Hollywood style. The success of Spike Lee's passionate social melodramas, such as *Do the Right Thing* (1989), *Jungle Fever* (1991), and *Malcolm X* (1992) have led the way for directors of color like John Singleton (*Boyz N the Hood*, 1991; *Poetic Justice*, 1993; *Higher Learning*, 1995; *Rosewood*, 1997) and Julie Dash (*Daughters of the Dust*, 1991, the first American feature by an African American woman).

The rise of minorities and women to directorial prominence has not been a total success. Some strong women directors, with a marked style and point of view, have not faired so well, while others have slipped into rather straightforward commercial production. Susan Seidelman, whose *Desperately Seeking Susan* and *Making Mr. Right* proposed strong and engaging feminist points of view, tried more commercially palatable films and lost her edge. Penny Marshall has moved from television sit-com actress to the highly bankable director of engaging films like *Big* (1988), *Awakenings* (1990), and *A League of Their Own* (1992). Penelope Spheeris has carved out a comfortable place making clever comedies based upon television skits and programs, like *Wayne's World* (1992) and *The Beverly Hillbillies* (1993). Jane Campion, a New Zealander, who made a few very strange, interior feminist films in her native country, broke into the American market by mixing soft-core pornography with some stylistic peculiarities in *The Piano* (1993) and then overreached, attempting to adapt Henry James in *Portrait of a Lady* (1996). Other minorities are being represented in small-budget films, such as Robert Rodriguez's *El Mariachi* (1992), or large-budget studio films such as *The Joy Luck Club*, directed by the Hong Kong–born Wayne Wang in 1993, who also did a small, ethnic film, *Chan Is*

Missing in 1982, and an intricate, understated film about men and families called *Smoke* in 1995.

Whether or not any of these filmmakers will break through the restraints of the Hollywood style is open to question. They are likely to remain content making good films within the system that may or may not reflect their specific cultures. The tendency is for a filmmaker not to remain pigeonholed as a maker of African American or feminist films. There is simply too much at stake. Too much money, too much fame, too much power.

The commercial and cultural realities of filmmaking largely overpower the desire to be an individual creator with a subjective style and a personal, passionate world view. The economic realities of production worldwide and the tastes of the majority of filmgoers mitigate against it. An unusual style takes money but rarely makes it. It costs more to create an elaborate tracking shot than to execute an ordinary series of over-the-shoulder shots. A passionate world view usually comes from a passionate ego, and there is little room for a big ego in directors, whose job is usually to carry out the orders of the ego with the money, the producer. And audiences are often uncomfortable with flights of cinematic imagination, a problem made clear in the spate of recent "independent" films, most of which are neither independent of studio money and distribution or of the conventions of the Hollywood style.

And that, finally, is what this book has been about, the development of a comfortable style that negotiates with its audience a series of predictable, and flexible, responses. Flexibility, however, only yields so far. The work of negotiation has its limits. Too much experimentation, too much irony, and a film is in danger of losing its audience. A filmmaker must always be concerned with her audience. We admire the idea of the artist, even though we're too often uncomfortable when an "artist" exercises an unusual imagination in film.

I don't wish to end this chapter on a pessimistic note. For almost ten years, from the late sixties to the late seventies, a vital, sometimes experimental film culture thrived in the United States and abroad. Many of the filmmakers we have discussed here began their work during that period, and new ideas thrived. Many, many people throughout the culture were thinking and talking and writing seriously about film. The serious study of film was developed and established in this period. Given the great cyclical nature of culture and creativity, such a period is bound to come around again—though perhaps in different forms.

NOTES AND REFERENCES

Individuals and Creativity   An excellent, though challenging, source for information on the individual subject and its shifting positions is Kaja Silverman's *The Subject of Semiotics* (New York: Oxford University Press, 1983).

The Ideal Viewer   A brave reader may want to tackle Jean-Louis Baudry's essay, "Ideological Effects of the Basic Cinematographic Apparatus" in *Film Theory and Criticism*.

Film and the Individual Talent   The best and clearest theorizing about the existence of the author is Michel Foucault's "What Is an Author?" trans. D. F. Bouchard, *Screen* 20, no. 1 (1979).

Cinematographer   One of the finest works on cinematographers is a film called *Visions of Light,* available on VHS and (preferably) laserdisc. It contains good commentary and excellent visual examples.

Editor   One of the best books on film editing is by the director Karel Reisz, *The Technique of Film Editing* (New York: Hastings House, 1968).

Composer   Because few people combine the talents of a film critic and music expert, there has not been a great deal of work on film music. One recent book is Kathryn Kalinak's *Settling the Score: Music and the Classical Hollywood Film* (Madison: University of Wisconsin Press, 1992).

For the use of popular music in film, see Jonathan Romney and Adrian Wootton, eds., *Celluloid Jukebox: Popular Music and the Movies Since the 50s* (London: British Film Institute, 1995) and I. Penman, "Juke Box and Johnny-Boy," *Sight and Sound* 3, no. 1 (April, 1993), 10–11.

Stories of Stravinsky in Hollywood can be found in Otto Friedrich, *City of Nets: A Portrait of Hollywood in the 1940's* (New York: Harper & Row, 1986), pp. 38–39, and John Baxter, *The Hollywood Exiles* (New York: Taplinger, 1976), pp. 220–221.

Screenwriter   Here is a story that demonstrates how difficult it sometimes is to arbitrate a screenwriting credit. In 1995, a film named *Bulletproof* appeared. The screenwriting credit was given to one Gordon Melbourne, a Canadian. In fact, the film was written by Mark Malone, an American. The bogus name was put on the film in order to register it for a Canadian tax shelter. (See *New York Times,* May 21, 1995, pp. H11–12.) For a good survey of Hollywood screenwriters, see Richard Corliss, *Talking Pictures: Screenwriters in the American Cinema* (New York: Penguin Books, 1975). For some stories about writers in Hollywood, see Tom Dardis, *Some Time in the Sun* (New York & Middlesex, England: Penguin, 1981).

Actors   There have been two recent books on acting: James Naremore's *Acting in the Cinema* (Berkeley and Los Angeles: University of California Press, 1988) and Christine Gledhill's edition of essays, *Stardom: Industry of Desire* (London and New York: Routledge, 1991). See also Richard Dyer's *Stars* (London, British Film Institute, 1979).

The cultural historian Garry Wills has written an important book on John Wayne: *John Wayne's America: The Politics of Celebrity* (New York: Simon & Schuster, 1997).

Producer   The biography of Welles is by Frank Brady, *Citizen Welles: A Biography of Orson Welles* (New York: Scribner, 1989). Welles's *It's All True* has recently been found and edited together. It was released in 1993, more than fifty years after it was shot, seven years after its director's death. Welles's original material for *The Magnificent Ambersons* has still not come to light.

The Auteur, The Birth of the Auteur   The quotation from Godard is from *Godard on Godard,* ed. Jean Narboni and Tom Milne, trans. Tom Milne (New York: Viking, 1972), pp. 146–47.

The Auteur Theory   Sarris's essay "Notes on the Auteur Theory in 1962" is in *Film Theory and Criticism,* pp. 585–88. Peter Woolen's work on auteurism is in his book *Signs and Meanings in the Cinema* (Bloomington and London: Indiana University Press, 1972). Sarris's *The American Cinema: Directors and Directions, 1929–1968* (Chicago: University of Chicago Press, 1985) is the classic survey.

T. S. Eliot's "Tradition and the Individual Talent" is widely reprinted and can be found in the collection *The Sacred Wood* (New York: Barnes and Noble, 1960).

Martin Scorsese   If you look for Scorsese's reflection in the mirror in *Raging Bull* you may not see it because the edges for the frame are cropped in the videotape version. Try the laserdisc.

6

OTHER SCREENS: THE FUTURE OF THE IMAGE

The central idea of this book is that film is not reality. What we see on the motion picture screen is a mediation, a representation, an image or series of images that have been made for specific economic and cultural reasons and are interpreted in specific ways. These images represent ideas, ways of seeing and thinking, doing and feeling. They represent culture, not reality. They are not simply *there*, out in the world, like a natural object. They are created, distributed, and received. They represent the work of the imagination and an economic process as well.

The very phenomenon of an image on a screen speaks about the power of mediation. What we are looking at is hardly the thing itself, but a projection of an image on a surface. Careful planning, thought, labor, heavy apparatus, and massive financing went into its creation. All the complexities of our culture and our individual experience go into interpreting it. A movie is a cultural construction and an economic event, a projection and an act of reception. The screen is its site. The screen is an apparently neutral surface, a passive receptor of the images that light it up. But we understand now that nothing created by people is neutral, and that the screen becomes not only the receptor of images but itself an image of ways of representing and displaying things, ways of seeing and knowing. It becomes a kind of metaphor.

Film is a dying vestige of an old technology. Spreading of photosensitive chemicals on a plastic surface, running the plastic through a camera, developing the negative in a chemical bath, editing the resulting images together, printing a positive, and then projecting it on a screen are all work of the nineteenth century. These old technologies had not changed until recently. Neither had their economics. In the middle of the twentieth century, image recording and delivery—the ways in which the images and their narratives reach their audience—underwent some modifications. By the end of the century, the basic technologies and economies of the screen began changing in radical ways.

TELEVISION

Television, of course, was the second new screen after movies. But TV was less a technological change than it was a cultural and economic upheaval. Like film, television is an analogue process. That means that the light waves reflected from a surface, such as the human face, are recorded on a chemical surface in intensities that are proportional to the original light source. But in television, instead of processing the surface with chemicals, the light is transformed into electronic signals. These signals are transmitted through the air, received by the television set, and reconverted into electrons that activate the phosphorous surface of the television tube, which responds to them by reproducing images whose electronic wave forms are analogous to those that originated the process.

The technology of television parallels the technology of film, and film is, more often than not, the primary material that television transmits. But beyond that, TV and film are very different. Film represents the outside world. Not because a film narrative necessarily takes place in the outside world. But before the late sixties, in order to see a current film, you had to travel into the outside world. Going to see a movie meant going out of the house. It was a communal, urban experience. After World War II, urban communities began to change. Middle-class people left the city in great numbers. At the beginning of this migration, before the growth of suburban malls where movie houses were relocated in miniaturized form, going out of the house to see a film declined as a social event. Television became the means to satisfy the driving need for visual narratives.

Film was always available on television—old movies, filmed series, and movies made for television were there almost from the start. Live television drama had a relatively short life, and Hollywood-made production took over by the late fifties. In the brief period of live drama—from the early to the mid-fifties—television produced a number of writers and directors—Rod Serling, Paddy Chayefsky, Arthur Penn, John Frankenheimer, and Delbert Mann, for example—who went to Hollywood and were important influences in the movies. Some live television dramas were turned into films that took a hard and tightly composed look at working- and lower-middle-class characters: *Marty* (Delbert Mann, 1955), *12 Angry Men* (Sidney Lumet, 1957), *The Bachelor Party* (Delbert Mann, 1957), *Days of Wine and Roses* (Blake Edwards, 1966). This direct interaction was short lived.

But no matter what the source of the programming, our reception and perception of television are very different from what happens to us in a movie theater. The space is different: domestic rather than public; inside rather than out. The focus of concentration is different: Television is situated as a piece of household furniture to be stared at; it is usually watched in the light and with other things going on in the room. The screen is different: it is small and lit from behind; its resolution is low; the image is fuzzy and full of noise. Television does not elicit the concentration demanded from us in a dark movie house. On commercial channels, programming and advertising contend for our attention.

Commercial Structures

The commercial structure of movies is, in a sense, subtle and deep. As we have seen, there is a quiet, profit-driven negotiation between filmmaker and film viewer that is maintained through all the processes of production and reception. In television, a kind of pay-as-you-go process was instituted very early on. Instead of individual funding for individual productions, money would come from advertisers. They would invest in a program not on the promise of delayed returns in the form of gross receipts, but in the hope that viewers would buy the products that were advertised on the shows. In the early days of television, until the late 1950s, advertisers minimized their risks by producing the very shows they sponsored. The television program was another product of Kraft Foods or Firestone Tires or General Electric and was used to advertise those products.

By the late fifties, most production was turned back to the networks and their independent suppliers. Advertisers bought time on particular programs, or simply bought time periods, and their commercial presence thrived. But no matter the mechanism, the presence of the advertiser and the production of programming to support the advertised product constitute the essential dynamic of television. The programming does not stand on its own but is interlaced with commercials. In these commercials, the viewer may be exhorted to buy a product by a spokesperson or a disembodied voice that accompanies images of people using the product. Or the viewer may be engaged by miniature narratives, small stories of sexuality, of loss and desire, of inadequacy and fulfillment, of false cynicism and real manipulation, often in a style that is quite different from the classic continuity structure of the main program.

The Television Gaze

Watching a film is a self-contained, integral narrative experience. In a sense, it advertises itself through the continuity style that propels us forward and keeps us engaged. Watching a film or other programming on television is not integral, but fragmented. As a television viewer, one watches and takes part in multiple narratives: the main program, the commercial interruptions, and the domestic dramas going on in the room, all of them folded one within the other. In this way, television becomes a kind of communal experience, though different from film and the movie theater. You go out to a movie, and choose a specific film to go to. You stay in for television, and you are less likely to aim for a particular show than simply to "watch television." The light television creates on its screen may be there for many other purposes than simply making its images visible.

Stylistically, television is sometimes more eclectic, even more adventurous, than film. While most of the narrative material follows the rules of the continuity style, there are exceptions and there are structural conventions that are unique to television itself. News programming and some commercials, for example, have developed a style of audience address unlike anything in narrative film. News readers face and look into the camera, making eye contact with the audience (who are, of course, mediated by camera and screen). This is largely denied to practitioners of the classical style in film. The gazes of film work by indirection. The straight-on gaze of the news reader or advertising spokesperson, however, is instituted to create another kind of intimacy.

The television screen was promoted, from the early fifties, as the window on the world, the place where isolated suburbanites or besieged city dwellers could see into the outside without having to be there. Movies ask people to come out to the theater where they could see the melodramatic, fantastic, and the uncanny and be moved. Television delivers the friendly and the informative directly. The person who delivers the information, whether of a man-made disaster or a new refrigerator, looks right out at you, confidently. In your private, domestic space, the face on the screen can pretend intimacy and evoke a narrative of participation and proximity, an invitation into a fantasy world of threat and violence (the news) or desire and pleasure (the commercial).

The News and the Gaze

As television and the world it pretends to represent progressed and the need for ratings and advertisers overcame good programming sense, the information it delivered got uglier, more vulgar, violent, and desperate. The look remained, becoming a demand for attention, a conspiratorial invitation into the shocking and dismaying. In commercials it became a mock-ironic, a beseeching look, asking us to consider that the value of one product was greater than another. The gaze of the news presenter, the host of a tabloid program or talk show, or the spokesperson for a commercial product are perverse examples of Walter Benjamin's theory of the loss of aura. Few things in life should be as intimate and moving, as subjective and unique, as direct eye contact with another person. But the eye contact of a television talking head is without uniqueness, without intimacy. His or her stare is for everyone and for no one in particular. It is, finally, a stare for the camera, which is translated to the screen. The viewer stares back not at the head, but at the screen. The result is a narcissistic interaction of mutually noncomprehending gazes.

Benjamin hoped that loss of aura would mean increased access, an ability to see more deeply and communally into the world. Removing the sacred presence of the artist and the ritual aspect of looking at "great works" might allow proximity, even active insertion of social imagination into works of all kinds. But television's lack of aura creates a wider gulf between the viewer and the world than film does, precisely because the direct gaze of the talking head and the constant supply of information *seem* to provide a look into the wide world. Quite the opposite occurs. The view is shallow not deep. It is directed by a belief—on the part of news producers—that violent and antisocial events interest the largest number of people. It is a paranoid and antisocial view and rather than provoke people to look deeply into the world, as Benjamin hoped movies would do, television, especially the television of news, talk, and tabloid programming, promotes a paranoid view. Television wants people to stay home and watch television.

Narrative Programming

Narrative programming on television can sometimes have a different effect. Dramatic programs and made-for-television movies sometimes tackle current social problems, the latter occasionally from a woman's perspective. Theatrical film addressed social issues, long ago (capital, credit, and community were themes of *It's a Wonderful Life*); television has taken up the responsibility. Cable and broadcast movies are sometimes concerned with political issues, even moral problems. Serials (programs with an open narrative line that continues from one episode to another like soap operas) and series (programs with a continuing set of characters in somewhat different narrative situations in each episode like situation comedies) may not address social issues, but often offer interesting exceptions to the classical continuity style and the stereotypes so often present in theatrical film.

Soaps   Closure is a key element of the classical Hollywood style. In finally pulling closed all open narrative threads, recuperating any transgressive actions back into the cultural mainstream, the classical style creates a sense of uniqueness, the impression that what we have seen is a contained and one-of-a-kind story. It offers satisfaction, the assurance that everything is now OK.

Television serials, soap operas especially, work in quite the opposite manner. Their main narrative work is to keep the narrative going, to never let it end! Every installment of a soap opera opens more questions, spins out more narrative threads, generates more trouble for its characters than it can ever close or solve. Another part of soap opera's work is done through its slow narrative rhythm and its concentration on female characters, intimately engaging its viewers. Soap opera is an extension of melodrama, which, as we saw, is often constructed around a woman repressed by her family, inhibited, unhappy, briefly liberated, and then, through an act of great sacrifice, brought back into the domestic fold in harmony with the moral demands of the culture. Soap opera greatly expands the liberation and sexual questing of the female characters by delaying their recuperation into the normal scheme of things for as long as it can. It allows a considerable latitude in the behavior of its characters and demands a long-term attention and commitment from its viewers beyond that required for any film and most other television programming. The slow pace of soaps, their lingering on character and details of the gaze, their exaggeration of goodness and villainy help integrate them into the lesser melodramas of daily life. They become part of life's routine.

Series   Series are the mainstay of evening television programming. They demand a peculiar kind of "now you see it, now you don't" response. Although they are broadcast every week, with the same characters, who regularly demonstrate the same characteristics in the same physical surroundings, both the characters and the programs also present the illusion of being reborn in each episode. In situation comedy, the events in one episode rarely recall the events in the previous. The only continuing thread is the way characters will respond to a given stimulus. The characters and their narratives seem to live in a closed universe. Their narratives are like miniature genres, which can be depended upon, in episode after episode, to deliver variations on the same ideas, the same lines, the same physical and emotional responses, the same viewer reaction. The same each week, only different. The breaks in this convention are rare enough to be striking, as when a character on *Seinfeld* mentions something that happened on another episode. *The Simpsons*, the postmodern animated series that embraces and mocks popular culture in complex ways, parodies the amnesia effect of television series. Homer's boss never remembers who his employee is, no matter how many close experiences they have had.

More than movies, series, sitcoms especially, attempt to address the world many of its viewers live in. They are family or work oriented—though when they deal with work, they try to turn the workplace into a surrogate family—and they look at small issues, small "situations." They can, these days, be very vulgar and exploitative in their references to sexuality, but they can also be comforting, in their familiarity and their repetitive pattern, their sense of sameness and difference, their reassurance that, whatever happens to their characters, they will respond always in the same way.

Flow

It is possible to think of the whole of television as a genre, and its sitcoms, melodramas, commercials, news, tabloids, music video, and nature programs as subgenres of a general, overriding structure in which images and the viewer's attention are casually locked into an assenting gaze. This is a structure of enormous elasticity where disparate images and stories, facts and factoids, representations of sexuality and merchandise, or merchandise as sexuality, the steady gaze of the news anchor or the nervous, twitching camera movements that, borrowed from MTV videos, are now commonly used for commercials and coming attractions all flow together. These bits and pieces are mediated by the television screen, which is gazed at by millions of people, all of whom seem easily to absorb the flow. The British cultural theorist, Raymond Williams, developed the concept of "flow" when he was trying to make sense of American television's homogenized disorder, the seemingly random, jarring movement of styles and stories, sameness and difference and constant interruptions, a movement that invites intimacy and refuses it at the same time. Flow is the coherence of the incoherent, a representation of life in bits and pieces. A reflection of the postmodern world.

Williams' notion of flow is somewhat analogous to the continuity style in film, a way to make coherent sense out of the fragmentary. But in the case of television, any illusion of continuity must come from the viewer with little assistance from the structure of what is being viewed. Unlike film, whose self-contained pattern of fragments follows the clear rules of continuity, television breaks programming down and interrupts it continually with few apparent rules of continuity. For the flow of parts to cohere, the viewer has to will it into coherence or accept the fragments as they move past his nonattentive eye. Curiously, television viewers seem not to want the flow to cohere as completely as a movie, and, in fact, they sometimes add another layer of disruption. Channel surfing, in which the sixty or so channels of an average cable hookup are moved through in random disorder by means of a remote control, is a popular act of televiewing that is both a sign of desperation and a welcoming of the incoherent. Channel surfing allows the viewer to impose a subjective disorder on the chaotic flow of images and information, narratives, and advertising supplied by the producers of television. It creates a curious intimacy by turning externally produced chaos into personal chaos—another kind of negotiation between the viewer and the text.

Nothing like channel surfing is available when watching a film in the movie theater (perhaps, moving from one theater to another in a multiplex). My guess is that surfing rarely occurs when a film is viewed on cassette or laserdisc. Film is conventional in its demands for linear attention no matter what the venue, whether mall theater or domestic space. When we watch a film on cassette, it can recede into the background the way television often does. But when we give it our attention, it holds us through its length, if it's not boring, the phone doesn't ring, and no other domestic demand occurs that would be absent in a movie theater. The television screen becomes a convenient surrogate for the movie screen when the self-defining, self-cohering images of a film narrative are projected onto it. When *television* is projected onto it, however, that coherence disappears, and the screen reflects as much our own restlessness as it does the fragmented programming and mix of styles sent over the air or through cable.

Cultural studies has embraced television as the form that is most amenable to viewer negotiation. Because the television screen is placed in an intimate, domestic space, the desire to make it a part of our subjective lives is strong, as we've just seen. Because television is the major diversion of the culture, watched by almost everyone, it becomes both private and communal intellectual and emotional property. Of course in reality no one owns television but its owners—General Electric (NBC), Rupert Murdoch (Fox), The Disney Company (ABC), Time Warner (HBO), Viacom (Paramount Pictures, MTV, Comedy Central), Westinghouse (CBS)—and most of these are involved in many other communications operations such as filmmaking and publishing. These companies sell their broadcast time to advertisers—except for HBO and other cable networks that get their fees from subscribers—and programming decisions remain far above viewers, who are represented in the abstract by viewership numbers, the Nielsen ratings, based upon relatively small viewer samples. But the desire on the part of viewers to make an accommodation, a negotiation, is very strong, and a kind of ownership grows at the home end. People talk about "my shows," fans appropriate *Star Trek* and rewrite episodes, sometimes as pornography. Celebrity trials become major, cultural preoccupations. Watching soaps and sitcoms becomes part of a life's routine and some of us may feel deprived without them.

Televisual Pleasure

The television screen becomes a cultural mediator far different from the movie screen. Film delivers large emotions in intense bursts. The television screen reflects and refracts small, lingering, persistent, even obsessive concerns. Its fictional programming goes on and on, and viewers' capacity to look at a series of programs over and over again seems as limitless as the broadcast outlets these programs find. *I Love Lucy, MASH, Star Trek* (in its many incarnations) are shown and watched with a fascination that indicates a desire to own the pleasures and imaginations of these programs and reexperience them endlessly. Situation comedies build their own dominant fictions of a closely knit family or, more often, a contentious but ultimately warm workplace community that's like a family, but without its oppressive blood ties. These are stories that speak to people about desires that are hard to fulfill in life.

But it is not sufficient to explain the popularity of such programs by reducing them to substitutions for the experience we want but can't seem to find any place else but on television. More important are the touches of humor and imagination, the characters that represent traits we find endearing or those we imagine we could emulate, the narrative structures that play intricate changes on some basic themes—the way films that belong to a genre do—these are the determining characteristics of the form and structure of television narratives. So is their intimacy, their omnipresence in the space of domestic life, and their ability to be retrieved, almost at will, from local stations, cable channels, and videotape. Television is available, emotionally as well as physically. It is with us and of us. We ignore it and embrace it. We shore up its fragments for our pleasure.

FROM ANALOGUE TO DIGITAL

The play of intimacy and industry remains a key to understanding television and why its screen has become the site of the obsessive gaze of millions of individuals and of multimillion dollar mergers and high corporate aspirations. Intimacy also plays a determining role in the most recent screen to occupy domestic space, the computer screen, where new kinds of representations, some nonnarrative (in the conventional sense), some with peculiar, suppressed, or labyrinthine narratives, are addressing and even creating new audiences, communities, and cultures. In order to understand what this means, and to begin a transition from our discussion of the analogue to the digital screen, we must first recover some terrain.

Film and television are analogue processes: the light and sound waves that originate from the subjects being photographed are, on a physical level, related to the light and sound waves that light the screen and that vibrate the loudspeaker. The digital image does not have physical continuity with whatever originates it. Light or sound from the source object is translated into information that is *not* analogous to the source. Input—light and sound, a request for a withdrawal from an automatic teller machine, or a search through a library catalogue—is translated into the common language of the binary. This is code, represented at its base by zeros and ones that operate the electronic switches that make computers work and act upon any information fed into them. That is why the very word "information" has stretched the limits of meaning, signifying not knowledge or ideas, but the almost ineffable process of input to output, what goes into the computer and is digitized, compressed, and sampled and what comes out, the characters and graphics displayed on a screen.

Digitized information, because it is reduced to a relatively simple binary language, stripped of all excess and redundant material, is easily manipulable and can be copied repeatedly with no degradation. This makes it perfect for moviemaking. Let's for a moment go back to our discussion about how filmmakers construct a shot. Wherever possible, a shot is built up from a number of elements that do not have to be in front of the camera at the same time. In predigital times, a human figure would be photographed against a blue screen. Later, a painter would make an elaborate, real-looking image of a backdrop. In the effects laboratory, these two shots would be projected onto another strip of film, resulting in a composite image of a character on a road, a cliff, in a cityscape, moving, flying, and so forth. This is a complex, multistep process in which, among other things, the image is degraded as it is rephotographed over and over.

Digitizing images reduces the steps and does not degrade the final result. Digital manipulation of images allows anything to be done by artists and programmers at graphics terminals. Real movement can be created out of still figures and figures can be created that exist nowhere in reality. Digital artists can place a figure in any kind of environment. In Spielberg's *Jurassic Park* (1993) and *The Lost World* (1997) all the dinosaurs that are not mechanical models are digital designs matched with human figures. Almost everything seen in the sky in *Independence Day* (1996), including the flying saucers and the airplane sorties against them, is digitally created. Films use digital design in more subtle ways as well. Crowd scenes can be created by simply duplicating figures digitally; the head of one actor can be pasted upon another; stunts can be constructed on a computer terminal with a minimum of actual human activity. Digital image manipulation and replacement has pretty much replaced optical special effects, just as digital "automatic dialogue replacement," ADR, has replaced sound dubbing, so that filmmakers can construct the best reading of lines after the film is shot, perfectly synchronizing sound to lip movements. The result of all of this is that what you see and hear in a film is even less authorized by the exterior world than it was before. The feather, that image of grace and simple-mindedness, drifting down to Forrest Gump's foot, is a digital effect.

Storage and Distribution What can be done on the micro level of the shot can be done on the macro level of the film itself, and so digitization becomes a distribution as well as a creative process, changing the way films are seen and where. Entire movies can now be digitized into electronic files, the way a term paper is digitally stored on a word processor. To be sure, the process is more complicated, and the computer resources that are needed for the process are enormous. But in the realm of the digital, storage and transmission problems are rapidly solved. With the solutions will come different kinds of ownership, availability, and access. If dozens, or hundreds, of films can be digitally stored on a computer, and if that computer can be accessed over a television or phone company cable or via satellite, viewer habits will undergo a major change. The introduction of DVD—Digital Video or Digital Versatile Discs— which are the size of CDs and can store enormous amounts of digitized material, will make movie watching even more of a portable experience than it is now with videotape.

Availability and access will expand. On a more profound level, the aesthetics of the image will change. Digital HDTV (high definition television), currently under development, creates an image made up of 1,125 lines of scanned resolution, as opposed to the current resolution of 525 lines. Although the HDTV image is still made up of scanned lines, as opposed to the fine chemical grain that makes up the film image, the number of those lines, along with the digital sampling that removes any extraneous visual "noise," renders an extremely well-resolved image that is capable of reproducing a gradient of color and brightness quite astonishing in its subtlety. It does not look like film. The quality of light and shadow is different; it has another kind of visual presence. When HDTV becomes available, a new kind of cinematography, or videography, will emerge that will allow imaginative film or video makers to create images as intricate and subtle as any on film.

People with a business imagination will understand the economies that can be realized in broadcasting HDTV images directly to theaters rather than the current practice of striking prints of a film and shipping them around the country to local theaters. The result will be that, when we go out to the movies, we will, in effect, be going to see television, though with a projected image of more visual subtlety than is now available on television. The content may very well remain film content. There may not be commercials that interrupt the narrative, though they will continue to exist inside the film, in the form of recognizable products, easily identified, a practice that has been going on for some time. But the image will be a video image, projected on a large, wide screen.

HDTV promises a video image of high resolution and large size, but neither it nor any other new delivery and distribution systems promise anything radically new in content or any experimentation in narrative structure. Indeed, all previous technological developments in film and television suggest that the old narratives will remain pretty much the same. The pessimistic view is that the movie screen and the television screen will become almost identical. What is projected on them will increase in spectacle, because the creation of large, explosive effects seems to be the direction that digital rendering is going in commercial film. What the images and narratives speak to us about, however, may exist within the old generic contours, driven by the same master narratives that have controlled film from its beginnings. The economics of large technological change almost always result in a conservative approach to the content delivered by new media.

THE THIRD SCREEN

Pessimism is countered, however, by the computer screen itself, which is rapidly finding its way into the home and often competing with television as the primary screen in the domestic space. The computer screen affords the greatest amount of control, the most solid interaction between the viewer and the material viewed. This is a direct, intimate control, unlike the process of negotiation that goes on with the unyielding images of film and television. The computer monitor looks a lot like a small television. Technically, part of its operation is like a television set, in that electrons activate phosphors on the back of the picture tube and images of text or pictures appear on its viewing surface. However, here the similarity ends. The way those representations get to the monitor, what they represent, who owns and controls the creation and reception of them is quite different from film and television.

Because computing requires technical knowledge and active participation, it can be argued that it should not to be considered a popular art or part of the mass media. Unlike film and television, access to personal computers is still determined by economic class and by education. Although the numbers of machines in use grows yearly, their penetration into the home is nowhere near that of television. As of 1998, 48 percent of American homes had computers with Internet access, as compared to nearly 99 percent that had television. However, these figures change when put in economic contexts. Far fewer poor and minority families own computers, but nearly all groups own one or more television sets. Still, working or playing at the computer is becoming a major preoccupation for many, and it makes up in intensity what it lacks in numbers of people whose lives it directly affects. The computer screen and all it represents has become a cultural force; it has changed us in some profound ways, some of them not for the better; and it will change more as more people get access.

Other Narratives

The computer screen offers creativity and inclusion in a process. Unlike a television program or a movie, what is displayed on the computer is not an ongoing story that positions us to respond emotionally at just the right moments, but an invitation to work, to be included in, or placed in control of, a process. The conventional film or television narrative sutures us into its forward momentum. Our interaction with the computer screen lacks the linearity of a classically constructed story with dramatic characters. The drama is made by us; we are the character interacting with the machine and with the words and images it helps us generate.

Human–computer interaction is ongoing, in process, and demands an active participation as opposed to a simulated one. It involves knowledge, specifically attained as opposed to passively absorbed. We learn the codes and conventions of film by watching films; we know how to interact with the computer by learning specific skills. This knowledge and the processes involved in working with the computer and its screens are subdivided into different kinds of interactions. These vary from relatively passive ones to the complexity of programming new screens, creating new computer applications and multimedia projects. Surrounding all this activity is the phenomenon of cyberspace, the ability of one computer screen to access thousands of others, on which different processes, different representations of data can be observed and different interactions can be performed.

Computer Games   Computer games are on the passive end of the scale, requiring more reflex than thought. In many ways, they constitute the closest analogy to movies and television. Games are, in fact, the computer venue in which movies studios are investing much time and money. They are often created as tie-ins with movies, and original computer games are made with movielike narratives. These are based on the action-adventure genre—often with second-string actors appearing in digitized videos within the games, some of which are mere blood sports, with destructive responses expected from the user and representations of violence shown on the screen.

There is an interesting correlation between these games and the primitive period of film. One of the legends about early cinema—a story told over and over regarding the Lumière brothers' film of a train leaving a station—was that the audience, so inexperienced with cinematic images, pulled back in fear at the sight. There is, of course, no likelihood of this reaction occurring in the face of the digitized, pixilated figures of a computer game. In fact, there was probably no likelihood that the Lumières' audience reacted in this way either. The legend is more important than the reality. But computer games do attempt to simulate a kind of primitive reflex reaction by allowing the viewer to contend with elements of a program (represented by images of warriors or monsters on the screen) that will do various things in response to various kinds of input. If you click the mouse or move the joystick at the right moment, in the right place, the program will respond by graphically representing on the screen a digitized figure spouting blood. There is emotion involved, based on the anxiety of timing the response at precisely the right moment, and satisfaction of sorts at seeing a figure seem to drop dead because of your action (or disappointment at seeing the figure representing you expire). But the interaction goes no deeper, takes no part of the complex structures of interactivity that the computer offers. Game playing is simultaneously a little more and a great deal less than a movie experience, reduced in size, with a crippled mise-en-scène, and a considerably restricted internal narrative. It is the nickelodeon version of computer interaction.

Myst and its sequel, *Riven*, created by Rand and Robyn Miller, use the computer game model—moving around the screen to find the answer to a riddle. But it removes most of the violence, adds a mise-en-scène that owes something to cinema, makes use of complex computer graphics capabilities, and elaborates a pattern of process, uncertainty, probability, logic, and open-endedness that is as close as we currently are to a program that expresses native computer potential. *Myst* and *Riven* speak a language and engages us in a narrative that is possible only on a computer screen. And this is an important event. Computers began as machines to replace and make easier jobs that used to be done by other means—typing, decoding, managing data, doing math, moving money (which is just another kind of data). Now computer–user interaction can produce images and events that are not substitutes but original creations in a discourse that can only be spoken by the machine in relation to the user.

From the idea of a native discourse come answers to some important questions about computers and narrative. Can computers tell stories at all? Can they narrate as opposed to being part of a larger cultural narrative? That is, can they represent a series of events in time in which characters are created, given a context, placed in a world, have things happen to them, which are then resolved back into equilibrium that allows their world to be closed off? Can they provoke us, as viewing subjects, to enter this narrative web, evoke in us anticipation and desire? Make us want things to happen simply to see how they will be resolved?

Conventional computer games do some of this. They set up a chase and pursuit model with a set of rules. By and large, they do this within a limited loop: chase, kill, be killed. The variations on the genre are limited. The narrative is bound not by what the computer is capable of but by the limits of the genre of the game and the restrictions set by the assumed desires of their players—mostly adolescent males. The computer is capable of doing much more. More accurately, imaginative designers and programmers are capable of making the computer do much more and require the user to do more, as well.

Computers are, at their binary fundamentals, makers of narratives. A computer program is a kind of script, a set of instructions that makes the machine perform, take user input and calculate it based on the information available to the program, move through that information, do recursive actions so that some things happen over again and others don't, branch, loop, and finally display the results of calculations on the screen.

A script for a film is interpreted as the director, editor, actors, production designer, composer, and cinematographer translate the words into images. A second interpretive act occurs when the film is viewed. Each viewer responds according to the cinematic and cultural codes structured into the film's narrative and his or her subjective reactions. These reactions have little effect on the narrative being constructed on the movie screen, except in the way it is interpreted. The script that is a computer program, on the other hand, can respond in varying ways. It can, within the limits of its construction, incorporate user response and change its calculations—where it branches, loops, whether something done in one place has repercussions on another part of the program—and represent the result of its calculations on the screen. These images can be addressed in turn and can make the program respond in different ways.

This should be obvious if we consider something as ordinary as a word-processing program. The program on the computer I used to write this book helped dictate the book's form, structure, and to some degree even content. It allowed me to type in whatever text characters I wanted and put them in the form of chapters, paragraphs, caps, italics, notes, and so on. It responded to my needs, acted the way I wanted it to act. It can do many things, except supply the words I need (even here I can open the computer's thesaurus database and find analogous words for a word I highlight). When I manipulate images on the computer, the program does much more. It samples colors down to the smallest visual unit on the screen—the pixel—and can alter it. I can clip a figure from one image and paste it into another. Here, the computer is in a complex mode, reading its program (its script), the information I give it, and working out new images as a result.

Computers and the programs that drive them do not have intelligence in the sense that they can originate ideas. But they are manipulable in that they can take one piece of information and, if they have been instructed how to do so, produce a number of different results. This is the basis of computer program structures that operate on logical elements: if . . . then . . . /and . . . or . . . /true/false/yes/no. Within these and other parameters, they can manipulate user input to produce a variety of different results. The results themselves can then be changed to create new results, which can then loop back to alter the foundation of whatever created the original results in the first place. The more intricate the program, the more articulate the graphical representations on the screen, and the more latitude given to the user to alter them, the more complex the interactions can be.

These are some of the principles that lie behind *Myst* and *Riven*. The structure of the program represents what appears to be an endless series of alterations, each one having a ripple effect so that a choice in one place creates consequences in other places. This would be interesting in an abstract, mathematical sense were it not for the fact that these games work their changes through graphical representations that are the closest the computer screen has come so far to creating a mise-en-scène. Images of imaginative worlds (in their design, they bear a visual relationship to the art of 1950s science fiction magazine covers) are articulated in the blue/green colors best suited to the limited range of some personal computers and articulated with objects that can be addressed by the user: switches, buttons, dials, cranks, books, pictures—the moving of any of which has an effect in some other screen, some other structure of the program, another imaginary, graphical space. As in a movie, musical themes are associated with various places, rooms, and worlds, spaces and times through which the viewer moves in search of the answer to a riddle, which itself has to be discovered before we know where we can begin to look for the answer.

This mise-en-scène is remarkably humanized, though without representations of human figures. A video of a man, talking incoherently, can be located in one of the books in the library of *Myst*. Winged figures, reminiscent of the mythic Icarus, who flew too close to the sun, can be seen floating from the sky on some of its screens. But the worlds of *Myst* are unpeopled landscapes, a fact that becomes part of the mystery. (There are a few more figures in *Riven*, but there, too, the player is the most important presence.) The mystery—the plot of this particular digital world, about kidnapping and ancient family feuds—is of considerably less interest than its process. The "people" of *Myst* are its players. The main character, the subject of the work, is the person operating the program during any particular session. The main narrative movement is the exploration of images and devices. Like some movies, the plot is simply less intriguing than the narrative process that creates it. The best part is the process of investigation, inventing a narrative within the wide-ranging bounds provided by the program, moving through the graphic images of imagined worlds.

Hypertext/Hypermedia   Process, in which the viewer/user is both subject and object, in control of the screen, searching for data, images, connections, following branches and links, pursuing paths, being led down blind alleys, coming up with specific or diffuse results, is something almost inherent in the form and structure of the computer. In 1965, a Harvard graduate student named Ted Nelson coined the word "hypertext" to describe an idea he had of computer-generated nonlinear connections or links between data. Such links would allow the user to connect disparate parts, connect big and small chunks of text and images, open one set of text to reveal others, move in ways other than straight lines, link data continuously and extensively. He called his project Xanadu, after Samuel Taylor Coleridge's magical kingdom in the poem *Kubla Khan*, and after the unfinished castle, filled with the world's art treasures, in Orson Welles's *Citizen Kane*. True to its conception, the project was never completed.

But the idea of hypertext and hypermedia caught on. *Myst* is a kind of hypermedia creation. Some writers have attempted a new fiction in which blocks of prose are linked in apparently arbitrary ways that alter the conventional linearity of the literary narrative, providing alternative ways of reading, alternative possibilities of how and where texts and textuality may exist. Hypertext fiction has not quite reached the status of a literary movement, and it is more provocative of interesting theory than good literature. Outside of word processing (in which the user is actively creating words), plain text is not the most inviting of representations to look at on the computer screen for long periods of time, even if it can be manipulated into curious patterns that allow the reader to create variable narrative structures.

Hypertext fiction needs to be linked into the larger concept of hyper- or multimedia, the ability to represent relationships between images, text, and sounds in a design that provides links between them, allows the user to discover or make connections, and displays contiguities of ideas that might not be obvious or possible in traditional linear, page-bound presentations. Multimedia is a methodology for exploring insides and outsides, of seeing into the margins, of opening the linkages between different kinds of representations, and explaining one class of representation (a visual image, for example) by means of another (a sound or words). In a multimedia project, a word or a block of text can be linked in various ways to other words and can be associated with an image. Parts of an image can be divided and linked to verbal description; a sound or voice-over narrative can accompany, embellish, or contradict the elements on the screen.

Film, Form, and Culture, The CD-ROM

If *Myst* is a kind of multimedia presentation that calls upon complex, covert links between image, language, and sound, the CD-ROM that accompanies this textbook is an example of multimedia used for analytic purposes. The study of film has always been hampered by the difficulty of access to illustrative material. Before the computer, it was next to impossible to quote from film, the way a literature teacher and critic can quote from a novel or poem. The cinematic text is physically removed from the viewer; it can't be held in the hand like a book; its sequences are difficult—and on the printed page, impossible—to access. Although videotape and laserdisc media have made it easier to control the visual text, showing a sequence on a printed page, the way lines from a poem or a reproduction of a painting can be shown, has remained elusive.

This is an elusiveness that constrains our ability to understand how the form and structure of film work. Still images don't do the trick and are hard to authenticate. Unless they are clearly frame enlargements—that is, photographs made from an actual frame of a film, as they are in this book—they are usually production stills, posed photographs of a film's stars that may have been made outside the main production. These were common throughout the studio period and are still made. They are not quotations from the films.

The ability to digitize film images, to turn their rich, analogue visuals into the common binary language of computers, puts them in the same class as any other computer file. They become the equal of text file and can become integrated with it. They can be addressed, altered, programmed, and designed into a larger textual entity. Earlier, we spoke about the ways in which Hollywood filmmakers are using computers to do the kinds of image manipulation that was formerly done by optical printing. Similar kinds of manipulation can be done on smaller, desk-top computers, and the result is a new kind of control of the moving image that leads to a new and more authoritative analytic and critical understanding.

Digitized motion picture images can be incorporated into most advanced word-processing programs. Although they can only be seen with the document on a computer screen, there they provide instant examples, clarifications, and authentifications for the prose analysis. In the CD-ROM that accompanies this book, digitized sequences from films become one part of a larger, interactive design; they are used as examples and their mysteries revealed. Taken out of the ongoing narrative flow of the film, isolated and broken down, they become part of another text, a hypermedia text in which image is linked to image, to analysis, example, and redefinition. As you will see, it is possible to open a critical dimension within the image so that by interrogating it (by a mouse click), information is divulged. Images in the CD-ROM from Eisenstein's *Battleship Potemkin,* Welles's *Citizen Kane,* Pare Lorentz's *The Plow That Broke the Plains,* (1936) have animated lines diagrammed within them—the way a football commentator on television diagrams a play—to show how the filmmaker uses space and mise-en-scène to define character and narrative. All the moving images can be paused and stepped through, as if a VCR were incorporated into the computer screen. Abstract principles like point of view, and general concepts like continuity cutting, montage, lighting, and the work of the camera are made visible. Idea and image are put in the reader's control.

The Computer and the Text

The multimedia event, no matter what its subject, is a creation of dimensions, an elaboration or invention of contiguities and connections, a way of creating an intertextuality of word, image, and culture in space by opening up linkages and associations that move in many directions. At the same time, it concentrates diverse materials in accessible ways. A central tenet of cultural studies is that people and the things they do never stand in isolation from each other. Texts are large, coherent events that include not only a single book, a film, or a television show, but the various events going on around them, all directly or indirectly connected. Social attitudes and situations, ideological currents, newspaper reports, fashions, music, the history of the moment, and our own responses are all part of a larger textuality that is, in turn, a part of the culture. Multimedia enables the creation of a text that can pull together these various textualities and explicitly or implicitly make links between them. It is a text of texts that makes range and depth part of its properties, and access an ongoing, interrogative process.

The creation and use of multimedia put the viewing subject in a situation unlike any other textual event. It gives the viewer control of a variety of large amounts of data that can be structured in intriguing and imaginative ways. It creates a sense of connection and exploration, and, in its networked, global form, it is creating a new kind of community, a kind of universal culture, in which subjectivity, identity, and participation are in the process of being redefined.

Modernity and the Internet

In Chapter 3, we discussed the concept of modernity and defined it as the movement of technological advancement, increased urbanization, rapid fragmentation of dependable, cohesive structures (such as family, religion, a dominant race or ethnicity, and government), and the falling away of individual agency. Modernity can be figured as a movement away from a center, and that "center" can be understood through a variety of representations: religion, the extended family, the small community, the ideology of free will and independent action. Computer technology is a bridge from modernity to post modernity. It allows us a way to experience and manage the transition. It shows ways to break away from the centers and create new configurations of the individual in the world that are both liberating and nostalgic, freeing and constraining. Film and television make us nostalgic about the simpler times that exist only in its images, offering us ways to dream ourselves out of the confusions of the modern world. Computer networks let us see modernity and offer us ways to navigate through it.

Modernity is developed on the ground of communications. The ability of people to be in immediate contact with each other offers ways to transcend local community and construct the global one that is essential to the processes of decentralizing culture. The invention of printing in the fourteenth century was a primary event in the spreading of information and ideas, the diffusing of the authority of the individual by making his words take the place of his presence, spreading those words beyond his voice, his ideas beyond his control. Printing helped conquer space by making ideas and information moveable and independent of an individual. This was when aura began to diminish.

In the nineteenth century that the process received another boost. During the last half of the nineteenth century, the railroad became a way for physical decentralization, allowing people relative ease of movement across a country. In the twentieth century, the car and the airplane took the place of the railroad and provided international access for many and local mobility for almost everyone. At about the same time, the cinema became an imaginative and emotional means of expansion, a means to access images of other spaces, other kinds of behaviors. Telegraphy and the telephone created—like the book and the film—a curious hybrid of movement and stasis. Through them, a person could reach another, distant place while remaining physically rooted in her original location. The telephone permitted the voice, the most forceful of communicative agents, to transmit its presence and intimacy. It broadened community and, like the railroad, increased commerce. Telegraphy and the teletype allowed the transmission of writing and images and therefore the communication of detailed information, structured, authoritative, and official, in the way speaking never could.

Telephone and telegraphy, like movies and television, are part of the analogue realm—continuous waveforms of information, transferred from point to
point. The transportation, quality, management, and storage of this kind of communications was bulky and limited, subject to the constraints of space and to the
"noise" that is introduced by factors as various as sunspots, poor equipment,
and distance. "Noise" is a concept in communications theory that stands for any
kind of interference in the transmission process, physical, ideological, corporate.
The digital reduces noise on many different levels. By transforming the analogue into the binary, image, sound, and text can be sampled and compressed as
numbers rather than waves. Physical noise can be removed and, as we've seen,
degeneration in quality is eliminated. Most important, because large parts of the
digital repository of information are open, accessible to all who have the rather
simple (if still somewhat expensive) equipment necessary to find and see them,
the ideological "noise" of ownership and information control becomes somewhat diminished. Computer communication is hardly as universal as the telephone, but where it is available, it offers opportunities of access and content, individually controlled, that no other communicative form has.

The great repository and distribution system of digital communications is
the Internet. Although it is a product of modernity, it is also a model of what
postmodernity is about. The Internet is an idea without a location, a thing
with no single physical presence, a way of moving ideas, visual images and
sounds, and a lot of text around the world, from screen to screen, with as little noise as possible. The Internet continually defies capitalist rules of ownership, because it isn't owned. It was originated by the U.S. Department of Defense in the 1960s, taken under the partial stewardship of the National
Science Foundation, and is now governed by a loose confederation of universities, government agencies, and corporations. Ownership does not define the
Internet, access does. The Internet is, in its simple reality, many computers—
called servers—linked together through a complex addressing protocol that
makes each one of them identifiable and addressable by any other. An individual who can access a network directly or by a phone hookup can connect
to some or all of the Internet, find those servers, and look at what they have
to offer.

This, of course, is its major limitation, the place where noise enters the system in the form of economic and class barriers to access. Though unowned in
the normal corporate senses of the word, the Internet costs money. Those costs
are usually borne by universities or corporations. Any student who is assigned
an address and has access to a machine with a modem or direct connection
can access the network. For around twenty dollars a month, anyone else with
a computer and a modem, and a local company that provides an Internet connection, can get access. Many of the pay-for-use dial-up services, like America
On line, provide some Internet connections. In many communities, public libraries, churches, and community centers are providing access. But the poor,
minorities, those living in the inner city or outer rural areas still find access
very difficult.

For those who can access the Net, there are various genres, various ways of representing, communicating, and receiving data, each with its own conventions, structures, and protocols. Newsgroups provide a large and sometimes bizarre variety of ongoing discussions, from computer programming to paramilitary rant. Some newsgroups constitute the male-only barroom of the digitized world, where aggression, vulgarity, and old rituals of gender exclusion are played out with uncensored ferocity. More propriety is shown on listservs, which are also discussion groups, but made up of subscribed members, grouped usually by academic interests. Listservs are easily formed and made local, so that your class, for example, can create a listserv in which members can discuss related topics with one other.

These means of personal communication, combined with electronic mail, which uses the Internet to send individual messages between people with server access, make the digital a personalized realm, and a comfortable one as well. Although, as in any community effort, loud and angry voices sometimes threaten to overtake conversations, niches have quickly developed, giving them a place where they can be either attended to or ignored. The spaces that remain are filled with people exchanging information, making contact, talking, a faceless, spaceless community in which subjectivity is redefined by intellectual and emotional interests, where one can simultaneously be audience and participant.

Were these the limits of the Internet, it would remain the province of university researchers and people who like to chat about everything from politics to sex and guns. What has brought it into prominence, made it a part of the cultural landscape where it is vying with film and television for the attention both of individuals and the corporate world, is another means of depositing and retrieving data across thousands of servers, called the World Wide Web. The Web was developed by computer scientists as an easier means of transmitting images and sound along with printed text across servers around the world. So easy, in fact, that almost anyone who has Internet access can design a "home page" and put it up for the world to see. The home computer can become a distribution site.

Web sites work in hyperlink fashion. Sites are linked to other sites, often continents away, through a mouse click; images yield texts and texts images. Experimentations with every kind of material occur. Individuals put up pictures of their children; there are online collections from most of the major museums in the world; advertisements for local flower shops; scientific and humanities research; large corporate sites that supply everything from moving images of recent film releases to software updates. These exist along with literary texts, photographs, and avant-garde art and literary experiments, pornography, government and medical information.

Every university, most of its departments, and many of their students and faculty have a Web site. Special public services, such as a Forum for children with diabetes, groups and companies attempting to bring Internet access and information to African American communities, and a Canadian group attempting to bring the network to old people, have sites. Rock groups, film festivals, and government agencies have Web sites. Using special sites that provide search mechanisms, you can find the most general or particular information on the Web. It is an enormous, unruly assemblage, a place where many people go to look around and find, with time and patience, what they need. Because of its unruliness, it is sometimes an untrustworthy place. Much of the information is very thin; some inaccurate. Some literary texts posted on the web are inauthentic. Many essays that appear to be scholarly may not have stood the test of review by academic peers. In a structure with no central authority—where almost anyone can be a producer—the facts and the narratives may be wrong or devious.

Any number of judgments can be made about the Web: the lazy person's shopping mall; a community for shy people; a passing fad for those bored with television; a useful, if limited, research resource and a very poor replacement for the library; a place for businesses, large and small, to make another buck; a space to exhibit and exchange images of all kinds—a postmodern space of sense and nonsense, the banal and—though not often—the profound. It might be useful to think about it on a slightly more abstract level. The Internet, and the World Wide Web in particular, are the current outposts of the postmodern, where subjectivities—the sense and the place of the individual self—shift and change. The Internet is an enormous and a small space where a person can assert herself by connecting to and communicating with—in no matter how limited a way—almost every computer in the world. Or a person can be absorbed by the images and words shifted around the globe from server to server and screen to screen. It is a place, like the movies, of myriad representations but, unlike the movies, of few stories in the conventional sense.

Like almost everything on the computer screen, the World Wide Web is a place of process in which everything happens but nothing is resolved. Unlike the movies, its images and words do not fall into closed, knowable fictional worlds (when fiction appears on the Internet, it is either of the hyper variety, which means that it is fragmented and without closure, or it is a reproduction of a traditional text, difficult to read in its entirety). As we said earlier, what is narrated on the Web is the story of investigation and participation, the subject's progress through an open-ended system.

The representations on the computer screen are open, ongoing, and their constraints are much different from those of conventional story-telling media. Because of the interactive nature of the computer and its screen, the individual subject is turned into an active participant and agent. And with that turn, rules are changed. Mass media, as we've said many times, require a largely passive response. Despite the validity of the cultural studies argument about negotiating interpretations and engaging the text according to our determined desires to read what we want to read, much of our interaction with film and television is a passive reaction to its codes and conventions. Little passivity is possible in our interactions with the computer screen. We need to know what we are doing, actively seek things out, and often interact with what we find.

More than film and television, our engagement with the images on a computer screen is without aura. That startling idea of Walter Benjamin's, stated in the 1930s, is even more applicable now. With the advent of digital cultures, we are freer than ever to enter a community of ideas, of words and images—of representations—and find our way with less constraints than the older media. Benjamin wrote in "The Work of Art in the Age of Mechanical Reproduction":

> Every day the urge grows stronger to get hold of an object at very close range by way of its likeness, its reproduction. . . . To pry an object from its shell, to destroy its aura, is the mark of a perception whose "sense of the universal equality of things" has increased to such a degree that it extracts it even from a unique object by means of reproduction. . . . The adjustment of reality to the masses and of the masses to reality is a process of unlimited scope, as much for thinking as for perception.

For "masses" read "ourselves." We are the ones extracting images and ideas, our own subjectivities, and testing them in the digital, networked world in ways the makers of popular culture could have never imagined. Through the digital, reality is being adjusted, just as it was with the movies at the turn of the century. And, just like then, we are searching for new languages of expression, new ways to create the new realities.

The structure of the World Wide Web, the possibilities inherent in multimedia authoring, the resources available to computer programming, may yield a language of inquiry, of humanity, of emotional resonance that could speak to us—or to which we may speak—with complexity and insight. This language will be of a different order of resonance and responsibility then the great works of film, the movies of Hitchcock, Kubrick, Welles, Scorsese, Godard, Antonioni, Bertolucci, Altman, Fassbinder, and all the others who have used their medium to probe and ask questions. But it will address and articute our curiosity and desire.

All the tools we have to act, perceive, and create have the potential to ask questions and find new meanings, new realities, and the languages of the computer and the possibilities of its screens have no more inherent limits than any other. The limits exist only in those who use the languages, who make the images and read them. Someone once said that the computer is still looking for its D. W. Griffith. What that means is that we still await the imagination that can turn the language of the computer program and the images of the computer screen into articulate and coherent statements that speak to our selves, our history, our culture.

NOTES AND REFERENCES

Television   The best source for a cultural study of how television infiltrated the home is Lynn Spigel, *Make Room for TV: Television and The Family Ideal in Postwar America* (Chicago: University of Chicago Press, 1992).

Commercial Structures   A good history of the development of commercial television is William Boddy's *Fifties Television* (Urbana, Illinois: University of Indiana Press, 1990). Mike Mashon's *A Word from the Sponsor: Madison Avenue and the Evolution of American Television,* forthcoming from University of Texas Press, clarifies television's early history.

Narrative Programming   For a good differentiation of "series" and "serials," and a discussion of narrative form in television, see John Ellis, *Visible Fictions: Cinema, Television, Video* (London: Routledge, 1992).

Soaps   For soap operas, there are two collections of essays: E. Ann Kaplan, ed., *Regarding Television: Critical Approaches* (Frederick, Md.: University Publications of America, 1983); and Suzanne Frentz, *Staying Tuned: Contemporary Soap Opera Criticism* (Bowling Green, Ohio: Bowling Green State University Popular Press, 1992).

Flow   The citation for Raymond Williams is in Chapter 3.

From Analogue to Digital, Storage and Distribution   Here is a story about a film that combines digital replacement with advertising. *Demolition Man* (Marco Brambilla, 1993), a film set in the future, with Sylvester Stallone and Wesley Snipes, has sequences that take place in a Taco Bell fast-food restaurant. There were no Taco Bells in Europe—where American producers count upon a film making a lot of money—but there are Pizza Huts, which are owned by the same company, Pepsico. Pepsico paid to have Taco Bell appear in the film. The filmmakers simply did a digital replacement so that Taco Bell now appeared as Pizza Hut. No refilming was necessary, and Pepsico got advertising in its European markets. (See *The Wall Street Journal,* Dec. 2, 1993, p. B1)

The Third Screen, Hypertext   The original group of hypertext authors were published on disc by Eastgate Systems. Their work includes Michael Joyce's *afternoon, a story,* Stuart Moulthrop's *Victory Garden,* and Carolyn Guyer's *Quibbling.* Some of the best recent hypertext has been published online in the journal *Postmodern Culture.* See especially the hypertext issue, vol. 7, no. 3 (May 1977) and Matthew Miller's "Trip" in vol. 7, no. 1 (September 1996). *Postmodern Culture* is an online, subscription journal available at http://muse.jhu.edu/journals/postmodern_culture/.

Hypertext theory is outlined in J. David Bolter, *Writing Space: The Computer, Hypertext, and the History of Writing* (Hillsdale, N.J.: L. Erlbaum Associates, 1991). Bolter's *Turing's Man: Western Culture in the Computer Age* (Chapel Hill: North Carolina University Press, 1984) is an interesting attempt at a cultural history of computing. There is a discussion of Ted Nelson and the theory of hypertext called "The Electronic Labyrinth," by Christopher Keep and Tim McLaughlin, found at http://jefferson.village.virginia.edu/elab/elab.html.

The Seniors Computer Information Project is at http://www.mbnet.mb.ca/crm/. The diabetes site is at http://www.castleweb.com/diabetes/.

One site that contains many links to African American resources is at http://www.cambridge.edu/hsubpages/Reseach_html/Afro-Am.html.

A Hispanic resource listing is at http://latino.sscnet.ucla.edu.

Film, Form, and Culture: The CD   One must always be aware of copyright issues when digitizing movie clips.

Modernity and the Internet   Two collections of essays address the cultural contexts of the Internet: David Porter, ed., *Internet Culture* (New York and London: Routledge,

1997); and Mark Stefik, ed., *Internet Dreams: Archtypes, Myths, and Metaphors* (Cambridge, Mass.: Massachusetts Institute of Technology, 1996).

The quotation from "The Work of Art in the Age Mechanical Reproduction," cited in Chapter 3, is on page 223.

For the comparisons of the computer screen with early developments in film see Brenda Laurel, *Computers as Theater* (Reading, Mass.: Addison-Wesley, 1993).

INDEX

ABC, 183
Abrams, M. S., 14
Abstract painting, 5
Abstract photographs, 9–10
Access Hollywood, 157
Acting styles, 103, 158
Actors, 156–159
    function of star system, 80–82
    in television and movies, 80
Actualités, 18
Address, 95
Adorno, Theodor W., 66, 67, 96
Advertising photography, 10
Age of anxiety, 83
Age of Innocence, 167
Air Force, 156
Akerman, Chantal, 140
Albino Alligator, 167
Aldrich, Robert, 127
Alexander Nevsky, 44
Alfred Hitchcock Presents, 76–77
Alice Doesn't Live Here Anymore, 167
Alien 3, 130
Allen, Dede, 151
Allen, Woody, 45, 150, 173
All That Heaven Allows, 116, 136–138
All the President's Men, 130
Alphaville, 133
Also Spake Zarathustra, 75
Altman, Robert, 119, 142, 153, 165, 173, 198
    film editing, 50–51
American Tragedy, An (Dreiser), 46
America Online, 195
Amy, George, 151
Analogue processes, 185
Angelopoulos, Theo, 47

Animal Locomotion (Muybridge), 12
Antonioni, Michelangelo, 28–29, 150, 153,
    173, 198
    films of, 134–135
Aparajito, 27
Apocalypse Now, 149
Apu trilogy, 27
Arbitrary cutting conventions, 41–2
Arkin, Alan, 158
Arnheim, Rudolph, 14
Art, aura of, 70
Art director, 148–149
Aura
    and computer screens, 198
    definition, 70
    of state intervention, 71
    and television, 180
Austen, Jane, 62
Autant-Lara, Claude, 163
Auteurs
    birth of, 162–163
    current, 173–175
    European origins, 162
    examples of, 172–173
    and Martin Scorsese, 167–173
Auteur theory, 163–173
Automatic dialogue replacement, 185
Awakenings, 174

Bachelor Party, 178
Ballad of Little Jo, 102
Balzac, Honoré de, 103
Bananas, 45
Barthes, Roland, 14
Barthlemess, Richard, 109

Basic Instinct, 115, 140, 156
Batman, 106, 149, 154
Batman and Robin, 106
Batman Forever, 106
Batman Returns, 106
Battleship Potemkin, 44, 45, 193
Baudry, Jean-Louis, 176
Bazin, André, 7, 9, 14, 59
Beckett, Samuel, 30
Before the Revolution, 47, 56
Belton, John, 97
Bend of the River, 81
Benjamin, Walter, 66, 69–71, 73, 180, 198
Bennington, Geoff, 141
Bergman, Ingmar, 150, 164
Bertolucci, Bernardo, 47, 56–57, 158, 173, 198
Betrayal, 44
Beverly Hillbillies, 174
Bicycle Thief, 131–132, 133
Big, 174
Bigelow, Kathryn, 140
Big Sleep, 47, 126, 156
Biograph Company, 36
Birmingham Centre for Contemporary
      Cultural Studies (UK), 72, 73
Birth of a Nation, 108, 147, 150
Blade Runner, 130
Blind Date, 80
Blond Venus, 121
Blow-Up, 28–29, 135, 150
Blue Angel, 122
Blue Danube Waltz, 51
Blue-screen matte, 26
Boddy, William, 198
Bogart, Humphrey, 105, 123, 126, 158
Bolter, J. David, 199
Bonnie and Clyde, 102, 148
Bordwell, David, 15, 58
Borges, Jorge Luis, 30
Bottomore, Stephen, 58
Bouchard, D. F., 176
Boyz N the Hood, 174
Brady, Frank, 176
Brambilla, Marco, 88
Brando, Marlon, 85, 158–159
Braudy, Leo, 58, 59, 141
Braun, Martha, 15
Breathless, 133
Brecht, Bertolt, 137–138
Bresson, Robert, 173
Brewster, Ben, 58
Broken Blossoms, 109–112
Brooks, Peter, 96
Browning, Todd, 121

Bruckman, Clyde, 21
Brunelleschi, Filippo, 6
Buddy films, 92–93
Buffalo Bill and the Indians, 50
Bukatman, Scott, 15
Buñuel, Luis, 173
Burch, Noel, 58
Burks, Robert, 150
Burton, Tim, 106, 142, 149

Cabinet of Dr. Caligari, 121
Cagney, James, 105
Cain, James M., 123, 124
Camera obscura, 4–5
Cameron, James, 72, 74, 140
Campion, Jane, 174
Candy, John, 158
Cape Fear, 167, 169–170, 170
Carey, James W., 96
Carmina Burana, 3
Carné, Marcel, 149, 162
Cartoon violence, 88
Casablanca, 99, 116
Casino, 167
CBS, 183
CD-ROMs, 192–193
Censorship, 100–102
Chabrol, Claude, 163, 166
Chandler, Raymond, 53, 123–124, 126, 134
Chan Is Missing, 175
Channel surfing, 183
Chaplin, Charles, 147, 158
   film-making of, 21–23
Chayefsky, Paddy, 178
Chen, Kuan-Hsing, 96
Children of Paradise, 149
Chinatown, 130, 156
Chronology, 43
Cimino, Michael, 173
Cinécitta, 130
Cinemascope, 78–79
Cinematic image versus photographic image,
      10–14
Cinematic texts and cultural studies, 76–86
Cinematographers, 149–150
Cinerama, 78–79
Citizen Kane, 33, 118, 120, 124, 150, 152, 161,
      191, 193
   filming of, 48–50
   and film noir, 122–123
Clarissa (Richardson), 63
Class-difference stereotypes, 118
Classical style; *see* Hollywood classical style

Cleopatra, 151
Cliff Hanger, 88
Clift, Montgomery, 85
Clockwork Orange, 173
Close, Glenn, 159
Close Encounters of the Third Kind, 153
Closure, 99–100
Cohan, Steven, 97
Cohen, Leonard, 153
Cohen, Marshall, 58
Cold War, 83
Coleridge, Samuel Taylor, 191
Collaboration, 146, 159–162
Come Back to the Five and Dime, Jimmy Dean
   Jimmy Dean, 165
Comedy Central, 183
Commercial television, 179
Communication media, 194–195
Composers, 151–154
Computer games, 188–191
Computers, 187–198
   CD-ROMs, 192–193
   hypertext/hypermedia, 191–192
   Internet, 194–198
   narrative in, 187–192
   and text, 192–194
Computer screen, 187
Conrad, Joseph, 53
Consciousness/unconsciousness in style, 57–58
Content, 31–32
Continuity cutting, 35–37, 41–43
   economics of, 42–43
   emphasis on shot versus, 46–47
   versus montage, 45
Cook, David A., 15, 141
Coppola, Francis Ford, 118, 148–149, 167, 173,
   174
Corliss, Richard, 176
Cosgrove, Stuart, 97
Craftspeople, 148
Creativity, 144–147
   collaboration as, 146
Cross cutting, 35
Cross-tracking, 164
Crow, The, 106
Cultural constraints, 100
Cultural differences, 63–64
Cultural studies, 74–76
   and cinematic texts, 76–96
   description of, 72
   judgment and values, 74
   negotiation process, 73–74
   and television, 183–184
   text and context in, 73

Culture
   and cultural differences, 63–64
   definitions of, 61–64
   ideological norms, 117–118
   masscult and midcult, 68–69
   modernity, 82–88
   of 1950s, 82–88
   of postmodernity, 90
   and subcultures, 62–63
   as text, 61–66
   theories of, 65–72
   theories of Frankfurt School, 66–68
   theory of Walter Benjamin, 69–72
Cumming, John, 96
Curtiz, Michael, 116
Cut, 34–43
   arbitrary conventions, 41–42
   continuity cutting, 35–37, 41–43
   dialogue cutting, 38–40
   emphasis on shot versus, 46–47
   montage, 44–46
   shot/reverse shot, 37–38
   sight lines, 40–41
Cyberspace, 71
Cycloramas, 11

Dadaism, 9–10
Dallas, 116
Dangerfield, Rodney, 145, 158
Daniels, William, 149
Dardis, Tom, 176
Dark City, 130
Darkman, 106
Dash, Julie, 174
Dassin, Jules, 132–133
Daughters of the Dust, 174
Davies, Terence, 47
Davis, Bette, 112–113, 123
Dayan, Daniel, 58
Days of Wine and Roses, 178
Dean, James, 85
Decline of the American Male, 84
Deep focus, 49
Deer Hunter, 173
Deitch, Donna, 140
Delsarte, François, 141
Demolition Man, 88
De Niro, Robert, 53–54, 158, 168, 171–172
Department of Defense, 195
Der Golem, 121
Dery, Mark, 15
Desert Hearts, 140
DeSica, Vittorio, 131, 132

Desperately Seeking Susan, 140, 174
Detective fiction, 123
Devil Is a Woman, 121
Dialectic of Enlightenment (Horkheimer), 66
Dial M for Murder, 79
Dialogue cutting, 38–40
Dickens, Charles, 103
Dickson, William K. L., 12, 17
Die Hard, 26, 88, 90, 91, 94–95
    and buddy films, 93
    compared to *Vertigo,* 76–81
    and men in film, 85–87
    race in, 91–92
Die Hard with a Vengeance, 77
Digital imaging, 27–28, 185
    for movies, 192
Digital reproduction, 71–72
Di Palma, Brian, 45
Di Palma, Carlo, 150
Directors, 174
    mise-en-scène, 47–48
Disclosure, 115
Dishonored, 121
Disney Company, 183
Dmytryk, Edward, 124
Documentary films, 26–27
Dominant fiction, 99–100
Donnie Brasco, 167
Do the Right Thing, 174
Double Indemnity, 124–126
Douglas, Michael, 115
Dovzhenk, Alexander, 44
Dr. Strangelove, 26, 173
Dracula, 121, 122
Dreiser, Theodore, 46
Drier, Hans, 148
DVD, 186
Dyer, Richard, 176

E. T., 153
Ealing Studio, 162
Early Spring, 135
Earthquake, 151
Eastwood, Clint, 119
Eclipse, The, 135
Economics
    of continuity cutting, 42–43
    of early movies, 12
    of HDTV, 186
    of movie images, 19–23
    of realism, 12–14
Edge of the City, 92
Edison, Thomas Alva, 12–13, 17–18, 21, 35, 147

Edison Company, 17
Editing, 34–35, 150–151
    expressive use of, 50–54
    by mise-en-scène directors, 48
Editors, 150–151
Edwards, Blake, 178
Eisenstein, Sergei, 51, 193
    filming techniques, 44–46
Eisner, Lotte, 142
Elfman, Danny, 154
Eliot, T. S., 127, 166, 176
Ellis, John, 199
El Mariachi, 174
Elsaessar, Thomas, 15, 58, 142
Emmerich, Roland, 106
Entertainment Tonight, 157
Ephron, Nora, 102
Epics, 104
Eroica symphony, 38
Eszterhas, Joe, 156
European cinema, 162
European culture, 63
Expressionism, and origin of film noir,
    120–122
Eye-line match, 40

Fairbanks, Douglas, 23, 147
Far Country, The, 81
Farewell My Lovely, 124
Fascism, 130
Fassbinder, Rainer Werner, 164, 173, 198
    Brecht's influence on, 137–138
    films of, 136–139
Fatal Attraction, 91, 115, 140
Faulkner, William, 126, 156
Fear Eats the Soul, 136, 137
Fellini, Federico, 153, 173
Film
    compared to computer games, 188–189
    in television, 178
Filming; *see also* Movies
    in auteur theory, 164–167
    away from studio, 25–26
    blue-screen matte, 26
    the cut, 34–43
    deep focus, 49
    departures from classical style, 43–50
    digital imaging, 27–28
    editing, 34–35, 48
    emphasis on shot versus cut, 46–47
    expressive use of mise-en-scène and
        editing, 50–54
    ideology of, 30–31

on location, 27
long take, 48–50
mise-en-scène directors, 47–48
montage, 44–46
out-of-sequence, 28–29
rear-screen projection, 25–26
the shot, 24–25, 33–34
tatami position, 135
Film noir
and *Citizen Kane*, 122
climax of, 126–128
examples of, 123–128
Expressionist roots, 120–122
and hard-boiled fiction, 123
origin of, 120
rebirth of, 128–129
Fincher, David, 130
Firestone Tires, 179
Fiske, John, 96
Fitzgerald, F. Scott, 156
Flaubert, Gustave, 166
Flavor of Green Tea over Rice, 135
Flow of television programming, 182–184
Fonda, Bridget, 159
Fonda, Henry, 158
Ford, John, 87, 119, 135, 163, 164, 165, 167, 170
film editing, 50
Forest Gump, 102
Form, 31–32
Fort Apache, 87
Foucault, Michel, 14, 176
Fox network, 183
France
auteur theory, 162–163
and film noir, 120
new wave films, 133–134
Frankenheimer, John, 178
Frankenstein, 121
Frankfort School, 69, 73, 75
in America, 67–68
in Germany, 66–67
French New Wave, 27
Frentz, Suzanne, 199
Freund, Karl, 122
Friedberg, Anne, 14
From Caligari to Hitler (Kracauer), 66
Fromm, Erich, 66
Fuller, Samuel, 163
Furst, Anton, 149
Fusco, Giovanni, 153

Gangster films, 105, 133–134, 171–172
Garbo, Greta, 149

Gaudreault, André, 58
Gaumant Studio, 162
Gay stereotypes, 118
Gender
buddy films, 92–93
and Cold War, 83
decline of the male, 84
and ideological norms, 118
men in film, 85–87
vulnerable males, 84–85
women's role in society, 82–83
Gender-specific stereotypes, 42–43, 55–57
General, The, 21
General Electric, 179, 183
Genres
analysis of, 107
film noir, 120–129
and gesture, 103
limits to, 102–103
melodrama, 107–119
and narrative economy, 105–106
neorealism, 130–133
new wave films, 133–138
origin of, 103–105
patterns of, 104–105
resilience of, 129–130
and subgenres, 102
types of, 102
women filmmakers, 139–141
German Expressionism, 120
Germany
Nazi regime, 67
in 1920s, 66
Germany, Year Zero, 131
Gerstel, Sharon, 12
Gesture, 103
Gibbons, Cedric, 148
Gilbert, James, 97
Gitlin, Todd, 97
Gledhill, Christine, 142, 176
Godard, Jean-Luc, 18, 21, 43, 120, 138, 163, 166, 167, 173, 198
filming technique, 34
films of, 133–134
Godfather films, 173
Godfather I, 130, 149, 158
Godfather II, 118, 130, 148, 149
Goldwyn, Samuel, 154
Good, the Bad, and the Ugly, The, 153
Goodfellas, 48, 54, 153, 167, 170, 171–172
Gramsci, Antonio, 71–72
Grand Illusion, 47
Gray, Hugh, 14
Great Train Robbery, 26, 35, 172

Greaves, Roger, 142
Greenwald, Maggie, 102
Griffith, D. W., 23, 106, 147
  and Eisenstein, 44
  filming technique, 36
  films of, 108–112
Grimsted, David, 96
Grossberg, Lawrence, 96
Gunning, Tom, 58

Hall, Stuart, 96
Hammett, Dashiel, 123
Hanson, Curtis, 130
Hard-boiled fiction, 123
Harlin, Renny, 88
Harrelson, Woody, 3
Hathaway, Henry, 128, 142
Hawks, Howard, 47, 126, 156, 163, 166
HBO, 183
HDTV (high density television), 186
Hearst, William Randolph, 122
Heart of Darkness (Conrad), 53
Heaven's Gate, 173
Henreid, Paul, 116
Hepburn, Katherine, 158
Heroes, 87–88
Herrmann, Bernard, 152, 153
Heston, Charlton, 128, 142
High culture, 65, 69
Higher Learning, 174
High-speed photography, 12
Hitchcock, Alfred, 32, 33, 49, 50, 53, 56, 72, 89,
    92, 110, 135, 150, 151, 152, 153, 163, 164,
    167, 168, 169, 171, 172, 198
  film editing, 51–52
  filming of *Vertigo*, 76–81
  filming technique, 37–38
  and Jimmy Stewart's films, 81–82
  The Wrong Man, 126
Hollywood
  producers, 160–162
  Production Code, 101
  studio system, 20–23, 147
Hollywood classical style, 24–32
  in continuity cutting, 42–43
  departures from, 43–50
  elements of, 54–55
  fabricating the image, 24–28
  visibility/invisibility of, 56
Home page, 196
Horkheimer, Max, 66, 67, 96
Horror films, 121
House Un-American Activities Committee, 83
Howard, Richard, 14

Hudson, Rock, 116, 117, 138
Hudson Hawk, 88, 102
Hunt for Red October, 77
Huston, John, 123
Hyperlink, 196
Hypermedia, 191–192
Hypertext, 191–192
Hypertext fiction, 191–192

Ideal viewer, 145–146
Ideological norms, 117–118
Ideology
  of filming, 30–31
  in Soviet films, 44–46
  and westerns, 118–119
Il Grido, 135
Illusion, in painting, 5–6
I Love Lucy, 122, 184
Images
  Benjamin's view, 69–70
  created by Keaton and Chaplin, 19–23
  digital, 27–28, 185, 192–193
  economics of, 19–23
  Godard's views, 18–19
  on HDTV, 186
  manipulating, 9–10
  moving, 11
  and narrative, 16–19
  versus objective world, 2–3
  from photographic to cinematic, 10–14
  in photography, 7
  versus reality, 1–4
  reality as, 8–9
Impressionist painters, 5
In a Lonely Place, 126, 127
Independence Day, 185
Indiana Jones and the Last Crusade, 106
Indiana Jones and the Temple of
  Doom, 106
Individuality, 144–147
Individual talent, 146
Inevitability of photography, 7
Intercutting, 35
Internal tensions, 98–99
Internet, 71, 194–198
Intertextuality, 74–76
Intertitles, 104
Intolerance, 44, 108
Italian neorealism, 130–132
Italian Renaissance, 63
It's All True, 161
It's A Wonderful Life, 81, 180
  internal tensions, 98–99
Ivan the Terrible, 44

Jackson, Samuel L., 43, 159
James, Henry, 30, 61, 174
Jaws, 31–32, 153, 173
Jeanne Dielman, 23
Jefford, Susan, 97
Jenkins, Henry, 96
Johnny Guitar, 166
Johnson, Nunnally, 84
Johnston, Claire, 142
Jones, David, 44
Journalism photography, 10
Joyce, James, 30
Joyce, Michael, 199
Joy Luck Club, 174–175
Judgment, 74
Jungle Fever, 174
Jurassic Park, 185

Kahn, Michael, 151
Kalinak, Kathryn, 176
Kaplan, E. Ann, 142, 199
Kapsis, Robert E., 97
Kazan, Elia, 158
Keaton, Buster, 158
  film-making of, 20–23
Keep, Christopher, 199
Kennedy, John F., 87
Killing, The, 27
Kinetograph, 12
Kinetoscope, 12
King, Martin Luther, Jr., 87
King, Rodney, 1, 3–4, 8, 16
King of Comedy, 168–169
Kinopravda, 45
Kinsey Reports, 84
Kiss, The, 18
Kiss Me Deadly, 127
Kolker, Robert Phillip, 143
Korngold, Erich Wolfgang, 152
Kracauer, Siegfried, 66
Kraft Foods, 179
Kubla Khan (Coleridge), 191
Kubrick, Stanley, 27, 56, 110, 135, 173, 174, 198
  film editing, 51
Kuleshov, Lev, 44, 58
Kundun, 167
Kurosawa, Akira, 173
Kurtnik, Frank, 142

L.A. Confidential, 130
La Chinoise, 18
Lady in the Lake (Chandler), 53
Landy, Marci, 142

Lang, Fritz, 122, 125, 162, 166
Langlois, Henri, 120
Language, 2
La Notte, 135
Last Action Hero, 77, 88, 102
Last Laugh, The, 122
Last Tango in Paris, 158
Last Temptation of Christ, 167, 170
Last Waltz, The, 167
Last Year at Marienbad, 44
Late Autumn, 135
La Terra Terma, 131
Late Spring, 135
Laurel, Brenda, 200
Laurel and Hardy, 158
L'Aventura, 135
Lawrence, Viola, 151
League of Their Own, 174
Lee, Spike, 173, 174
Left-Handed Gun, 85
Left-wing ideologues, 68
Lehman, Michael, 88
Leonard, George B., Jr., 97
Leone, Sergio, 153
Leroy, Mervyn, 105
Lethal Weapon, 88
Lewis, Jerry, 20, 158
Leyda, Jay, 59
Linear convergence, 6
Little Big Man, 119
Little Caesar, 105
Loizeaux, Elizabeth, 14
Long Day Closes, The, 47
Long Goodbye, The, 50, 165
Long-shots, 47
Long take, 48–50
Lorentz, Pare, 46, 193
Lorrain, Claude, 4
Losey, Joseph, 173
Lost World, 185
Lovell, Terry, 142
Lumet, Sidney, 178
Lumière brothers (Auguste & Louis), 6, 17–19, 21, 35, 147, 188
Lyne, Adriane, 91, 115
Lyotard, Jean-François, 141

MacDonald, Dwight, 68–69, 95, 96
Machine animale (Marey), 12
Macy, William H., 159
Madonna, 74
Magic lanterns, 11
Magnificent Ambersons, 34, 47, 161
Making Mr. Right, 140, 174

Malcolm X, 174
Malone, Mark, 176
Maltese Falcon, 123, 126
Maltz, Albert, 133
Mancini, Henry, 154
Man from Laramie, 81
Man in the Grey Flannel Suit, 84, 85
Mankiewicz, Joseph, 92
Mann, Anthony, 81
Mann, Delbert, 178
Man Who Knew Too Much, 77, 81
Man Who Shot Liberty Valance, 165
Man With a Movie Camera, 45
Marcuse, Herbert, 66
Marey, Etienne-Jules, 11–12, 14–15, 17
Marshall, Penny, 174
Marty, 178
Marx Brothers, 158
Masaccio, 6
MASH, 50, 165, 184
Mashon, Mike, 199
Masscult, 68–69, 95
Mass culture, 61
    emergence from popular culture, 64–65
Massumi, Brian, 141
Mast, Gerald, 58
Master narratives, 99–100
Mayer, Louis B., 160
McCabe, Colin, 58
McCabe and Mrs. Miller, 50, 119, 153, 165
McCarthy, Joseph R., 128, 783
McLaughlin, Tim, 199
McMurray, Fred, 142
McRobbie, Angela, 97
McTiernan, John, 77, 88, 94
Mean Streets, 54, 153
Mechanical reproduction, 71–72
Melbourne, Gordon, 176
Méliès, Georges, 17–19, 21, 22, 26, 35, 147
Melodrama, 63
    in *All That Heaven Allows*, 116
    characteristics of, 104–105
    by D. W. Griffith, 108–112
    examples of, 107–119
    ideological norms, 117–118
    in *Now, Voyager*, 112–116
    purpose of, 110
    repressed sexuality in, 113–114
    self-sacrifice in, 116
    soap operas, 181
    westerns, 118–119
    in *Written on the Wind*, 116–117
    by Yasujiro Ozu, 135–136
Melville, Herman, 166

Men; *see also* Gender
    deline of the male, 83
    vulnerable males, 84–85
Mercury Players, 152
Metropolis, 122
Meyer, Carl, 121
MGM, 23
Midcult, 68–69, 95
Mildred Pierce, 123
Miller, Matthew, 199
Miller, Rand, 189–192
Miller, Robyn, 189–192
Milne, Tom, 176
Minnelli, Vincent, 166
Minorities, 174
Miracle in Milan, 131
Mise-en-scène, 20–21
    in computer games, 191
    expressive use of, 50–54
    and film noir, 120–122
    in Scorsese films, 52–54
Mise-en-scène directors, 47–48
Modernity, 82–88
    and Internet, 194–198
Modern Times, 21
Monaco, James, 143
Monroe, Marilyn, 158
Montage, 44–46
Montgomery, Robert, 53
Moonlighting, 80
Morley, David, 96
Morocco, 121
Morricone, Ennio, 153
Morrison, Toni, 30
Moskin, Robert, 97
Mother and the Law, The, 108
Moulthrop, Stuart, 199
Movie conventions
    elements of classical style, 54–55
    gender specificity, 55–57
    notion of consciousnes, 57–58
Moviemakers
    actors, 156–159
    auteurs, 162–175
    cinematographers, 149–150
    collaboration, 159–162
    collaboration as creativity, 146–147
    composers, 151–154
    craftspeople, 148
    editors, 150–151
    individuals and creativity, 144–147
    Martin Scorsese, 167–173
    producers, 160–162
    production designers, 149

screenwriters, 154–156
in studio system, 147
Movies; *see also* Filming; Genres; Hitchcock,
    Alfred; Scorsese, Martin; Welles, Orson
address and response, 95
of Alfred Hitchcock, 51–52
black/white versus color, 129
buddy films, 92–93
compared to television, 178
cultural criticism of texts, 76–96
versus cyberspace, 71
digital imaging, 185, 193
digitized into electronic files, 186
early history, 13–14
early popularity of, 13
economic processes, 12
economics of images, 19–23
Edison's contribution, 17–18
of Eisenstein, 44–46
European cinema, 162
form and content, 31–32
gender-specific stereotypes, 42–43
genres, 102–107
hero's role, 87–88
ideal viewer, 145–146
images versus reality, 1–4
from image to narrative, 16–19
intersection of photography and film, 11–12
invisibility of style and structure, 29–30
of John Ford, 50
of Keaton and Chaplin, 19–23
of Martin Scorsese, 52–54
men in, 85–87
of modernity, 82–88
of 1950s, 82–88
and patent wars, 13
and popular culture, 60–61
of postmodernity, 90–92
previewing, 106
Production Code, 101
of Robert Altman, 50–51
screen size, 78–80
sequels, 106
of Stanley Kubrick, 51
stars of television and, 80
storage and distribution, 186–187
target audiences, 69
technical nature of, 24–32
and television, 78–80
view of Frankfurt School, 66–68
vulnerable males in, 84–85
women filmmakers, 139–141
women's roles, 82–83
Movie violence, 88

Moving images, 11
Mozart, W. A., 34
MTV, 2, 182, 183
Mulcahy, Russell, 106
Multimedia, 192–194
Mulvey, Laura, 59, 138, 143
Munch, Edvard, 120
Murder My Sweet, 123–126
Murdoch, Rupert, 161, 183
Murnau, F. W., 25, 47, 121, 122, 162
Music, 29
    composers, 151–154
    in melodrama, 104
Music Hall entertainments, 64
Musser, Charles, 14–15, 58
Mussolini, Benito, 130
Muybridge, Eadweard, 11–12, 17
Myst, 189–192

Naked City, 132–133
Naked Gun 33⅓, 45
Naked Spur, 81
Narboni, Jean, 176
Naremore, James, 176
Narrative economy, 105–106
Narrative, 16–19, 31–32
    backwards, 44
    cinematic texts, 76–96
    classical style, 43
    closure, 99–100
    on computers, 187–192
    film noir, 120–128
    internal tensions, 98–99
    in modernity, 88–90
    in movie genres, 102–107
    movies of 1980s, 82–88
    in neorealism, 130–133
    new wave films, 133–138
    of postmodernity, 90–92
    types on television, 181–182
    visual pleasure in, 139–141
    and women filmmakers, 139–141
    work of screenwriters, 154–156
Narrative constraints, 100–102
Nashville, 50, 165
National Public Radio, 62
National Science Foundation, 195
Natural Born Killers, 1–4, 16, 46, 102
Nature, 8
NBC, 183
Neale, Steven, 141
Negotiation process, 73–74
Nelson, Cary, 96

Nelson, Joyce, 142
Nelson, Ted, 191, 199
Neorealism
   in America, 132–133
   in Italy, 130–132
Newell, Mike, 167
Newman, Paul, 85
New wave film, 133–138
   Antonioni, 134–135
   Fassbinder, 136–138
   influence of Brecht, 138–139
   Yasujiro Ozu, 135–136
New York, New York, 167
Niagara, 128
Nichols, Bill, 14, 58, 142
Nielsen ratings, 183
Nightmare on Elm Street, 74
Night Moves, 129
1980s, 90–91
1950s, 82–88
Nixon, 46
Noise, 195
Nomads, 77
North By Northwest, 77
Nosferatu, 121
Novels, 63
Now, Voyager, 112–116, 117
No Way Out, 92
Nykvist, Sven, 150

Objectivity, 3
Old and New, 44
180-degree rule, 41
On the Waterfront, 158, 168
Orff, Karl, 3
Othello, 149
Out-of-sequence filming, 28–29
Over-the-shoulder cutting pattern, 41
Ozu, Yasujiro, 135–136, 173

Pacific Heights, 91
Painting, 4–5
   perspective and illusion, 5–6
Paisan, 131
Pakula, Alan J., 129
Pamela (Richardson), 63
Panavision, 78–79
Panofsky, Erwin, 14
Parallel editing, 35
Paramount Pictures, 46, 79, 183
Paris Cinématheque, 120
Parker, David, 97

Pastorals, 104
Patent wars, 13
Pather Panchali, 27
Pathé Studio, 162
Peckinpah, Sam, 119
Penn, Arthur, 85, 102, 119, 129, 148, 151, 178
People Magazine, 157
Perception, 8
   of cinematic narrative, 24
Perspective, 29
   in painting, 5–6
Peterson, L. S., 142
Photographic image versus cinematic image,
      10–14
Photography
   high-speed, 12
   manipulating the image, 9–10
   and painting, 5
   and reality, 6–7
   and the thing itself, 7–8
   varying forms of, 9–10
Piano, The, 174
Pickford, Mary, 23, 147
Place, J. A., 142
Place in the Sun, 84–85
Player, The, 165
Playhouse, The, 22
Plow That Broke the Plains, 46, 193
Poetic Justice, 174
Poetic realism school, 149
Point-of-view techniques, 53–54
Polanski, Roman, 130
Popeye, 165
Popular culture
   Benjamin's theory, 69–72
   consumers of, 73
   and Frankfurt School, 66–68
   and intertextuality, 74–76
   MacDonald's view, 68–69
   negative views of, 60–61
   origin of mass culture, 64–65
Porter, David, 200
Porter, Edwin S., 26, 35, 172
Portrait of a Lady (James), 174
Posey, Parker, 159
Postman Always Rings Twice, 123
Postmodernity, 74–76, 90–92
Powell, Dick, 124, 142
Powell, Michael, 167
Preminger, Otto, 163
Presley, Elvis, 69
Previewing, 106
Prince of Tides, 140
Print culture, 64–65

Printing, 194
Producers, 160–162
Production Code, 101, 155
Production designers, 149
Prose writing, 29–30
Proyas, Alex, 106, 130
Psycho, 41, 53, 72, 77, 92, 110
    editing of, 52
    shot/reverse shot in, 37–38
Public Enemy, 105
Pudovkin, Vesevolod, 44
Pulp Fiction, 43, 127, 167

Quai du Commerce, 138–141

Race, 91–92
Radio, 64–65
Raging Bull, 54, 167, 168–171, 171
Raiders of the Lost Ark, 77, 106, 153
Railroads, 194
Raimi, Sam, 106
Rains, Claude, 116
Rap music, 61
Rapper, Irving, 112, 113
Ray, Nicholas, 85, 126, 163, 166
Ray, Satyajit, 27
Realism
    of black and white films, 129
    economics of, 12–14
Reality
    as image, 8–9
    versus images, 1–4
    and photography, 6–7
Rear-screen projection, 25–26
Rear Window, 77, 81–82
Rebel Without a Cause, 85
Red and the Black, The, 163
Red Desert, 150
Reisz, Karel, 176
Renaissance, 63
Renoir, Jean, 47, 162, 163, 164, 165, 173
Representation, 4–10, 9–10
    in painting, 4–5
    perspective and illusion, 5–6
    in photography, 5
    photography and reality, 6–7
    photography and the thing itself, 7–8
    reality as image, 8–9
Repressed sexuality, 113–114
Resnais, Alain, 44
Response, 95
Richardson, Samuel, 63

Right-wing politicians, 68
Ritt, Martin, 92
Riven, 189–192
River, The, 46
Rivette, Jacques, 163
RKO, 160–161
Robinson, Edward G., 105, 125
Rock and roll, 61, 69
Rodriguez, Robert, 174
Rohmer, Eric, 163
Romance fiction, 61
Romancing the Stone, 106
Rome, Open City, 131, 133
Rope, 81
Rosewood, 174
Rossellini, Roberto, 131, 163
Rota, Nino, 153
Rozsa, Miklos, 152
Russian Revolution, 44

Sarris, Andrew, 163–164
Scarlet Empress, 121
Scarlet Street, 123–126, 127
Schlesinger, John, 91
Schoonmaker, Thelma, 151
Schrader, Paul, 142, 173
Schroeder, Barbet, 140
Schumacher, Joel, 106
Schwarzwenegger, Arnold, 87–88
Scientific American, 12
Scopophilia, 2, 13
Scorsese, Martin, 48, 129, 143, 151, 153, 174,
    198
    film editing, 52–54
    filming technique, 34
    innovations in film, 167–173
Scott, Ridley, 102, 130
Scream, The, 121
Screen size, 78–80
Screenwriters, 154–156
Screen Writers Guild, 155
Script, 189–190
Searchers, The, 87, 119, 165, 170
Search for Bridey Murphy, 89
Seidelman, Susan, 139, 174
Seinfeld, 44, 182
Seldes, Gilbert, 96
Sequels, 106
Serie Noir, 120
Series programming, 181–182
Serling, Rod, 178
Seven Year Itch, 158
Shadow, The, 106

Shangai Express, 121
Shepperton Studio, 162
Sherlock, Jr., 22
Shining, The, 110
Shoot the Piano Player, 133
Short Cuts, 50, 165
Shot
  deep focus, 49
  in Eisenstein's work, 44–46
  emphasis on, 46–47
  long take, 48–50
  out-of-sequence filming, 28–29
  zoom shot, 50, 165
Shot/reverse shot, 37–38
Shub, Esther, 44
Sight lines, 40–41
Silverman, Kaja, 141, 175
Simpsons, The, 75, 154, 182
Singer, Bryan, 167
Singleton, John, 174
Single White Female, 140
Sirk, Douglas, 116–117, 119, 136, 166
Situation comedies, 182, 184
Skal, David, 142
Sleepless in Seattle, 102, 150
Snake Pit, The, 151
Soap operas, 181
Socialist narratives, 100
Socialist realism, 46
Solas, Humberto, 173
Some Like It Hot, 158
Soviet Union, 44
Spacey, Kevin, 159, 167
Special effects, 26
Spencer, Dorothy, 151
Spheeris, Penelope, 174
Spider's Strategem, 56–57
Spielberg, Steven, 31–32, 77, 106,
    151, 153–154, 167, 172, 173,
    174, 185
Spigel, Lynn, 198
Stagecoach, 151
Stalin, Josef, 46, 71
Stallone, Sylvester, 87–88
Stam, Robert, 141
Stanford, Leland, 12
Stanwyck, Barbara, 142
Stargate, 106
Stars
  function, 80–82
  of television and movies, 80
Star Trek, 74, 184
Star Wars, 130
State intervention, 71

Steamboat Bill, Jr., 20
Stefik, Mark, 200
Steiner, Max, 152
Stendahl, 163
Sternberg, Joseph von, 121–122
Stevens, George, 84
Stewart, James, 158
  career of, 80–82
Stone, Oliver, 1–4, 16, 46, 130
Storyline, 31–32
Strange Days, 140
Strangers on a Train, 169–170
Stravinsky, Igor, 154
Streetcar Named Desire, 158
Streisand, Barbra, 140
Strike, 44
Studio system, 147
  development of, 20–23
  operation of, 24
Subcultures, 62–63
Subgenres, 102
Sunrise, 25, 47
Surrealism, 9–10
Suture effect, 37

Tarantino, Quentin, 43, 127, 167
Tarkovsky, Andrei, 173
Tatami position, 135
Tavoularis, Dean, 148–149
Taxi Driver, 53, 57, 129, 153, 167,
    168–170, 171
Technology
  of digitizing, 184–187
  of movies, 24–32, 148–151
  of television, 178
Telegraphy, 194–195
Telephone, 194–195
Televised pleasure, 184
Television, 178–184
  commercial structures, 179
  and film, 78–80
  flow of programming, 182–184
  HDTV, 186
  as mass culture, 65
  narrative programming, 181–182
  program quality, 180–181
  screen size, 78–80
  stars of movies and, 80
  viewers, 179–180
Television gaze, 179–180
Ten Days That Shook the World, 44
"Tender Trap," 153
Terminator, The, 72, 87, 129

Text
    and computers, 192–194
    and context, 73
    in cultural studies, 72
    culture as, 61–6
    and intertextuality, 75–76
Thalberg, Irving, 160
Thelma and Louise, 102
Theory of Film (Kracauer), 66
Thin Man, 123
Thompson, Kristen, 15, 58
"Three Coins in the Fountain," 153
3-D films, 79
Time-Warner, 183
Tiomkin, Dimitri, 152
Titanic, 74
To Catch a Thief, 77
Toland, Gregg, 122, 150
Tomasani, George, 151
Touch of Evil, 127–128, 129
Towne, Robert, 156
Tragedy, 104
Transportation, 194
Trauner, Alexandre, 149
Traveling matte, 26
Traveling Players, 47
Travolta, John, 43
Treichler, Paula A., 96
Trip to the Moon, 19
Truffaut, François, 120, 133, 163, 166,
    167, 173
TV Guide, 129
12 Angry Men, 178
Twentieth Century Fox, 79
2001: A Space Odyssey, 51, 75, 173

UFA Studios, 148
Umberto D, 131, 132
United Artists, 23
Unpacking, 73–74
Untouchables, The, 45
Usual Suspects, The, 167
U-Turn, 130

Values, 74
Vaudeville, 64
Verhoeven, Paul, 115
Vermeer, Jan, 4–5
Vertigo, 92, 94–95, 172
    compared to *Die Hard,* 76–81
    and culture of 1950s, 82
    editing of, 52

    and men in film, 85–87
    modernity in, 88–89
    race in, 91–92
Vertov, Dziga, 44, 45
Viacom, 183
Villains, postmodern, 90–91
Visconti, Luchino, 131
VistaVision, 79–80
Visual pleasure, 139–141
"Visual Pleasure in the Narrative Cinema"
    (Mulvey), 139
Vulnerable males, 84–85

Walsh, Raoul, 163
Wang, Wayne, 175
Warner, Jack, 156
Warner Brothers, 23, 123
Warshow, Robert, 96, 141
Watering the Gardener, 17
Waxman, Franz, 152
Way Down East, 108
Wayne, John, 87, 88, 158
Wayne's World, 174
Weekend, 34
Wegener, Paul, 121
Welles, Orson, 47, 53, 56, 133, 135, 142, 149,
    150, 152, 153, 160, 161, 163, 164, 191, 193,
    198
    and *Citizen Kane,* 122–123
    filming of *Citizen Kane,* 48–50
    filming techniques, 33–34
    Touch of Evil, 128, 127
Wellman, William, 105
West, Mae, 99
Westerns
    heroes in, 87
    as melodrama, 118–119
Westinghouse, 183
Whale, James, 121
Wheeler, Lyle, 148
White-telephone movies, 130
Who's That Knocking on My Door, 167
Whyte, William, 97
Wiene, Robert, 121
Wild Bunch, 119
Wilder, Billy, 124, 149, 158
Wild One, 85, 158
Willett, John, 143
Williams, John, 153–154
Williams, Raymond, 72, 96,
    182, 199
Williams, Tennessee, 69

Willis, Bruce, 26, 86, 88
  compared to James Stewart, 80–82
  in *Die Hard*, 76–81
  film/television career, 80
Willis, Gordon, 148
Wills, Gary, 176
Wizard of Oz, 129
Wollen, Peter, 165
Women
  in American society, 82–83
  and decline of the male, 83
  directors, 174
  filmmakers, 139–141
Wood, Christopher S., 14
Wood, Robert, 58
Wood, Robin, 141

Word-processing programs, 190
"Work of Art in an Age of Mechanical
     Representation" (Benjamin), 69, 198
World of Apu, 27
World Wide Web, 196–198
Written on the Wind, 116–117
Wrong Man, 77, 126, 127
Wyman, Jane, 116

X-Files, 74
Yentl, 140
Zemeckis, Robert, 106
Zohn, Harry, 96
Zoom shot, 50, 165
Zoot suit riots, 82